I Married
A Best Seller

I Married A Best Seller

SHEILA HAILEY

Michael Joseph in association with Souvenir Press

First published in Great Britain by Michael Joseph Ltd
52 Bedford Square, London WC1B 3EF
in association with Souvenir Press Ltd
43 Great Russell Street, London WC1
1978

ISBN 0 7181 1734 4

Photoset, printed and bound
in Great Britain by
REDWOOD BURN LIMITED
Trowbridge & Esher

To my husband, ARTHUR HAILEY,
*in the faint hope that this will shame
him into dedicating a book to me*

P.S. I am not holding my breath.

Contents

CHAPTER 1

A Helluva Way to Start a Romance

In 1976 Arthur Hailey and I celebrated our silver wedding anniversary. We had four parties: a dinner-dance for 160 in the Bahamas, where we live; a luncheon for 100 in the Napa Valley, California, where we used to live; a dinner-dance for fifty in Toronto, Canada, where it all began; and a small dinner for ten in Auckland, New Zealand, on the actual date of our marriage. As a friend remarked, 'Sheila, aren't you milking this a bit?'

'You're damn right,' I replied.

For to stay happily married to anyone for twenty-five years is an achievement. To stay happily married for that length of time to a writer is a miracle.

Why? Because a writer is temperamental, ruthless, sensitive, impatient, emotional, unreasonable, demanding, self-centred, and excessively hard-working. That is, he has to be most of these things if he is to be a successful writer. My husband is all of them.

He is also precise, pig-headed, fastidious, fanatically clean, maniacally tidy. *And* he works at home. In fact, he's done so for twenty-one years. (This alone would send many women running to the nearest divorce court.) Yet here we are . . . still in love, still each other's best friend, still laughing at each other's jokes.

But it hasn't been easy. I mean, can you imagine your old man complaining because the stamp you stick on an envelope is slightly crooked? Or being peeved because you've handwritten a batch of cheques instead of typing them?

Arthur once came home from a two-week trip and, after settling down at his desk, buzzed me on the intercom.

'Sheila, did you use my scratch pad over here while I was away?'

'Oh, yes,' I said. 'I was taking down all those instructions you were giving me when you phoned from London.'

'Well,' he said, 'you left part of several pages attached to the pad. They're all ragged at the top.'

'My God,' I cried. 'How *could* I? Will you ever forgive me?'

A slight chuckle at the other end . . . and I heard no more about it. Once again, I have survived 'an incident'.

You think I'm kidding?

I should have been warned the first time we met, in August 1949. I was working in the typing pool of a magazine publishing company, Maclean-Hunter, in Toronto, Canada. Much to my chagrin, it was the only job available when, fresh out from England two months before, I made the rounds of book publishers, touting four years' London experience in the publishing field.

I had left England looking for adventure. Postwar Britain was dreary, its citizens already deprived of financial freedom. A traveller was allowed to take out of the country £35 which, in June 1949, was barely enough for a modest two-week holiday. I longed to see other lands, so a one-way £35 ticket to Canada, and an emigrant's status (which enabled me to seek a job) seemed the best way to start travelling. I didn't intend to stay longer than eighteen months, in which time I could earn enough money to see the country. Then I vowed either to return to England, or journey on to somewhere else.

A day in the M-H typing pool consisted of transcribing Dictaphone cylinders, the heavy black wax forerunner of the lightweight recording belts and cassettes used today. I had to charge my time to whatever magazine had been unlucky enough to get my services. My services were a disaster. Half the time I couldn't make any sense out of the broad, unfamiliar Canadian accents on the cylinders. Once I described an editor as an 'odd coarse man' when he was explaining in a letter that he was 'an ardent horseman'. Then one day I picked up a cylinder marked 'A. F. Hailey, Editor, *Bus & Truck Transport*'. What came out was a beautifully clear, clipped English voice, dictating letters deliberately and precisely, with every name spelled out and all the punctuation carefully specified. It was impossible for even me to go wrong. I typed the letters in record time, and they were comma-perfect. I was overjoyed. At last a voice I could understand. So a little hand-written note went back with the batch of typed letters, a note which said: *Thought I would let you know how much I enjoyed hearing the first homeland voice since I started this job.*

I was hoping he would seek me out and ask for a date or something—especially when I learned that A. F. Hailey, too, had emigrated from England two years earlier—for I rebelled at the impersonal atmosphere of the typing pool, where I never met any voice I worked for. But I was disappointed. Nothing came of it except a note to the head of the pool asking if I could please handle all Hailey correspondence.

Eventually, though, we did meet—in one of the editorial offices where I was standing-in for a secretary who was on holiday. We were unimpressed with each other. He was overweight and glum. I was overweight and tweedy. I discovered later that Hailey was unhappy because his marriage was breaking up. My excuse for being overweight was that I liked to eat a lot; I still do, but over the years I have learned some self-control.

Promoted at last, in January 1950, to a junior editorial job, I received a note: *Congratulations, and even though it now means I shall have to read my dictated letters before they are mailed, I wish you well in your new job. How about lunch sometime?*

Looking back at this beginning, I think I must have been attracted first by his voice, second by his energy, and thirdly by his highly-organized mind. It was obvious that Mr. Hailey was attracted by my ability to type perfectly, to spell correctly, and to follow instructions implicitly. Without answering back. A helluva way to start a romance, one that could have been the beginning of a smooth, dull life for both of us. But Arthur found out, when he got to know me, that I was exceptionally gifted at arguing and answering back. It's been his cross ever since.

Arthur was sad and cynical on our first date. He told me over dinner—not lunch—that his wife and three small sons had left him. He was obviously suffering a real sense of failure, and seemed to want to castigate himself for it. I remember thinking, 'Why is he telling me all this? I couldn't be less interested. I don't need to know.' I must have communicated this feeling on our second meeting, because more than two months went by before he asked me for a third date.

Small wonder. Neither one of us looked great. Arthur was heavy, with a big moon face, a big mouth, and big teeth. His hair was outrageously short in the North American 1950s style, which made his face look even fatter. He had a penchant for light, spivvy suits. He once escorted me to a Toronto Byline Ball (an annual wingding for the newspaper crowd) in a turquoise-coloured suit. I thought his taste was atrocious.

I was no catch either. Apart from being chunky, I wore heavy English woollen clothes that were far too warm for overheated Canadian buildings. (They were all I had.) As a result I sweated a lot, and my face was often shiny. Spectacles had a tendency to slide down my nose, hair hung limply around my shoulders. At five feet eight inches, I always thought I was tall enough and so wore flat-heeled shoes. They looked fine in England, unchic in the New World.

It was not, in fact, love at first sight. But it must have been something. Maybe it was because we had the same kind of English background, or the same passion for books and printing, or the same burning ambition to 'get ahead'. Certainly we had the same sense of humour. I discovered his earlier gloom was not typical. I laughed a lot when we were together, and to this day I find the most attractive men are the ones who make me laugh. Whatever it was, we gradually grew on each other. *I* never called it love, because I was determined not to get permanently involved with anyone in Canada. I was going back to England, get a job on Fleet Street, and become a famous journalist.

And so I might if it hadn't been for the camping trip. By the summer of 1950 Arthur was, I knew, deeply in love. One day he asked if I would go on a camping trip with him and another couple, Bill and Glenys Stevenson. (Bill later became the author of many books, including *A Man Called Intrepid*.) I said yes. I was eager to see the glories of northern Ontario, particularly Algonquin National Park—so the four of us excitedly made plans. Two weeks before our scheduled jaunt, the Korean War broke out, and Bill—then a talented reporter for the *Toronto Daily Star*—departed at once to cover it. The camping trip was out, as far as Glenys was concerned, and since it was the Stevensons' car we were to use, I was sure it was out for us too. Arthur was so crestfallen and disappointed, he pleaded with me to go anyway. Although he had no car, very little money, was also paying for a divorce and helping to support three young sons, he told me he did have some vacation pay coming and he would rent a car. He knew where he could borrow a tent and a Coleman stove, and he was sure it wouldn't be difficult to borrow sleeping bags. He was most persuasive and I hesitated only momentarily. I was twenty-two, living away from home, and I thought—why not? In 1950, it wasn't strictly proper, but then, in those days daughters didn't often leave home to live abroad.

It was the most idyllic bittersweet vacation we have ever had. I had told Arthur I could never marry a divorced man, although I knew by this time I loved him. Still, I had been in love before and had survived. I learned to cook in a hurry—over wood fires—and discovered that a good meal was the easiest way to make a man mellow. We found secluded spots, beside breathtakingly beautiful lakes, on which to pitch our tent. I had been a Girl Guide between the ages of eleven and fourteen, so I seemed to take over this chore naturally, giving directions to Arthur which he carried out correctly, perfectly, without answering back. We swam naked in the cool northern lakes, and made love every day and night, several times. We laughed a great deal, loved a great deal, and learned that we could live together. Soon I realized he was more emotional and sensitive than I had thought, and soon he discovered my quick temper. At one point, we ran into a rainstorm and abandoned any idea of camping outside that night. We checked into an ancient motel—ramshackle cabins with iron bedsteads and lumpy mattresses and worn linoleum—and I found out how utterly depressed Arthur can get when the weather is bad and his surroundings shabby.

(Years later, in an interview for the inflight magazine of American Airlines, Arthur said: 'It was during that glorious camping trip that I decided I wanted to marry her. And one of the reasons was, I found that over just a fire of twigs and stone she was a superb natural cook. We had great fun in the tent, too, but maybe my reasoning told me that would level itself out, but the cooking would stay for a long time.' I spoke up in the same interview: 'Arthur says it was my cooking. It was because I was a big, strong girl, and I could see that folded tent and know exactly what had to be done, and say, "You take that end and I'll do this." And that's why he married me, because I could cope.')

13

On the way back to Toronto, he pleaded anew for me to marry him. Surely those two weeks must have convinced me how right we were for each other. I said simply, 'I have to go back to England.'

And so we continued to see each other—constantly, in fact, through the remainder of 1950, with a two-month separation when I joined a girl friend for a tour of Canada and the United States.

In December I was to take a train from Toronto to New York before sailing for England. At last the moment of parting had come, and as the train started to chug out of Union Station Arthur looked up at me, openly weeping. 'You *will* come back, won't you?' I looked down, crying also, and whispered, 'I don't know!'

I locked myself in the lavatory, looked in the mirror, and watched the tears rolling down my face. Then I blew my nose and looked again and said out loud, 'You stupid fool! If you feel like this, why *don't* you come back?' But at the back of my mind, I wondered: How would my parents take it? I was the youngest of four daughters in a close-knit family. Canada was a long way from London. On a magazine editor's salary, I wouldn't be hopping back and forth visiting every year. And what about Arthur's having been married before, with three sons to support?

Trying to push these thoughts out of my mind, I enjoyed three wonderful days in New York. Among other things, there was a standing-room-only ticket to see Mary Martin and Ezio Pinza in *South Pacific*. I was enthralled and deeply moved. Suddenly Sheila was Ensign Nellie Forbush, the nurse from Little Rock, Arkansas; Arthur was Émile de Becque, the handsome, middle-aged French plantation owner, with two Polynesian children. I had tried to 'wash that man right out of my hair'—but it was no good, I was hooked.

The Atlantic crossing from New York to Southampton on the *Queen Elizabeth* was cold and grey, and I arrived in a cold and grey London on December 13, 1950. After the vastness of North America, with its huge skies, England seemed tiny and quaint, with little toy trains puffing through a miniature countryside.

The family was clearly delighted to be welcoming me home, and it was a warm and exciting reunion. But the next day I had to tell my mother that I was going back to Canada—for good. She was brave and understanding. 'You've always known what you wanted and gone after it,' she said. 'And you've always liked older men, and there are few men who reach thirty without having been married ... or something. But,' she added in a puzzled way, 'if this chap is English, why don't you live in England?' I had to explain the wonderful country that was Canada, the opportunities there were, how I could envisage the kind of life we never could achieve in England.

So I had my dear mother's blessing, and I wrote a letter to Arthur Hailey saying yes, I would marry him. And he, typically, sent a cable back saying my letter was the best Christmas present he'd ever had.

CHAPTER 2

Youthful, Stumbling Steps to Writing

What is talent? Where does it come from?

Is one born with the spark to become a musician, an artist, a writer? I think the answer is: Yes—but one still has to work at it. For somewhere along the line the will to succeed takes over, and it is this single-mindedness of purpose that ultimately brings the rewards of fame and fortune.

It also helps to have a mother with similar goals.

In the case of Elsie Hailey, her ambition was for her only child, Arthur, to be a clerk in an office—which she regarded as a high-class occupation—instead of a factory worker. She herself had left school in 1897, at the age of ten, to go into domestic service—one of the few choices in England for a young working-class girl of that era. Yet she had within her a flair for storytelling that I believe she passed on to her son. Arthur has often told me that when he was a small boy she would make up stories to tell him. In later years her letters to us were always long and lively; true, they were sometimes ungrammatical and misspelled, but it didn't matter. When our children saw their paternal grandmother on their visits to England, she would tell them, too, stories which she made up as she went along. Perceptive as children always are, they recognized the similarity between their grandmother and their father.

(During a tedious car trip—to our cottage in northern Ontario, for instance—one of the children would ask a simple question: 'Daddy, why is that telephone pole leaning over like that?' Instead of answering as most people would, 'I don't know,' he made up an impossibly long, crazy story that involved a complicated plot and dozens of characters. The children listened delightedly, even while protesting, 'Oh, Daddy!')

Around 1916, Elsie Mary Wright was engaged to marry a soldier, Arthur Frederick Hailey, as soon as he came back from World War I. Like so many others in that tragic war, he did not return. His older brother, George, then thirty-six, a veteran of the Boer War, a British Army regular in India, and a survivor of the Battle of Mons, did come back from the trenches in France. He offered to marry his dead brother's sweetheart. The thirty-two-year-old Elsie, already twelve years past the average marrying age of that time, said yes.

'George and I were strangers, Sheila,' she told me many times. 'But I grew to love him over the years.' Indeed she did, and when I saw her at eighty-five, energetically and uncomplainingly looking after her frail and senile husband, one could have no doubt of it. Arthur and I would urge her to get some nursing help. 'No,' she'd say determinedly. 'I can do it—and I *will*. George is happier with me. No one understands him like I do.'

Back in 1919 the newlyweds settled in Luton, known for its manufacture of hats and motor cars.

It seemed a miracle to Elsie that she should 'fall in the family way' so soon after her marriage. When the boy was born on April 5, 1920, she named him after her dead lover. Young Arthur was the centre of her life. She was devoted to him.

The Hailey family lived in a typical working-class house. The front door opened directly onto the pavement. There were two tiny bedrooms upstairs, two rooms and a cold-water scullery downstairs, and an outside toilet in a pocket-size backyard. George paid nine shillings and sixpence a week as rent—out of his weekly wage of three pounds. There was gas lighting throughout, but at night one used a candle to go from one part of the house to another. Arthur and I have compared notes, for I lived in similar surroundings as a small girl, and we both remember the nights when one would lie in bed, wanting to go to the toilet, but putting off that walk downstairs and out to the cold backyard, holding a flickering candle.

Arthur became a great reader. He visited the local public library, borrowing as many books each week as he was allowed. While other boys were out playing, he read. His paternal grandmother clucked: 'All that reading's not good for the boy. He should be helping you in the house, Elsie. He doesn't do a thing.' (Years later, I often thought to myself that—yes, Grandma had a point.) And when Arthur talked of his future, George—a factory worker himself—would scold, 'Elsie, you mustn't encourage such nonsense. We're working-class people. It's no good aiming too high.'

For Arthur wanted to be, not a clerk, but a newspaper reporter. He loved to write and liked getting involved in the local scene. He wrote little plays for his Sunday school, and letters to the local paper, the *Luton News*, on issues of the day. An enthusiastic swimmer by the age of thirteen, he was upset that the public swimming pool was closed on Sundays, and wrote to the editor to tell him so:

Sir: This town is comparatively forward in the matter of Sunday entertainment. Sunday concerts are organized both by the municipal authorities and the Grand Theatre. Only a few weeks ago tennis in the Parks on Sunday was innovated. Outside the town are greyhound racing tracks.

Yes, we are comparatively fortunate except for one thing, and that is, the opening on Sunday of the Public Swimming Baths. Through the passing years swimming has achieved more and more popularity with the man-in-the-street. Now it is a sport with which every man, woman and child is acquainted. As well as offering an undeniable appeal and attraction, it is one of the healthiest sports in which it is possible to participate.

I was pleased to read in your paper some time ago that the proposed new swimming bath is intended for Sunday opening. But why wait until the new swimming pool is erected? Why cannot the present swimming bath be opened for, say, one hour each Sunday morning, from seven o'clock to eight o'clock? At the present time, when we look at Sunday from a saner point of view than did our Victorian ancestors, we must realise there is no sin in swimming. It is a clean, healthy, natural sport in which God gave man the ability to participate. Did He then intend us not to swim on the Sabbath? I am of the firm opinion that swimming can in no way deteriorate religion. Swimming is a thing that I think symbolizes purity and cleanliness, and, above all, helps one in a true Christian manner to aid and save the drowning. Another thing, if, as I have suggested, the Public Baths were opened from seven to eight o'clock, it would in no way affect the congregations of the churches at that early hour.

I would like to say one more thing. There are many people in Luton who, through force of circumstances, are unable to

attend the Swimming Baths during the week and who, conse-
quently, if they require to bathe, are compelled to do so in other
districts—Yours, etc. A.F. Hailey

When Arthur saw his prose in print for the first time, it was a heady
experience. He wrote more and more letters to the editor. Along the
way, fortunately, he learned to write more succinctly.

At first he conducted these activities in a windowless cupboard
under the stairs, lit by a candle. My guess is that it was as neatly
organized and logical as his study is today. A notice was tacked outside: 'A. F. HAILEY—OFFICE HOURS: HEAVEN ALONE KNOWS.' He
reminisces, 'It was hot and stuffy in there, but it was also quiet and
peaceful, and I could read or write undisturbed.'

His passion for efficiency demanded a telephone, but that was
unheard of in an English row house—so he settled for a home-made
intercom system. He bought two ancient telephones for a few pennies
from a local junk stall, and connected them by wires to a primitive
battery. He installed one unit in an upstairs bedroom, the other in his
'office'. But the buzzer on the telephone was temperamental, and his
mother would not always hear it. Then Arthur would have to open
his cupboard door impatiently and yell upstairs, 'Mum, answer the
phone!'

The proud mother finally decided to let Arthur move out of the
tiny cupboard and use the front parlour which was seldom used,
immaculately tidy, but cold and draughty. This was a considerable
concession, a tribute to the prestige that the young would-be writer
commanded in his household.

Although Arthur denies it ('Don't let too much accuracy spoil a
good anecdote,' he sometimes says), he did well at school in most
subjects, but was a blockhead in mathematics. Forty-odd years later,
the owner of five electric calculators, he recalled the people who
taught him; in an article for the yearbook of the Lyford Cay School,
of which he is a board member, he wrote:

I remember the first teacher I ever had. Her name was Mrs.
Smith. She wore a grey skirt, did her hair in a bun, and she
taught me to spell 'dog' and 'cat', words which have remained
useful across the years. Mrs. Smith made the chalk squeak on
the blackboard—which didn't seem to bother her but sent shi-
vers up and down me, and still does, just thinking about it.

19

That was in England, and I was aged five. Soon after, I had another teacher who insisted our class learn the names of the books of the Bible and recite them aloud in sequence. We spent hours doing that and a fat waste of time it was! The experience taught me one thing—not to clutter the precious cupboard space of one's mind with piddling information which can be quickly looked up if needed. To this day, because of that teacher, I refuse to memorize addresses, dates, telephone numbers or my car licence plates. The mind has better uses.

It was a teacher named Miss Francis—I recall her as blonde and laughing a lot—who showed me, when I was seven, that memorizing *can* be beautiful. She had us all learn:

> *Where the bee sucks, there suck I*
> *In a cowslip's bell I lie;*
> *There I couch when owls do cry.*

Dear lady! Dear Miss Francis! Are you still alive, I wonder? Probably not. But I wish you could know that nearly fifty years later I wrote down those lines without having to look them up.

Another teacher I recall—this was several years further on—was referred to by his pupils as Crusty. He was an elderly, stern man with a big moustache which he waxed and rolled to points at both ends. Crusty was strict and frequently applied his cane to our reluctantly outstretched hands, but he was a good teacher and made learning interesting, especially geography. In fact, it was models we made of villages in far countries which gave me an urge to travel which I have never lost. Perhaps I would have had the urge anyway, but Crusty stimulated it.

Why did we call him Crusty? Well, during the year I was in his class he was summoned to court because he hadn't paid his bread bill. This was reported in the local newspaper and caused much tongue clacking and shaking of heads. Someone (it may have been me) cut out the news story and pinned it on the class notice board. It stayed there a couple of days before Crusty saw it. Then, while we waited, expecting an outburst, he quietly took it down, saying nothing. I remember hearing at the time he had an invalid wife and I've sometimes wondered what financial problems Crusty had at home which we never knew or thought about. Children can be cruel.

Which reminds me of another time. I was in a class of forty—all boys—and our teacher was a young, inexperienced Welshman named Mr. Jones. He wasn't a natural teacher, nor could he maintain discipline. As a result the classroom was often a noisy shambles. Twice the headmaster summoned Mr. Jones into his study to caution him, and word went around the school, as it always does. Nothing changed, though, until one morning

Mr. Jones simply didn't arrive.

Near noon the headmaster summoned the whole school to assembly and stood before us, looking shocked and pale. He said he was making an announcement of a kind he hoped never to have to make again. Mr. Jones was dead. Later we learned he hanged himself, presumably in despair.

That was tragedy. Another teacher provided—at times—slapstick comedy. He was known as The Mad Scientist and taught (what else?) elementary science. The work tables in his classroom were always in disorder, with bits of Leclanche cells spread around, and smelly chemicals, and old batteries broken open to extract the carbon cores. (We used them in building home-made microphones.) Nor were things helped by The Mad Scientist's habit of throwing the nearest book at any pupil who offended him. But we had fun and *learned, learned, learned.* I was aged twelve and the principles of electricity I picked up (Faraday's Law of Electrolysis, Ampere's electromagnetism discoveries, et al) are with me still.

But the teacher I remember most was a Mr. Swallow, who taught me mathematics during my final year in school when I was thirteen. At that time, in Britain, fourteen was the end of the line for schooling unless your parents had money. Mine didn't.

Mr. Swallow discovered two things about me early in our relationship. One, I was hopeless at maths. Two, I enjoyed writing stories. I suppose he recognized I had some kind of flair in the second direction so, while others in the class were doing algebra and long division, he encouraged me to write stories instead, giving me a pass mark in maths, though I didn't deserve it. He also guided my reading in the hours out of school and, looking back, I know that year with Mr. Swallow was the most important educational experience in my life.

We kept in touch, I'm glad to say, and I visited him in his later years, whenever I was in England. He also wrote to me from time to time, saying he was glad his instinct about my writing stories had worked out. Mr. Swallow died a few years ago. His widow wrote to tell me and, as I read her letter, suddenly I couldn't see it very clearly through my tears.

It has long been possible for a bright child in England to win a scholarship to a grammar school. But competition in the early 1930s was impossibly tough. In Luton (with a population of 70,500 in 1931), there was only one Junior County Scholarship for the whole town, given annually to the very best of the brainiest eleven-year-olds. Hundreds of children from poorer homes who automatically left school aged fourteen were more than capable of benefiting from higher education—but such was the system. When Arthur's turn came, he was one of the top two contestants. The last hurdle was a personal interview. He lost out to the other candidate—a girl. I think his profound respect for women was nurtured on that day.

On hearing the news of Arthur losing out to the girl, Elsie did the next best thing. She urged her boy to go to evening classes to learn shorthand and typing, and she scrimped and saved to pay for the tuition. His resolve to become a reporter heightened each time he attended the school: from the windows of that building he could see into the local newspaper offices.

Alas, when he left school soon after his fourteenth birthday—'one of the few sad days of my life'—and applied for a job on the newspaper, the receptionist gave it to him straight: 'We only take on boys who've been to grammar school.'

With his shorthand and typing, though, Arthur did get employment as an office boy with an estate agent. His first wage: five shillings a week. Soon he was typing letters. But he was not an accomplished typist, and was cautioned several times about mistakes he had made. One day he left off a zero in a price quotation of a big factory property for sale. The head of the company signed the letter quickly, without spotting the error. There was hell to pay when acceptance of the deal came in at the lower figure—one tenth of the real price. Telephones to and from London were busy all morning. The boss was late for his weekly Rotary luncheon meeting. Late as he was, though, he took time to stop by Arthur's desk and fire him.

Arthur managed over the next few years to earn a living of sorts and to stay out of the factory. He continued to read avidly and to write—poetry, letters, playlets, essays, short stories, all unpublished.

World War II changed his life.

It began on September 3, 1939. The previous day Arthur Hailey, aged nineteen, was mobilized. Recognizing that war was inevitable, he had enlisted in the Royal Air Force Reserve on August 8, 1939, rather than wait to be called up in the Army. Like thousands of other young men, he wanted to be a pilot. But AC2 Hailey (Aircraftsman, 2nd Class) discovered that the Air Force, like the newspaper business, required that applicants for pilot training should have a grammar school education.

His shorthand and typing, however, eventually funnelled him to a desk job and soon after, as a corporal, he was working as a clerk to the station administration officer—an elderly wing commander who loved nothing better than to fly. He loathed the time he had to spend in his office. Desk work has always been child's play to Arthur and he took over more and more chores—reading the mail, typing the letters in reply and presenting them as a *fait accompli* for his superior's signature.

The wing commander was delighted with this bright young chap who relieved him of so much time-wasting office work. He relied on Arthur more and more. Some days he barely glanced at letters he was signing—until one day his assistant over-reached. Arthur had typed the wrong answer to one of the incoming letters and it went out, signature and all, to the commanding officer. The wing commander was in deep trouble. How could he admit that it was his clerk whose judgment was in question?

He admonished Arthur with a never-to-be-forgotten line: 'Yes, Hailey . . . you're clever all right . . . but in a *night school* sort of way.'

During these early Air Force days, Arthur continued to write—mostly poetry, and lots of it. Some he kept, but most—he told me—he threw out.

There is one verse of a poem, 'Airborne, Climbing,' which he wrote in 1939, aged nineteen, that contained a toast he has used many times and still uses today. It was only recently, since writing this book, that I realized it was his own:

> *Let me remember old familiar faces*
> *Smiling again down half forgotten years,*
> *Shadows of laughter, friendship's lasting graces,*
> *Loves launched and lost—the boy god has no peers.*
> *Out of the past, and bearing no rejection,*
> *Distance and time shall bridge this final toast:*
> *'God bless my friends and all their imperfection!*
> *Of life's good gifts I counted this the most.'*

The poetry I liked best was unnamed and unfinished. He wrote it in spare moments while taking a jungle-survival course in Bhopal, India:

> *It is April in England now; the daffodil*
> *In golden muse has raised a curtain to the stage*
> *of Spring,*

> *And all her lovers, who are manifold,*
> > *Pause in that wonderment new life can never fail*
> > *to bring.*
> *Whatever time or tide shall bear upon their crest,*
> > *Whichever passions mark the twisty path of mortal*
> > *strife,*
> *Springtime shall never fail; how could it fail*
> > *While youth and birth and apple blossom hold their*
> > *sway of life?*
>
> *In the heat of a Burmese forenoon a gunner spoke to*
> > *another,*
> *'It is Springtime in England' he said and wiped out*
> > *the sweat from his eyes.*
> *Springtime, O God! for one glimpse of the meadows of*
> > *Sussex in morning;*
> *'They're coming again,' said the other as he pointed*
> > *into the skies.*
> *'Rapid fire'—the hell of the jungle made greater than*
> > *mind can conceive;*
> *Twin columns of death spit upwards as the business of*
> > *battle is on.*
> *Yet there in the ring sight he sees it: a pattern of*
> > *nodding tulips,*
> *Quiet gardens and shade of a beech tree: he slumps*
> > *and the vision is gone.*

Many young pilots, who had had the required education to learn to fly, were shot down and killed or wounded during the Battle of Britain. ('Perhaps that would have been my fate,' muses Arthur, 'if I'd got that scholarship.') It was a critical time and new pilots were desperately needed. The Royal Air Force lowered its scholastic requirements, and Corporal Hailey was accepted for pilot training. This was the time of Lend-Lease; as part of that programme, the U.S. Army Air Corps was training R.A.F. pilots in the U.S. So Arthur was sent to Americus, Georgia—little known at that time but now known better. President Carter's home is nearby.

Right from the beginning, he was chronically airsick. The students flew in open-cockpit planes—Stearman PT-17s—and wore heavy flying jackets. Each time Arthur put his on, the smell of stale vomit on the sheepskin collar wafted up to his nose, making him queasy even before climbing into a plane. Occasionally, he'd have to wash out the entire cockpit to clean up the mess. Air sickness slowed his progress in learning and he failed his first flight check. He was bitterly disappointed, because this automatically disqualified him from further training.

He was sent from the U.S. to a personnel depot in Nova Scotia, and from there to western Canada and, miraculously, another crack at flying. In a confidence only given pillow-to-pillow, he told me, 'A strong recommendation from my flying instructor reached my new posting. He said anyone who had spilled as much of his guts as I had, and then had some left over, should be allowed to take the course again.'

Occasional airsickness continued, but Arthur adjusted to it, finished his training successfully, and became a sergeant-pilot in 1943. Later that year he was commissioned. He reminisces: 'That was another turning point in my life. When I entered the Officers' Mess, I encountered a new world. From that day on, no one ever asked what my education was or where I went to school. It was assumed because I was an officer I was an educated person.'

In early 1944 Pilot Officer Hailey was on leave in Chicago. He was invited to a party given for visiting servicemen by the British Consul General. There he met Joan Fishwick, an English girl working at the Consulate. They fell in love over the weekend, and wrote letters to each other over the next three months. Then Joan flew to Prince Edward Island, where Arthur was stationed at that time, to be married on June 23, 1944.

It was a wartime romance—two young people who barely knew each other, looking for love and stability in a crazy, mixed-up world. Later they were to learn, sadly, they were not well suited. They were both amiable people who had little in common, and whose differences brought out the worst in each other.

Arthur's tours of duty took him back to England, and then on to the Middle East and Far East. He flew reconnaissance patrols in the Mediterranean which he now describes as 'unadventurous and unspectacular'. Never a daredevil, and unable to comprehend the pleasure men get from hunting, he is thankful that he never killed anyone during World War II. Later in the war he was tapped to fly top brass around—from the Army as well as the R.A.F.—and became known to some of his fellow pilots as 'Straight and Level Hailey'.

CHAPTER 3

Rip Cord

It was the luck of the draw that Arthur had the kind of war he had, never in the front line of action. This gave him the time to write; he continued to do so whenever he got the chance.

On one occasion, stationed in Perth, Scotland, he and his fellow flyers were cooped up for days in an R.A.F. crew room. They were waiting for the weather to break so they could get out and fly. Arthur had read everything in sight and was becoming bored. He decided to write a story.

'Rip Cord' was the result. It was published in *Courier*, a now-defunct British magazine, and later reprinted in *American Story Digest*.

Of all Arthur's early writing I believe this showed most clearly the promise of what was to come. The best of his talents—for story-telling, for suspense, for action-packed drama—is contained in this one short story, written when he was twenty-four.

RIP CORD

By Arthur Hailey

You'll understand I don't want to shoot a line, but if I am to make this story clear I must first explain that I pride myself on being a fairly efficient sort of cove. Not that I'm an admin type or anything like that, but what I mean is—in a personal sort of way. For instance, I always carry plenty of stamps, fill my fountain-pen every other night, and have the answer pat when someone asks: 'What's the date to-day?' I invariably possess string and brown paper and the latest bus and train timetables; in fact, scarcely a day goes by without someone in the mess requiring the use of one of these.

As I say, this isn't a line, but merely serves to highlight the essential difference between my own outlook and that of Forsyth.

Now, Forsyth's was not a commonplace character; in lots of ways I used to think he had a spark of genius somewhere inside. His was among the finer powers of leadership I have known; when you were tired or cold or scared stiff—as everyone is at times—he could send words over the aircraft intercom in that quiet, laconic voice of his which would summon up the blood and set you back on the job again, ashamed at your own weakness. He had endurance too, and high courage; we found that out the night we went to Essen. With the navigator out from a cannon shell, I was doing my best to plot our way home. We made it, but it wasn't until we'd landed and Forsyth had fallen forward over the control column that we discovered he too had caught a packet in the leg and shoulder.

All these qualities, and more, were Forsyth's. But against them was one failing. He possessed neither eye nor memory for detail. I know; you see, I was his second pilot.

We first met, he and I, when his own second dickie was down with 'flu. I was spare bod at the time so gravitated into the crew as a matter of course; after that, for one reason and another, we remained teamed up.

I remember his words at the beginning. 'The Wingco told me you're quite a nut on organization,' he said. 'That'll suit me down to the ground, because I'm not. Tell you what: you look after the details and I'll devote myself to grand strategy.' I laughed at the time, but in the end that was how things worked out.

There were occasions, as well, on which Forsyth's tongue could be scathing. I recall an air test one morning after a mess dance the evening before. I had disagreed with his opinion that an unserviceable synchroscope was not a vital replacement. Looking back I am inclined to think he was right and the immediate readiness of our machine more important just then. However, the torrent of abuse he heaped upon my head was inexcusable.

'The trouble with you, Brown,' he said towards the end, 'is that you have a conventional name and a conventional mind to go with it. Your sort lacks the imagination to improvise. Of course, I can fly without a synchroscope; in fact, I'll go on airspeed and compass alone if there's a job to be done.'

Later, at lunch, he apologised and afterwards, I discovered, spent the afternoon bullying an unfortunate instrument repairer into doing the job at maximum speed and in time for ops that night.

In that you have the man: impatient of detail, yet with eyes to see the vaster scheme beyond it: discerning—for I have often thought ruefully how true was his assessment of my own character—yet big enough to allay a doubt he did not share.

I have often wondered if he chuckled that afternoon while the synchroscope was being changed. Did he really believe that in a thousand-plane raid on Germany it mattered whether or not our own engines were turning over at equal revolutions, to a hair's breadth? I doubt it, but I wish I'd asked him to tell me his thoughts then. Now, I shall never know them.

In time, of course, as we came to know one another better, each was more tolerant of the other's ideas. I was content to accept Forsyth's captaincy and he became used to my concern with safety and keeping to the rules. 'Here comes old Mother Brown,' he used to tell the others in the crew. Then to me: 'I see a gleam in your eye, Browny. I'll bet there's a new Flight order out.' But for all this banter, I like to think that he relied on me a good deal.

It was on one of these occasions I first broached the question of an extra parachute. I had read several times of crews bailing out in a hurry and someone pulling his rip cord while still in the aircraft. Against this possibility I had conceived the idea of carrying a spare. When I suggested it to Forsyth he laughed, as I had known he would, but agreed. 'Go ahead,' he said, 'if you can fix it up.' At that I spoke honeyed words to a W.A.A.F. Corporal and it was arranged without much difficulty that one would be placed in our machine each day. So, from that time onwards, when we rode on ops there was a spare umbrella stowed beneath the navigator's table.

After a while I think the others almost forgot it was there; indeed they had no cause to remember. Until one night over the Ruhr.

We had been to Cologne to pay an unfriendly call, and on the way back Jerry tossed up everything he had. We had come to what we thought was the fringe of his defences when the flak hit us. There was a violent explosion to port and the starboard wing went down till it was well-nigh vertical. With the two of us on the controls we managed to straighten up and, as we did, the engineer came stumbling forward. He snatched back the port outer throttle and slapped down the feathering button. Then, pulling the helmet away from Forsyth's ear:

'We're on fire.'

As number one engine faltered and stopped, Forsyth reached

for the extinguisher handle, selected 'port outer' and pulled hard. We could see the glow of fire inside the aircraft now. I leaned across and tugged Forsyth's arm.

'Is it going out?'

He turned in his seat.

'No.'

Then I saw him switch on the intercom. His voice rattled in my head-set; it was unhurried and entirely calm.

'Pilot to crew. Abandon aircraft. Jump. Jump.'

The next few minutes are confused in my mind. I had my own harness to secure and pack to fasten. I do know that when I turned to Forsyth to help with his, his lips formed a query.

'I think there's a 'chute under the nav's table.'

I nodded.

'Pass it up, will you?'

I remember thinking disgustedly: 'Another detail; this time he's forgotten to bring a parachute.' However, there was no time for discussion, so I turned to move aft. I had taken a step when, midway down the fuselage, there was a bellying of white silk. In a flash I knew what was happening; the mid-upper gunner had pulled his cord prematurely.

I went back to tell Forsyth. For a moment he started and I think he paled. Then he laughed.

'Well, you're vindicated, Browny; I give you best. Let him take the spare.' I suppose I hesitated, for he lost his calm then and yelled. 'For God's sake give him it and get out! I can't hold her much longer; she's going to roll.'

At that I turned aft again and signalled to the navigator. Forsyth was Captain of Aircraft and I knew the rules of the game.

The gunners got away first, then the wireless op clamped his key and followed them—after that, the engineer. Normally I precede the navigator, but I waved him past. He went; a burning aircraft is no place in which to argue.

I fumbled my way forward into the cockpit. Forsyth saw me. I am sure he knew what was in my mind for his eyes blazed and frantic words rose to his lips.

'You thundering fool! Get out! Get out!'

Then—and although I am not certain, I like to believe this—his eyes softened and he nodded and grinned. It was then I knew I would go and leave him behind.

As I drifted down, I saw above me and away to the west, a great red glow which lighted the skies. Then it fell, with Forsyth inside, like a meteor, to earth. There was cloud below and I didn't see him go in.

Of the last I am glad.

*   *   *

The way home through occupied territory is tortuous and, what with leave as well, it was a few months before I returned to the squadron for duty. But one day, shortly after getting back, I ran into the W.A.A.F. Corporal who ruled the parachute section. She expressed pleasure at seeing me once more, then asked about our last trip.

'It's a long story,' I told her.

She thought for a moment, then: 'I was sorry to hear about Mr. Forsyth.'

'We all were,' I said.

I was moving away when she made a remark.

'It was a good job you didn't need the spare 'chute that night.'

I turned abruptly.

'What was that?'

'I said it was a good job you didn't need the spare 'chute. I suppose Mr. Forsyth told you about it.'

'No,' I said, 'I don't think he did.'

'Well, we had everything out that night and, what with a lot being up for packing, I couldn't put the usual spare in your machine. I explained to Mr. Forsyth when he came in for his own 'chute.'

'His own?' I interjected.

'Oh yes, he was in for it during the afternoon. It wasn't completely packed so he asked me to have it put in the aircraft.'

I drew in my breath. 'I suppose he didn't, by any chance, tell you to put it in a particular place.'

'As a matter of fact he did,' said the Corporal. 'I remember that. Under the navigator's table, he said.' She looked at me sharply. 'I hope he found it.'

'Yes,' I said thoughtfully, 'we found it.'

After the war, Arthur realized he had no trade or profession. He knew how to fly an aeroplane—that was all. And now he had a wife to support. Clinging to security, he sought a peacetime commission and worked in the Air Ministry in London, writing pamphlets to be used in air-crew training and also editing an R.A.F. magazine, *Air Clues*. With money saved from his wartime pay, he bought a small house in Morden, Surrey.

Joan and Arthur Hailey's first son, Roger, was born there in 1946.

Their life was comfortable. An Air Force officer's pay was good and, since his duties were not onerous, Arthur began earning extra money from free-lance writing—mostly about aviation. His skill at transforming technical material into simple language was already well developed, and demand for his articles increased. He even

found, in some Air Ministry files, a series of official memos which
gave him an idea. He condensed the memos, rewrote them slightly,
then sold the result to *Punch*. Here's how that piece appeared in the
May 1, 1946 issue:

FULL CIRCLE
MINUTE 1

S.14

The new offices into which this Directorate is to move next
week are very dirty. May they be redecorated, or at least thoroughly cleaned, before we go in, please?

W. H. BARROW, Wing Commander.
18 Feb.   *Deputy Director of Air Activity.*

MINUTE 2

W/Cdr. Barrow

It is regretted that due to shortage of labour and materials,
decoration within the Ministry cannot be undertaken at the
present time. It will also be impossible to make arrangements
for any cleaning other than that which is normally carried out by
the cleaning staff.

E. W. TORQUE,
21 Feb.   *Higher Clerical Officer.*

MINUTE 3

S.14

Very well; we will get together and do the place up ourselves.
Distemper is cheap enough, and we can borrow some brushes.
23 Feb.   W. H. BARROW, *W/Cdr.*

MINUTE 4

W/Cdr. Barrow
Your Minute 3.

Whilst not unsympathetic towards the 'Help Yourself" campaign, we are afraid we must enter a caveat against any such
measure being taken, as it is contrary to the policy of the Ministry of Works to allow any works services in Government
offices to be carried out by other than their own employees or,
alternatively, by contractors appointed by that department.

The fact that the Ministry of Works cannot undertake this
work at present is no excuse for members of the staff to take the
law into their own hands. Such a proceeding would be highly ir-
regular.

26 Feb.   E. W. TORQUE, *H.C.O.*

Minute 5

W/Cdr. Barrow
I am now informed that, in spite of the previous minute, the work under discussion has been carried out by officers on your staff. I shall be glad of your explanation.
5 March.   E. W. Torque, *H.C.O.*

Minute 6

S.14
Sorry. I forgot to cancel the order.
7 March.   W. H. Barrow, *W/Cdr.*

Minute 7

W/Cdr. Barrow
On this subject I have received very strong representations from the Ministry of Works that the offices occupied by you, and recently redecorated, should be restored to their former condition until such time as the Ministry is able to deal with this matter. I may add that the Ministry take an extremely serious view of the incident, and if a satisfactory solution is not reached within the near future there are likely to be serious repercussions.
12 March.   E. W. Torque, *H.C.O.*

Minute 8

S.14
There seems no doubt that the work must be undone, and the new distemper fetched off the walls. However, now we are aware of the delicate position, we feel we ought not to do anything more ourselves, but wait for the Ministry to do the job. Will you get in touch with them?
16 March.   W. H. Barrow, *W/Cdr.*

Minute 9

W/Cdr. Barrow
Your request at Minute 8 is noted. However, we regret that owing to shortage of labour and materials it will not be possible for this work to be put in hand for some considerable time. Nevertheless, the matter will be borne in mind and an endeavour made to effect removal of the distemper at some future date. Perhaps you will confirm that this arrangement is agreeable.
25 March.   E. W. Torque, *H.C.O.*

Minute 10

S.14

Perfectly. There's no hurry for a year or two; I'm having the file brought forward on 1st April, 1951.

31 March.   W. H. Barrow, *W/Cdr.*

Postwar England, however, soon palled in contrast to Arthur's memory of North America. In his work he was frustrated by an Air Ministry official censor, a retired senior officer, who blue-pencilled attempts to inject humour into the R.A.F. magazine. Even now Arthur describes him angrily as 'a dried-up split pea of a man who never had an original thought in his life'. Arthur was impatient, too, with the continuing British restrictions—the beginning of what he saw as a socialist bureaucracy which would stifle initiative and curtail freedom. Food was rationed. Life was dreary.

He wanted to put up a clothes-line in his backyard and needed a wooden post. He tried to buy the timber, only to be told he needed a permit, which he would have to apply for at the local municipal offices, then wait for a decision. His reaction was: 'This is authority gone mad! Is this what the war was all about?'

Impulsively he decided to emigrate to Canada and bought air tickets. Then he enquired how he could resign his R.A.F. commission—and promptly did.

Joan was delighted at the idea of a return to North America. She was deeply attached to her mother, sister, and two brothers, who lived in Chicago; she missed them greatly.

Arthur's parents were devastated. The idea of uprooting one's life to emigrate was completely alien to their cautious natures.

Elsie said: 'But you're doing so well.' And indeed, in her terms, he was. A desk job, a commission, good pay, and a small but steady income from free-lance writing; in all, he was earning about one thousand pounds a year, a princely sum in 1947 for a twenty-seven-year-old.

George said: 'I can't understand it. Why, you've just painted your house.'

New paint job or not, the house was sold. Arthur and Joan, with baby Roger, now one year old, emigrated to Canada. (It was Roger's first flight ever—on American Overseas Airlines. Years later, Roger went to work for American Airlines and also met his wife Linda there. They are both still employed by that company.)

33

When Arthur Hailey arrived in Toronto in November 1947, he felt he was returning to a country he knew. He had, of course, spent part of his R.A.F. wartime career there, training to be a pilot, and he had been in all nine provinces. (Note to the exact: Newfoundland became the tenth province in 1949.) This knowledge gave him a big advantage over other newcomers, particularly in the matter of becoming accepted by Canadians. For there is a tendency for many English immigrants to think they are God's gift to the world—and it is a rude awakening for them to discover this is seldom the case. In postwar Canada, in fact, Englishmen were not overly popular. With their rumpled suits, longish hair, and superior attitude ('Well, of course, we don't do it quite that way back home'), they were easily spotted and given short shrift.

In his thorough fashion, Arthur determined to shed his Englishness. He discarded his British clothes, delved into his savings and bought a new North American suit with wide shoulders and wide lapels, and—a wide-brimmed hat. He also adopted the North American custom of shortening first names and, with a bit of a shudder, began introducing himself as 'Art Hailey'.

He made the rounds of newspaper and magazine offices. They all said more experience was needed. However, a large magazine publishing company, Maclean-Hunter, was impressed enough to offer mild encouragement—but no job. So he joined a small real estate business—no salary, just commissions—and earned enough money to get by. He also made a habit of dropping in to Maclean-Hunter periodically to remind them he was still interested in working for them.

Three months later, persistence paid off. When the trade magazine *Bus & Truck Transport* needed a new assistant editor, he was hired.

He bought a small five-room bungalow in a new suburb of Toronto, and a used car. Then he put all of his energy into his job, the way many people do when they are unhappy at home. He and Joan were not getting along too well—though, obviously, it was not all bad. Their closer moments produced two more sons—John and Mark—while Arthur's conscientious efforts at work were rewarded when he was promoted to editor in the autumn of 1949. That was about the time I joined Maclean-Hunter's typing pool, having found it as difficult as he had to land a writing job.

Joan left Arthur just before Christmas of 1949 to go back to her mother in Chicago. She took with her Roger, now three; John, twenty-two months; and Mark, three months. It must have been a painful decision for her, but I can imagine her life was not happy. She probably felt cut off and imprisoned, living so far out of town with small children and no transport. She desperately missed her family, and Arthur's preoccupation with his work, which I came to know only too well later on, surely increased her loneliness.

On Christmas morning, 1949, Arthur Hailey—alone in his small house—thumbed his nose at the world by doing his washing and hanging it out to dry, when everyone else in the block was involved in Christmas festivities.

CHAPTER 4

'Someday I Will Live Like This!'

Arthur was almost eight years old when I was born—in London on December 5, 1927. But while *his* mother had been overjoyed at giving birth, mine was not.

My mother, Beatrice Maud (née Willbourn), already had three daughters—Doris, eleven; Gina, eight; Frances, six. I was not even an afterthought; I was a mistake. Mother had had two miscarriages after the birth of Frances. I could well have been the third, but fate was kind to me.

My father, James Watt Dunlop, was a mistake too. His father was a Scottish baronet, Sir Richard M. (I know the full name but, to avoid potential problems, am omitting it here.) The only flaw in Dad's ancestry was that his mother was one of Sir Richard's house-maids, and the whole affair was hushed up. As a small child, James Watt was sent from Edinburgh to London to live with a kind lady whom we later knew as Grandma Dunlop. She treated Jim as her own son and gave him her name. He grew up to be something of a loner, ever conscious of his background, which in that generation was considered a stigma. How different his life might have been as a legitimate son!

As the youngest of four, I was undoubtedly spoiled. At first, my sisters fought over who was going to push the pram when the family went out walking. A few months later, the novelty of a baby sister having worn off, they fought over who was *not* to take me out. I had become a damn nuisance. And when they grew older, and Saturday-morning housecleaning chores were divided between them, they protested loudly that it wasn't fair I did no housework. My mother said I was too young.

Dad was not what you would call 'a good provider'—a term Mother used in later years when assessing son-in-law qualities. By trade he was a tailor's cutter, but during my childhood he had a variety of jobs which paid him a weekly wage of three to five pounds. Out of this he gave my mother the smallest amount he could get away with, and squirrelled away the rest. Saving money was his passion in life; he would walk miles rather than spend a few pennies on bus fare, and in his view, everything but food was too expensive to buy. But he was a wonderful father of small children; he preferred their company to that of grown-ups. And he had a delightful Cockney sense of humour. With adults, however, he was shy and reticent. He scarcely ever took my mother out for an evening, yet he resented her friends dropping in to see her.

For Mother was warm, outgoing, generous. She loved company, and everyone adored her. She deserved a better life but cheerfully accepted her lot because she loved my father, as he did her. We were a happy, close-knit family. All of us had a real sense of fun.

Mother was an accomplished dressmaker who worked at home and spent all her earnings on her family—for clothes, good food, house furnishings, and seaside holidays. I grew up in a household littered with paper dress patterns, lengths of fabrics, scissors, pins and needles. Behind every door hung a half-finished garment ready for a client's fitting. I spent a large part of many school lunch hours running errands to buy threads, zips and ribbons. More often than not when I arrived home after school, there would be a posh car—a Rolls, Daimler or Bentley—parked outside our house and I would be introduced to another fashionable lady. One of these beautiful persons, a Miss Thomas, took a liking to me and asked if she could take me on a two-week holiday to Broadstairs where she had a summer home.

At the time I had just recovered from rheumatic fever. I had been six weeks in Paddington Green Hospital and a further four months in a convalescent home near Bagshot in Surrey. So my mother readily agreed.

How well I remember that Broadstairs house!—a far cry from our working-class London home. It seemed always full of sunshine and flowers. The drawing room was furnished with deep, soft armchairs and sofas covered in bright chintz. I recall sitting in that room, sipping a drink of Rose's Lime Juice and water. The sun glinted on the ice cubes; I could see the lime cordial swirling around them. Until then I had not known anyone who owned a refrigerator which produced ice cubes.

This is one of my early and more beautiful memories. I thought: someday I will live like this!

Winning the Junior County Scholarship, which gave me a free place in a high school, helped me move toward that goal. Unlike Arthur, who missed out on the one similar scholarship given in his hometown, Luton, I lived in densely populated London, which offered more opportunities. My own scholarship included tuition and an annual grant to cover the cost of school uniforms.

The declaration of World War II in 1939 coincided with the beginning of my high school education. Earlier that year, after Germany invaded Czechoslovakia, talk of war was heard everywhere. It was not, '*If* there's a war . . .'; people said, 'When war begins . . .' I remember it all vividly. I was eleven and eager to start my new school. But the school, like most others in the London area, was to be 'evacuated' to the country. The thinking was: *Get the children out of the target areas.* No one seemed to know where we would go, or when, but the Government decreed that we must be ready to depart at a moment's notice.

Each child had a suitcase, packed with clothing and essentials, which was kept at school. Every day for the whole week before war was declared I said goodbye to my family and went to school, not knowing if I would be back. I carried some food for lunch and, over my shoulder, suspended by a string, my gas mask in its cardboard case. I remember the look of relief on my mother's face when I returned each day, the dreaded moment of departure having been postponed once more. Finally on Saturday, September 2—the same day that Royal Air Force Reservist Arthur Hailey was summoned to serve his King and country—our departure was announced. We would leave by train from Paddington Station, for some unknown destination. Only after we were on our way did we learn that we were going to Camborne in Cornwall.

There were about two hundred of us—confused kids marshalled by a dozen or so equally confused and harassed teachers—and this scene was repeated all over London and in the large industrial cities of the Midlands. Looking back on that long-ago day, seeing myself take leave of my family—a stoic little girl caught up in a maelstrom she scarcely understood, with an identification label pinned to her clothing and carrying that pathetic gas mask—I realize how grateful I am that my own children have been spared the trauma and heartache of war.

The 300-mile train journey seemed interminable; I had never been so far from London before. But at the end of the long ride the good people of Camborne greeted us. We were herded into a local school hall and the haphazard operation of 'billeting' began.

Some preparations had been made, though not many, and the procedure was new and bewildering to everyone. Under a hastily enacted law, every family in Camborne and other reception areas which had a spare bedroom was required to take in one or two children. The official compensation was the small sum of ten shillings a week per child. What had not been organized was which child was to go to what family. I remember hundreds of people wandering around, choosing likely looking candidates—as farmers might select livestock—then registering their choice at a row of tables where billeting officers were seated.

I had teamed up with a girl named Edna. We agreed to be roommates, but Edna and I were among the last few picked, and for a while we felt like outcasts. I was tall for my age, and perhaps our Cornish hosts passed me over because I looked as if I had a big appetite. If so, they were right. But finally a pleasant-looking woman approached and asked if we would like to stay with her.

'Well . . . yes, please!' I said. What else could we say?

She was a schoolteacher—fortyish, strict, but kind. We called her Miss Ivy. She and her spinster sister, Miss Elsie, lived with their aged mother. None of them was used to having children in their home, so all of us had lots to learn. The house was comfortable and we had excellent food. I can drool now, remembering Cornish pasties, stuffed with meat and vegetables, and buns, warm from the oven, served with home-made blackberry jam and fresh clotted cream.

Edna and I were mostly happy, though occasionally one or the other of us would be homesick. The worst time was the day after our arrival in Camborne. We heard Prime Minister Neville Chamberlain in a radio speech telling the country and the world that war was now declared. I went upstairs to our room, threw myself on the bed and sobbed. In my imagination I visualized German aircraft raining bombs on London and my parents and sisters lying injured or dead beneath bombed ruins.

But as the weeks went by and the 'phony war'—the pre-Dunkirk period—settled into stalemate, I recovered from these blues. My mother and I exchanged letters regularly. Life in London was nearly normal, although food rationing was beginning and more air-raid shelters were being built. It must have seemed strange, though, to see so few children around.

Our school—Paddington & Maida Vale High—proved too large to be absorbed into the Camborne community. I remember classes held on stairways, the teacher at the bottom, while we—the students—sat on the stairs using notebooks balanced on our knees. So we were moved one hundred and four miles east, to Torquay. There we shared accommodation on a shift basis with a local secondary school. My billet was three miles from the school, and I wrote an impassioned plea to my mother for a bicycle. She bought one cheaply from a factory which was selling its stock before conversion to a munitions plant. All through my older sisters' childhood they had dreamed longingly of owning a two-wheeled 'fairy bike', but every Christmas they were disappointed. Now suddenly the youngest got a bicycle—just by asking.

Many years later Gina, then fifty-five, jokingly remarked that I was always the most favoured, and being given a bicycle proved it. I cried out in surprise: 'Are you still bothered by *that?* Do you know that bike cost less than four pounds?'

'Is that *all?*' she said. 'Oh, well, now I don't feel so bad about it.' We both laughed, but the incident reinforced a belief: don't underestimate sibling rivalry.

So for three years, living in six different strange homes, I stayed away from London. Thus I escaped the 1940–41 blitzkrieg bombings which destroyed so much of Britain's cities and caused so many casualties. My parents were bombed out of one home but luckily were unhurt.

My sister Frances was conscripted into the army—the women's Auxiliary Territorial Service. Gina was required to take a war-production job—wiring the circuits of small radios for the armed services.

Then London went through a quiet spell and I pleaded with my mother by letter to let me return and transfer to another school— Kilburn & Brondesbury High. I was fourteen and disheartened by the length of time I had already been away from home. She agreed. Thus the remainder of my school life was spent in London and I was there to experience the terror of the German V-1 and V-2 air raids. V-1 was short for *Vergeltungswaffen Eins*, or Vengeance Weapon One. I remember several times cycling to school and hearing the engine of a V-1 'buzz bomb' above suddenly switch off—a fearful silence because it meant that the flying bomb, which had been travelling forward, was now heading down. As had been drilled into me, I would jump off my bike, lie down on the pavement and wait for the explosion. All of those times I was lucky; lots of others weren't. Dusting myself off, I would resume my journey to school.

At the height of the V-2 raids, our family trekked from our house at nights to sleep in street air-raid shelters. Others slept in the tube stations. My mother was terrified of these new weapons of war— with good reason; they were long-range rockets, described as the aerial counterpart of a naval torpedo. Because V-2s travelled faster than sound, there was no warning. One heard them coming *after* the explosion. I know now that I was a great trial to Mother at this time. Aged sixteen and a smart-aleck, I wanted to stay in my own bed. My attitude was (and is still): *If you're going to get it, you'll get it.* So every evening I grumbled as I hauled my sleeping bag to the shelter. Though everyone else was in street clothes and slept under blankets, I insisted on wearing pyjamas and sleeping between a white sheet lining I had devised and sewn myself.

It was against this continuing wartime background that I took my Junior Matriculation exam in 1944. It took place in a basement corridor of our school, where desks had been set up behind heavily sandbagged interior walls. When air-raid sirens sounded, all of us dived under our desks, abandoning the exam until the 'all clear'.

Despite the interruptions, I did well and my scholarship was extended to include two more years at high school, plus three at university. Foolishly, I turned it all down. A university education seemed totally alien to our way of life; my sisters (just as Arthur did) had all finished school and begun to work for a living at the age of fourteen. Observing the others, I was impatient to earn some money of my own; I did not want to be even partially dependent on my mother for a further five years. So at the age of sixteen I chose what seemed then a more practical scholarship—a year's secretarial training at Hendon Technical College.

Also, in a youthful, unthinking way, I hoped the war would continue until I was old enough to join the Wrens—the Women's Royal Naval Service. I assumed, of course, I would be an officer and could visualize myself in a smart tricornered hat involved in some important mission which would win the war.

However, the war in Europe ended in 1945 without my help, and on VE night my parents, my sister Doris and I, along with thousands of others, stood outside Buckingham Palace cheering the King and Queen, who waved to the crowds from a balcony. Then we moved on to Piccadilly Circus and there, as elsewhere, London went wild. Strangers hugged and kissed each other. We joined hands with them and sang lustily, 'There'll always be an England!' No one could quite believe it was all over.

Doris was twenty-eight and the mother of a little girl, Susan, aged four. Her husband, Frank, had been in North Africa and Europe with the British Eighth Army for four long years. Only when I was much older could I begin to comprehend what that night meant to Doris, and how much she and thousands like her had had to endure. Even so, it was another year before Doris and Frank were reunited.

My business training at Hendon Tech landed me a job with a major London book publisher soon after the war ended. I was first a secretary, then an editorial assistant. I loved the editorial job because of its variety. I checked the galley proofs of books to be published, read submitted manuscripts and wrote reports on them, then composed my own letters to would-be authors.

In the course of all this, I fell in love with my boss, a forthright man with a strong sense of humour; he, too, grew fond of me. Compared with all we hear about yeasty love affairs nowadays, it was a near-innocent relationship and I had the sense to realize there was no future in it. He was twenty-seven years older than I and married. In some ways it was a Pygmalion friendship. He was a scholar and an author of books, and while I was no flower girl like Eliza Doolittle, I had a lot to learn. He guided my reading, encouraged me to write, and emphasized the importance of correct, simple language and careful speech.

He took me once to meet his father, a retired minister with the same brand of humour. We had a lively discussion about religion; I

declared I had none. His father mentioned the Bible. I wrinkled my
brow and quipped, 'I don't remember that title . . . Who published
it?' I recall their laughter still.

Arthur, with whom I later discussed that old relationship, believes
it to have been an important influence and one of the best things that
ever happened to me. I think so too.

During those years I suspect I was a bit of a pain to those around
me. I know damn well I was an intellectual snob at home, without
much reason. I was scornful of the fact that my family took the *Daily
Mail* on weekdays and the *News of the World* on Sundays, both—as I
saw it—plebeian newspapers, so I ostentatiously bought the more
cerebral *Daily Telegraph* and Sunday *Observer*.

In later years, after I met Arthur, I learned that he, too, struggled
in similar ways to climb out of the limiting, lower-class environment
in which we were both born. Another thing I discovered was that
while I was working for the publishers, he was an R.A.F. staff officer
at the Air Ministry in Kingsway, not far away. Although our paths
did not cross at that time—at least, that we were aware of—I like to
think we were two kindred spirits destined to meet eventually.

In 1948 I had what I thought was a great idea. I would go to
Canada for a year.

My family figured I was crazy. They were shocked at my venturing
so far, with little money and no certainty of a job when I arrived. But
my good friend and mentor encouraged me. 'I shall miss you, you
Cockney heathen. But you ought to go,' he said. 'It will give you a
chance to be on your own and spread your wings.'

So I walked down the Strand to Canada House in Trafalgar
Square and took the required medical for would-be emigrants. Then
I booked passage on the Cunard liner *Ascania* for the following June,
and began saving for the fare. Boy, did I scrimp and save! Eight
months later, by the time I sailed from Liverpool on June 13, 1949, I
had not only paid for my fare to Canada, but had enough money to
get me back to England.

At various times in my life—this was one—I have silently thanked
my father for teaching me about saving for a purpose. I was never
sure what *his* purpose was; he lived to be eighty-three and, at his
death in 1970, had spent scarcely any of the money he saved across
the years. Eleven years earlier, when my mother died—from cancer
at the age of sixty-four—I was visiting England. My mother's wish

was that she be cremated with no flowers and minimal fuss, so the simple funeral I arranged was inexpensive. My father was the bene-ficiary of Mother's small life insurance, so I gave him the under-taker's bill. To my astonishment, he counted out the exact amount in cash—mostly one-pound notes which had been wrapped in an old shirt produced from a locked suitcase. The suitcase was kept on the top shelf of his locked wardrobe in his locked bedroom.

Dear Dad. Who knew what went on in his mind? My guess is that just the knowledge of his little nest egg gave him the security he was seeking all his life.

But back to my Canadian adventure.

The Atlantic crossing at first was rugged, then romantic. The 15,000-ton *Ascania* had been a wartime troopship and was only par-tially converted to peacetime use; it had been pressed into service be-cause of heavy demands for space on Canada-bound ships. I shared a cabin with nine other women; the youngest was forty-five. All were 'British mums' visiting daughters who had met and married Cana-dian servicemen while the latter were in Britain. I was only twenty-one and desperately seasick, so they mothered me. While I was sick— for four agonizing days I still remember—most of the unmarried male and female emigrants on board were pairing off. My cabin-mates were distressed that—as they put it—I was being 'left on the shelf' or, more accurately, the topmost bunk.

Then two of the women reported to me: 'We've met a really nice young man. His name is John Smith (it really was), he's twenty-eight, English, tall, dark, good-looking. He's just right for you, Sheila, and we've told him about you.'

On the fifth day out, seasickness left me and John and I were intro-duced. We did, indeed, hit it off. So well that, five days later when we disembarked in Montreal, we were discussing getting married. A shipboard romance is unique. We were in limbo with nothing to do except get to know each other, which we thought we did by journey's end. He was returning from a vacation in England; earlier he had emigrated to Canada, where he was a second engineer on a cargo boat which carried bauxite from the Saguenay in Quebec to South America. He said that after his next voyage he would meet me in Toronto, where I was headed, and we would continue our romance.

We did meet about three months later, and we dined and danced. Later that night, alone, I thought: *Whatever did I see in him? He's not my type at all.* I guess John felt the same way, because our big passion fizzled in just a couple of days.

Once in Toronto, as I explained earlier, I took the only job I could get: as one of forty typists in a pool at Maclean-Hunter Publishing Company. I loathed it. I had to punch a time clock twice a day—in at 8:30 A.M., out at 5 P.M. and, in between, charge every minute of my time to the various departments I typed letters for. It was a jolting contrast to the relaxed, almost lazy atmosphere of the office I had been used to in London, with its numerous coffee and tea breaks.

As I have already related, it was during my six-month stint in the typing pool that I encountered one A. F. Hailey over a dictaphone cylinder. Readers know the rest except . . .

When a secretarial vacancy occurred in any of the Maclean-Hunter offices, it was usually filled by someone promoted from the pool. But I didn't want to be a secretary; I wanted to write. So I turned down two jobs, even though they offered higher pay, and kept badgering the head of the pool to consider me if a writing job came up. Eventually one did and I became an editorial assistant on *Canadian Homes & Gardens* at a salary of $150 a month—precisely what I was earning as a typist.

Still, I was seeking experience and was glad to make the change. My first assignment was to write an article: 'How To Make Good Coffee'. I remember the editor, Jerry Maccabe, laughing. 'Here, Limey! See what you can do with this. Everybody knows the coffee in England's god-awful, so maybe you can learn something at the same time.'

Looking back, I realize my article was pedestrian. I researched and wrote about types of coffee pots, the need to measure water and coffee accurately, why it was important to have a meticulously clean pot. I also described a strange experiment allegedly proving why one should use fresh cold water when making coffee. A restaurateur I consulted told me that if one put goldfish in a container of chilled 'old' water from a hot water tank, they would die. However, those that were dunked in fresh water always survived. To this day, I don't know if he was kidding me, or what it really had to do with making coffee. Anyway, I wrote it, and it was printed.

In my second article, published a month later, I told readers how to weather-strip their houses. That, too, was something new to me; in fact, I had no idea until then what weather-stripping was. This was ironic, since I was born and lived in English houses, which must be among the draughtiest in the world and in great *need* of weather-stripping.

I went on to edit a monthly garden column, even though I had not lived in a house with a garden since I was seven years old.

I was slightly more on track when I became associate editor of *Brides Book*, a magazine published twice-yearly; at least I had a steady boy friend by then—Arthur. My responsibilities included writing about wedding etiquette: how invitations and announcements should be worded, who pays for what, which family gives the rehearsal dinner, and so on. At the back of my mind during all this I was sure that, no matter whom I married, hardly any of it would affect me. A good deal of what I had to write I considered a lot of nonsense. I tried to sum up my feelings in an introduction to the etiquette section:

> Here for your guidance are eight pages of wedding etiquette. They cover everything from the engagement announcement to the party after the reception, and are as complete as we can make them. We hope they will be useful.
>
> But one word of advice. If you find that your budget won't stretch to the wedding of your dreams, don't worry. If you know deep down inside that a large formal wedding is outside your way of life, don't strive for it. Keep it simple and unaffected, and your wedding will be just as lovely.
>
> For you are marrying the man of your choice. That is the thing that matters. Have a lovely wedding—yes. Take care in its preparation and you will make it just that. But don't put greater importance on the wedding than on the marriage. The wedding is the first step toward a full and happy life with the man you love: the marriage *is* that life.

Although it was still my intention to stay in Canada only until the end of 1950, I was eager, while the opportunity existed, to see as much of North America as possible. So I decided to use August and September for a trip across Canada and the U.S., and persuaded a newfound Canadian friend, Madge Sloley (now Kerr), to accompany me. Having made that decision, it was obvious I would have to start saving again.

It seems incredible when I think about it now, but out of my $150 monthly salary, I saved $600 over the next six months. My landlady, Mrs. McCordick, helped by charging only $7 a week for half a room and board (I shared a bedroom with her daughter, Irene), provided I would do some of the household ironing. I eagerly agreed. I eliminated bus fares by scrounging rides to and from work with neighbours who drove cars, and Arthur helped too. Because he was in love he wanted to be with me during all of his spare time. He took me to movies, plays, frequently to dinners, and often paid for my lunches. On other days I brown-bagged it with a sandwich, buying a ten-cent cup of coffee. If I wanted to see my travel agent, as was sometimes necessary, I bought a bus ticket and passed up the coffee. Occasionally, something beyond my control loused up my savings programme. For instance, if there was a collection in the office for some gift or other, I'd reluctantly have to rob my holiday fund.

My travel agent was a Mr. Corrigan, who worked for Canadian Pacific Railway. Poor man—he organized the itinerary for our two-month trip and we were forever changing plans. Mostly our itinerary hinged on where we could get free accommodation from friends or relatives or *their* friends or relatives. When Madge and I could find no way of freeloading, we would stay at a YWCA. I remember one 'Y' in Victoria, British Columbia. The bill was seventy-five cents each per night, in return for which we had a comfortable, clean bed in a curtained-off cubicle.

My Toronto employers gave me a two-month leave of absence and wangled a free rail pass for the Canadian portion of my journey. This was good-natured of them, because I had already taken a two-week vacation in July to go on that glorious camping jaunt with Arthur.

It was a memorable trip. We travelled by train across Canada and the U.S., and for the first time I realized the vastness of both countries. I recalled my train journey to Cornwall the day before World War II began; it seemed trivial by comparison. I thought the Canadian prairies would never end. We travelled through wheatfields all day, then went to sleep in our berths, and next morning the landscape was precisely the same—nothing but wheat stretching to the horizon. And the majestic beauty of the Canadian Rockies was overwhelming. I already liked Canada; on that trip I fell in love with it.

Madge and I adapted to our surroundings wherever we went. Dressed in slacks, we drank beer with oil workers in Devon, Alberta, a boom town amid Canada's burgeoning oil fields. It was a frontier community with wooden pavements and a true western atmosphere. We were in a tavern and the only women there. By contrast, two days later, wearing our prettiest dresses, we sipped daiquiris as guests in Vancouver's elegant Royal Yacht Club.

We travelled through the state of Washington to Portland, Oregon, to visit a one-time school chum of mine, Beryl Davenport (now McDonald), who had married a G.I. in London after the war. In San Francisco we had pleasant accommodation at the YWCA for only $2.50 a night each, but in Los Angeles we stayed in a decrepit, seedy downtown hotel. Our room was next to the outside fire escape; we were glad of that because the place was a firetrap. As we turned on the lights, the switch sparked and we'd see cockroaches scampering on the floor. It was certainly cheap, but we were jolted by that crummy hostelry. Fortunately, we were there only two nights.

It was in Los Angeles that I realized how close we were to the Grand Canyon. I wanted to alter our itinerary to go there, but Madge, who had given in to my whims until then, was adamantly against it: 'Sheila, we cannot do *everything*. I'm not going to change plans any more, so there!' (I have been around most of the world with Arthur, but still haven't made it to the Grand Canyon. Someday I hope to.) Anyway, we continued on schedule to Lake Mead, Las Vegas, Salt Lake City, Chicago, Detroit, then back to Toronto.

Arthur greeted me on my return, looking trim and prosperous. He had cut down on his eating and his weight; and with some extra money he'd earned doing free-lance radio broadcasts, he had bought himself a smart new brown suit, with all the trimmings. He smiled happily, delighted that I was back. And I was glad to be back, feeling at home and comfortable with him. I thought: *This guy is going to be hard to give up.*

But there was never any doubt in my mind I *would* put Arthur behind me, for I was determined to go back to England. About a month after my return from the trip, Arthur phoned me one morning. At that point he was taking me to lunch almost every day, but I told him I was busy that noon hour. He was persistent; he wanted to know what I was doing. I hedged, but he didn't give up.

'If you must know,' I finally told him, 'I'm starting to make plans to go home. Today I'm going to the library to look up names and addresses of magazines in England, so I can write ahead to ask for interviews when I get back.'

There was a long silence.

'I'll come and help you,' he said at last.

And he did. As we walked to the library, neither of us spoke. I felt sad because I knew Arthur was upset and close to tears. Then we sat in the reference room and, while he located and read out the information, I wrote it all down.

I need not have bothered. In the end, my practical head lost out. Some six weeks later, when we said our tearful goodbyes in Toronto's Union Station, my heart told me I would be back.

CHAPTER 5

Getting Married—
the Hard Way

Once the decision to marry was made, and with my family reconciled to the idea, I felt exhilarated and wanted to rush back to Canada. But I stayed at home for four months and tried to compensate a little for my absence for the remainder of my life. I realized, as did my parents and sisters, that it might be a long time before I could visit England again—as it turned out, I didn't get back until six years later.

Meanwhile, Arthur and I lived for each other's letters. Among other subjects he kept me informed about the slow progress of his divorce. His wife, Joan, had already agreed to a divorce and had established the necessary one-year residency in Illinois where she was living, but each legal step was discouragingly slow. As to my activities, I reported to Arthur that I had undertaken a writing project. Though I needed money, it was difficult to get a job for such a short period and my old publishing flame came to the rescue. He suggested I write one of a series of children's schoolbooks he was editing. My book would be based on the story of a medieval French soldier, Pierre Terrail Bayard, who was knighted in 1495. The payment was an outright £25. I said okay and set to work reading about Bayard, then retelling his story in the needed format.

While all this was happening, my mother and I spent most of our days together, she at her sewing machine, me at a typewriter. During intervals from work we discussed what the family might give me as wedding presents. Mother wondered how much money we could pry loose from Dad. (He eventually came through with £30, enough to buy a set of china, with twelve of everything. Alas! by the time Arthur and I could afford to entertain twelve people at one meal, I was weary of the pattern, but it has since served our children well in various college lodgings.)

I remember one day when Mother met me for lunch after I had spent the morning shopping for china, linen and furnishings in department stores on Oxford and Regent Streets. She greeted me with a long face and said uncertainly: 'Sheila, I have to break the news to you. A letter came . . . and it's been turned down. I'm sorry I opened it . . . I know how much it means to you.'

Arthur's divorce! A sudden knot of dread tightened within me.

'What did the letter say?' I asked.

'Your manuscript isn't good enough.'

'Oh, is *that* all!' I almost cried in relief.

The letter, which I read later, advised me that the manuscript needed more work—which I did. Then I received my £25 and, in due course, *Bayard the Fearless* was published. (Seeing my name on a book did not go to my head; it's taken me twenty-seven years to produce another.)

At last, after a tearful family farewell, I sailed once more to Canada aboard the *Ascania*, only this time in better, refurbished quarters.

During my absence Arthur had saved enough money to pay for my Atlantic crossing and to buy an old 1938 Buick for five hundred dollars. He drove this museum piece from Toronto to Montreal to meet me, and was waiting outside Customs when we docked—to bail me out again, as it developed. I had failed to realize there would be import duty to pay on the wedding presents. Thus, after long separation from my betrothed, my first romantic words were: 'Have you got any money?'

In a grand gesture he threw his wallet over the barricade, then silently wondered if he'd have enough money left for petrol to get us back to Toronto. That was my man!—supremely generous, and with great style.

In 1951 it would never have occurred to either one of us to live together, a practice that has become commonplace in the seventies. I went back to stay with my adopted Canadian family. The McCordicks had been kinder and more generous than any people I had known. I truly loved them, and I think they had grown fond of me too. But Mrs. McCordick was deeply religious and easily shocked. It troubled her profoundly that I was going to marry a divorced man. 'Are you *sure*,' she said to me one day, 'that you know what you're doing? Arthur is still a married man, with three young sons. He's an older man too. (He was all of thirty-one by this time.) You're only twenty-three and, you know, Sheila, you're not bad-looking . . . there'll be *other* chances!'

The one thing that troubled me was—yes, Arthur *was* still married. I had already shelved girlish dreams of a white wedding in a huge cathedral filled with every person I ever knew. (As for the honeymoon . . . well, we had already had that. No one has ever had a better one than our camping trip.) I just wanted to get married, any way, any how.

Canada had the most impossible, antiquated divorce laws at the time and, strictly speaking, an Illinois divorce was not recognized. It was imperative, in order that our union be legal *somewhere*, that we marry in the United States. Finally, we heard from Arthur's Toronto lawyer, Sam Benedetto, that the divorce was granted on June 14, 1951, and that the papers would be in his office by Saturday morning, June 30.

Great! We would pick them up and drive across the Canadian—U.S. border at Niagara Falls and get married in Buffalo, New York, just like that. On Friday I told friends at the office that I was to be married the next day, packed all my belongings that evening, left the McCordick home, and moved over to Arthur's house. I was happy and excited.

The next morning we drove downtown to Sam's law office, and I waited in the car while Arthur went in to collect the divorce decree. He came out almost immediately, looking downcast.

'It hasn't arrived,' he said, and I burst into tears, desolate. When I had cried myself dry, Arthur kissed me gently.

'Listen, darling! We have our bags packed. Let's just drive up to Muskoka, stay at a nice lodge, and have a good weekend. And we'll just tell people that yes, we *did* get married. No one will be the wiser. Besides, as far as I'm concerned, we're married right now!'

Muskoka is a summertime lake resort, some ninety miles from Toronto. We checked into a lodge as Mr. and Mrs., and I wore the twelve-dollar gold wedding band we had bought, imagining that everyone we met would notice it immediately and stare at me accusingly.

After the weekend I was back in the office at Maclean-Hunter Publishing Co. When I had returned from England three months earlier, I had been re-employed by the company, this time as editor of *Newsweekly*, an employee publication. It was part of my job to collect news about other employees, so I knew a great many people and had many phone calls. I answered them all 'Sheila Hailey speaking' in a strong, bold voice; from that Monday morning onward, I was Sheila Hailey in every way. And I wrote a brief news item for that Friday's *Newsweekly*, announcing our 'wedding'.

Still, I desperately wanted that marriage certificate, and I was happy and relieved that the divorce papers finally arrived on the following Tuesday. We had known that New York State law required Wassermann (venereal) tests before a marriage licence could be granted, and the previous week—during a lunch hour—we had gone to St. Michael's Hospital in Toronto to get them. The next Saturday, July 7, we arose early and drove to Buffalo, armed with divorce papers and Wassermanns—which were negative.

We located City Hall and, bright-eyed and innocent, told the clerk we wanted to buy a marriage licence. Yes, we had all the proper documents. However, the clerk was sorry but, you see, he couldn't accept *Canadian* Wassermann tests.

'No, sir! You hafta get a Wassermann from a doctor licensed to practice in New York State. That's the law.'

With the help of the Yellow Pages, we phoned a few local doctors and located one who would give us the tests immediately. He promised to mail the results to us in Toronto as soon as he could; we must have them by the following weekend, we told him.

We drove back to Toronto, and on Monday morning we both went to work as usual. During the week, the American Wassermann test papers arrived, again negative, and the following Saturday, July 14, we drove to Buffalo—again.

This time, everything was in order. But traffic was heavy, and we arrived at the licence office in the Buffalo City Hall with three minutes to spare before the noon closing time. Glory hallelujah!, we got our licence.

'Where can we get married?' I asked.

Complacently the licence clerk pointed out that the bureau wasn't allowed to give that kind of information, since they couldn't be found favouring one judge or minister over another.

'Besides,' he drawled, 'you gotta wait forty-eight hours after buying the licence before you kin get married. That's the law!' And I wanted to punch him in the nose, he was so smug with his knowledge.

So . . . back to Toronto, because we both had to be at work on Monday morning.

Our car was the same old Buick which Arthur had bought a few months before. It ran on money. It drank almost as much oil as petrol, and to save nickels we bought oil by the case at the local supermarket. We kept the case of oil in the boot, and every time we'd stop for petrol we poured a can of oil into the crankcase. Those trips to Buffalo were not cheap.

And so it was that the next Saturday, when we were ready to pack the old car for the regular round trip to Buffalo and, feeling exhausted at the thought, we looked at each other, and I said, 'Honey, let's stay home this weekend.' We did. After all, we had now been Mr. and Mrs. to our friends for some time. What the hell did one week's difference make?

Our real, bona fide, absolute wedding day was to be Saturday, July 28. We had made arrangements to be married before Judge Michael E. Zimmer at 11 A.M. I had bought a new cream-coloured linen dress with matching jacket—a real luxury, because I made most of my own clothes at the time. Arthur stopped at a florist's and bought me roses.

Judge Zimmer's first words when he opened his front door at eleven o'clock sharp were modestly welcoming and ominous. 'Oh! . . . hello . . . come in. Er, haven't you any witnesses?' And after showing us into his living room, he disappeared.

Seconds later his wife emerged from the kitchen, wiping her hands on a towel. About ten minutes later their daughter came down the stairs, obviously having been roused from a Saturday-morning sleep-in. Mrs. and Miss Zimmer became our witnesses.

Forget the logistics; the words we finally heard were simple and beautiful:

> We have gathered here to unite this man and this woman in marriage, which is an institution conducive of the very laws of our being for the happiness and welfare of mankind.
> To be true, this outward ceremony must be a symbol of that which is inner and real—a union of hearts which the State makes legal.

Marriage is not meant for the happiness alone, but for the discipline and development of character. To that end, there must be a consecration of each to the other and both to the noblest purposes of life.

I promised to take Arthur as my lawful wedded husband, to live together in conformity with the laws of matrimony, to love him, comfort him, honour him, and keep him in sickness and in health, in prosperity and adversity, so long as we both should live.

I did not promise to obey him. Just as well.

It was all over in a few minutes. Arthur paid the judge, and then we drove to the Statler Hotel for a magnificent lunch that we could not afford. I remember the bill was $12—twelve dollars!—and Arthur left a one-dollar tip.

Who says it is easier to get married than divorced? It was so painful at the time, for I was sensitive about Arthur's divorce and our wedding fiasco. I carefully tried to keep the knowledge to ourselves. I even lied to my family in England, sending them a cable the first weekend we were 'married'. As the years went by, though, the memory of those weekends became funnier, and we gradually told the story of our two wedding anniversaries to close friends, amid much laughter. It was often confusing, because I'd forget which of our friends and acquaintances thought it was June 30, and which others knew it to be July 28. And when our children began to ask when we were married, I would have to stop and think . . . which date was the *real* one?

Now, twenty-seven years later, it couldn't matter less.

CHAPTER 6

'He Has
a Marked Flair
for the Dramatic'

To resume Arthur's story . . .

When he and I were married in July 1951 we were both well established at Maclean-Hunter. Arthur continued his job as editor of *Bus & Truck Transport*. He had become an authority on road transport. During the Canadian rail strike of 1950, for instance, he gave daily radio reports, explaining how the trucking industry was coping with the whole of the nation's transport needs. (It was the money he earned from these broadcasts that paid for the new clothes I had admired.) He championed the truckers by making speeches, waged editorial campaigns to change trucking legislation, won editorial awards. He was, in fact, a moderate-sized fish in a small pond.

I had switched to the new job as editor of *Newsweekly*, and secretary to the editorial director of the company.

Our combined salaries were adequate to live on, but we were in a hurry to refurbish our home—the same small house that Arthur's first family had lived in. I have always been a nest builder, and it is important to both of us to have comfortable, well-organized surroundings. We bought a refrigerator on hire purchase. Then we converted the coal furnace to oil, and for this we borrowed money from the bank. We were still driving the old 1938 Buick, and the repairs to it were a continual drain. After making all our monthly payments, there was little left to buy new furniture.

I remember one evening we wanted to see a movie. But it was a couple of days before our monthly salary cheques were due; we had only the smallest of change between us. We both searched through pockets, handbags, and down the sides of the old second-hand chairs and sofa which adorned our living room. We found a few small coins, but still there wasn't enough. So we ferreted out empty milk and pop bottles from kitchen cupboards and the basement, and exchanged them for cash refunds at a local market en route to the cinema. With pennies to spare, we laughed jubilantly as we bought tickets and settled in our seats.

With his transportation knowledge, Arthur wrote as many free-lance news stories on that subject as he could for a business newspaper, *The Financial Post*. He was paid about seventy cents an inch of printed copy. I will not go so far as to say he overwrote, but he did try to make each story as long as possible. When *The Financial Post* was published each Wednesday, the first thing he did was to take out a ruler and measure how many inches the paper had used, and figure out how much he would be paid.

During the first year of our marriage we shared household chores. Arthur prepared big hot breakfasts every morning, setting the table and doing the dishes afterward. All I had to do was make our bed. (This seems incredible to me now, because after living in our Bahamas home for seven years, he still doesn't seem to know where the dishes are kept.) I prepared dinner each evening and on weekends cleaned the house, while he did the laundry and shopping (but he always insisted I write the shopping list in the order that the items appeared on the shelves as he walked around the supermarket).

Together we started a free-lance writing business, producing two monthly news bulletins for trucking concerns.

We worked hard.

Shamelessly, we made use of the office facilities of Maclean-Hunter, and stayed at our desks until 8 P.M. two or three evenings a week. Arthur would do the writing, I did the display typing, ready for offset litho printing. When we arrived home, we were tired and hungry, a deadly combination that could have wrecked our marriage. But we were both ambitious, so most nights—without complaint—I prepared huge dinners, which we always ate with much enjoyment. (Small wonder that at that period of our lives, I was about fifteen pounds over my present weight; Arthur was more than thirty pounds overweight.)

Soon I left my job to write and produce these publications on my own, adding four more to those we already had. It was a profitable business and I could work when I pleased. More often than not, it was late at night—much to Arthur's displeasure. He could never understand how I could leave work until the last moment and then have to stay up late to meet a deadline. But old habits don't change. It's the way I have written parts of this book.

Arthur left Maclean-Hunter, too, in February 1953, and joined Trailmobile, a Canadian subsidiary of an American commercial trailer manufacturer, as sales promotion manager. At first he turned down the job when it was suggested by the president, a business friend, but yielded when the salary was upped to about $11,000 a year, an offer too good to refuse in 1953. I continued to write. By this time we had constructed an office in our basement, having installed the ceiling, planked floor and panelled walls, on weekends in our 'spare' time. It was a real luxury to work there after so many months at the kitchen table.

Arthur was not happy in sales promotion. The extent of his writing was advertising copy for new and used trailers. After a couple of years of such writing, it was difficult to come up with fresh adjectives to describe what he referred to privately as 'boxes on wheels'.

He was uncertain about the future. Although he was competent, decisive, well-organized, he didn't see himself as a captain of industry, and I'm not sure his superiors did either. He still longed to write but felt locked into his job by the salary, especially since we now had a daughter, Jane. At thirty-five, he was resigned to a life in the corporate world and decided to try for a higher rung on the ladder. He went to a management consulting firm, J. B. Fraser & Associates, which specialized in executive placement, to find out—as he put it at the time—'if all my nuts are tight and if I have what it takes to become president of General Motors'.

An industrial psychologist, Douglas W. Jones, gave him a battery of tests. A couple of weeks later, his profile analysis came back, uncannily accurate:

> The subject is a person of very superior intelligence who is in many ways practical and realistic . . . He has a vivid imagination which he uses extraordinarily well . . . He has a marked flair for the unusual and dramatic . . . He is very ambitious and possesses drive and determination to match this . . . His drive, at times, leads him to be impatient . . . He is willing to take

chances and to alter his life pattern in order to achieve his goals . . . He keeps himself under a good deal of pressure which leads to some strain and tension . . . He has a strong sense of humor . . . The subject is a strongly work-orientated individual who may not have developed enough real techniques of relaxation.

The most significant comments jumped off the page at the end of the report:

He has a great deal of creativity which seeks expression and he needs an outlet for this . . . He would do well as a writer and may be wasted in industry. He really should switch to a field of straight creative endeavour.

The report cost Arthur one hundred dollars. It was money well spent, for it encouraged him to think that perhaps it wasn't too late to get into the kind of writing he'd always wanted. But how? There was no easy solution, and his writing ambitions seemed destined to remain daydreams.

One of those 'Walter Mitty-type' dreams changed all that. It was the most significant single event in Arthur's career.

It was late 1955. He was returning to Toronto by air from a business trip to Vancouver. The aeroplane was a four-engine Trans Canada Airlines (now Air Canada) North Star—large by standards of that time. His mind wandered to the flight deck and he visualized the two pilots at the controls. He speculated: what would happen if they both got sick and couldn't fly the aeroplane? I wonder if I could fly it?

He was a rusty wartime pilot who hadn't flown for nine years, and even then, the largest aircraft he ever handled had only two engines. His mind raced on. What could put both pilots out of action? It was a Friday and there had been a choice of fish or meat for the evening meal. The answer flashed back: food poisoning from the fish.

Would there be a doctor on board? Yes—and he would also have to treat some of the passengers who had eaten the same food as the pilots. The others would have eaten the alternate choice—meat— including Arthur Hailey, who would have to fly the aeroplane, and the stewardess, who would help him at the controls.

For the rest of the trip he thought about his make-believe experience from beginning to end. By the time he reached Toronto he had worked out a scenario.

I met him at the airport.

His first words were: 'Darling, I have the most wonderful idea for a television play. Listen . . .' He was bubbling with excitement as he described the plot. I was caught up in his enthusiasm.

He wrote the play over two weekends and the five evenings in between. He had never seen a television script, so he wrote it like a stage play in three acts. The acts were broken down into 'scenes'—Act II had twenty-seven scenes. Only later did he learn to include camera directions such as CUT TO, CLOSE SHOT and DISSOLVE—though, as Arthur points out, none of that is really necessary. As he has sometimes told students, 'If the basic writing is there, a competent secretary can add the technicalities. In any case, most are superficial, because a TV or movie director will make his own camera decisions anyway.'

He conferred with a test pilot to make sure the technical details were accurate, then typed out his play and addressed the package to 'Script Department, Canadian Broadcasting Corporation, Toronto'. The Contracts Department phoned him about a month later. The CBC liked his play and wished to buy it. The fee for a new author was six hundred dollars.

We were thrilled by the news and hugged each other excitedly. A few days later Arthur was summoned to the office of Nathan Cohen, then head of the Script Department. He suggested a few minor changes and explained that the play was four minutes short for an hour's telecast. Could Arthur write the extra lines which were needed to fill that time? Incredibly, no other rewrite was needed. Arthur has never written anything since that required so little revision.

The teleplay was called *Flight Into Danger*, and it was presented on April 3, 1956.

There has never been such an evening of excitement in our marriage. The two of us sat in our living room as the live production of the play began. 'General Motors Theatre Presents . . . *Flight Into Danger* by Arthur Hailey . . .' The adrenalin started pumping; we squeezed hands nervously. Then as the action developed, Arthur and I became more and more excited. It was a superb production and we knew it. I also felt in my bones that this was no one-shot, no fluke, though Arthur was less sure. I was convinced that for him this was just the beginning. He had made it.

Our son Steven was two weeks old. I had brought him home from the hospital eight days before, thankful that he had chosen to be born early enough for me to see Arthur's play at home. I remember Steven let out a cry in the middle of the play. I had no intention of letting him interrupt my viewing, so I dashed to his crib and carried him back to the living room to nurse him. He guzzled happily and didn't give out another peep. We have always measured the years since Arthur's breakthrough by Steven's age. At the time of publication of this book Steven is twenty-two, over six feet tall, and a senior at Stanford University. He has, like his father, progressed a little since that magic evening.

At the play's conclusion the phone began to ring, and it rang continuously until well past midnight. The calls were all from friends, elated over the play. A group of neighbours gathered at our door to congratulate Arthur. Then they moved into our living room and helped us celebrate. The next day there were rave reviews in the papers. Later we learned this reaction was unanimous.

That single play, that single flight of the imagination, changed our lives. It was like winning the sweepstakes. I urged Arthur to leave his job at Trailmobile—and write, write, write. But he was not as convinced as I was that this initial, spectacular success would continue. With two small children, he was reluctant to depend on free-lance writing alone. So we compromised. He left the company and started his own advertising agency, Hailey Publicity Services Ltd. His major client was Trailmobile, which paid him a monthly retainer for handling all its advertising and public relations. He also received the usual agency commissions. Now he had the time in which to write, and the security of a small, steady income.

Arthur wrote a second play, *Time Lock*, which was snapped up by the CBC, followed by *Shadow of Suspicion* and *Course for Collision*, another aeroplane suspense story. In all, he wrote twelve plays that were produced on television.

During the summer of 1956 Arthur was introduced to a New York agent, Maeve Southgate, who promptly sold *Flight Into Danger* to NBC's 'Alcoa Hour'. Maeve was as convinced as I was that Arthur had a big future as a writer, but was not satisfied with the way the agency she was working for proposed to handle him. On the strength of her belief in Arthur, she left her agency job and went into business for herself with Arthur as her first client.

It was the beginning of a close relationship that continued for nearly twenty years. Maeve and Arthur never had a written contract, but each remained loyal to the other until her death in 1974. He was always her principal client, and as her ten per cent grew fatter over the years, she took delight in reminding me that she was a 'Hailey-kept woman'. She had great admiration for Arthur as a writer and as a man; and he, in turn, felt he owed so much to her encouragement, her faith in him, and her business acumen.

When, on September 16, 1956, the NBC production of *Flight Into Danger* was shown, it was an immediate hit. *Variety*, the show business trade paper, nicknamed it 'Hailey's Comet'. The BBC subsequently screened the kinescope of the original CBC production. The studio switchboard was jammed by enthusiastic callers. The *Daily Telegraph* described it as 'one of the most exciting dramas television has yet shown us', and the *News Chronicle* called it 'rare and outstanding'.

Suddenly Arthur was in demand as a television playwright. It was the so-called Golden Age of Television Drama—dramatic shows were performed live almost every night of the week. TV's appetite for new plays was enormous and Arthur was kept busy, writing every play under contract for the next two years. Along the way I finally convinced him he did not need the advertising business.

It was 1957 when Arthur received a letter from a Mr. Ernest Hecht, an energetic young man who was just setting up his new London publishing house, Souvenir Press. He had seen *Flight Into Danger* for the second time on BBC and felt it would make an exciting novel. If Arthur wrote it, he would be delighted to publish it. But Arthur was too involved with his television writing to entertain the idea. 'Besides,' he told me when we discussed it, 'I don't think I can write a novel.' He declined. Ernest Hecht is not easily put off. He wrote back, 'If I can get another writer to co-author the book, would you be agreeable to a fifty-fifty split of royalties?' We both felt we didn't have anything to lose, so Arthur agreed.

The co-author for the novel *Flight Into Danger* (or *Runway Zero Eight*, as it was called in the U.S.) was 'John Castle', a pseudonym for two writers, Ronald Payne and John Garrod. (A few years later, Ronald Payne was killed in a tragic traffic accident.) These gentlemen had already co-authored a successful novel called *The Password is Courage*, so the joint byline of John Castle and Arthur Hailey capitalized on both a previous success and a new up-and-coming writer. (Arthur's name came first in North American editions.)

For Ernest Hecht, *Flight Into Danger* became one of his early international best sellers, and Souvenir Press has burgeoned successfully and continually ever since. To ensure a wide distribution of *Flight Into Danger*, Ernest entered into an arrangement with the well-established house of Michael Joseph Ltd., which proved so amicable that both publishers continue to issue Hailey books jointly with advantages to both houses and to the author.

That early association between Ernest and Arthur began what I know will be a lifelong friendship. We never forget that it was Ernest Hecht who really set Arthur on the road to novel writing.

The subsequent chain of events happened this way: Arthur received the galley proofs of the short novel, *Flight Into Danger*, which 'John Castle' had produced. As Arthur read them, he confided to me that he thought he could have written the book after all. 'Most of my dialogue is here and the plot was already worked out.'

At the time he was deeply involved in his most successful TV production since *Flight*. It was *No Deadly Medicine*, a two-part, two-hour 'Studio One' hospital drama, starring Lee J. Cobb, William Shatner, and Gloria Vanderbilt. Directed by Sidney Lumet and produced by Herbert Brodkin, it won two Emmy nominations—one for the author, the other for Lee J. Cobb, who also received a Sylvania Award for his performance.

The editor-in-chief of Doubleday, Ken McCormick, watched the show in New York. He, too, was struck by the notion that the play would make a fine novel and phoned Arthur's agent to say so. Maeve Southgate relayed the conversation to Arthur who, because of his previous experience with Ernest Hecht, did not dismiss the idea and signed a contract with Doubleday.

He was incredibly lucky with the timing. Demand for original television dramas was dwindling and the weekly series formula was taking over the airwaves. Arthur did not feel this was his forte and soon after switched permanently to writing novels.

For the novel version of *No Deadly Medicine* he did additional research. He watched an amputation, open-heart surgery; listened to radiologists, pathologists, anaesthetists; talked with nurses, interns, hospital directors. After that it took Arthur only nine months to write the book, because the characters and main story line had previously been developed, and much of the dialogue was already written. He gave it a new title: *The Final Diagnosis*.

I shall never forget the look of wonder on his face when he received an early copy in 1959. Here was his work in a neat package that he could hold in his hand. He did not have to speculate, as he had with television writing, whether the directing or the acting had made his play seem better or worse than it actually was. There had been no story conferences of author, producer, director, actors—when sometimes even the girl who brought in the coffee suggested new lines of dialogue. There had been no tense scenes with a temperamental actor who wanted to change his whole characterization. This book was all his. He was solely responsible for it. Readers would buy it or not, as they saw fit. He would not have to meet a good friend who might greet him: 'Say, you had a play on TV last night, didn't you? Sorry I missed it.'

For a first novel, *The Final Diagnosis* was a remarkable success. It was well reviewed, and it sold steadily. Even today, nearly twenty years later, it continues to sell thousands of copies a year in many languages. The Literary Guild of America chose it as a selection, and it became a Reader's Digest Condensed Books choice. Eventually, it was translated into twenty-two languages. It also attracted filmmakers' attention and the rights were sold to United Artists.

Arthur's next book, *In High Places*, was published in 1962. It was a huge success in Canada, a more modest one in the U.S. Again, the Literary Guild selected it; it went into twelve foreign-language editions; it won the Doubleday Canada $10,000 prize novel award. This novel is a favourite of mine. Its theme of international politics—envisaging Canada joining the United States because of imminent war with the Soviet Union—is one that intrigued me then, and has continued to do so over the years.

Since that time, Arthur has brought out a new novel about every three years: *Hotel* 1965; *Airport* 1968; *Wheels* 1971; *The Moneychangers* 1975. His new novel, *Overload*, will be published in 1979. Each book was published in the same year in the country of his birth, Great Britain. All the books are still in print in hardback and paperback and, to date, have sold more than nine million copies in various editions within the British territories. The paperback versions of *Airport* and *Hotel* each sold over a million copies, for which Arthur received Golden Pan Awards. His books have all been selected for the Reader's Digest Condensed Books, and *Airport, Wheels* and *The Moneychangers* were selected for the British Literary Guild or other book clubs.

All his books have been on the major best-seller lists all over the world, not only in America and Great Britain. In America, *Airport* had the longest run—sixty-four weeks on the *New York Times* Best Seller List, thirty of those weeks in number one position. *Hotel*, the first of Arthur's books to be a top best seller, was on the *New York Times* list for fifty-two weeks.

I.et me say here, though, how misleading the best-seller lists can be. In those fifty-two best-seller weeks, *Hotel* sold 82,652 copies. *Airport*, over its sixty-four weeks, sold 262,587 copies. *Wheels* was snapped up fast and sold 207,983 copies in the thirty-three weeks it stayed on the *New York Times* list, seven of those weeks as number one. And *The Moneychangers* sold 171,138 copies in forty-four weeks and topped the list for fourteen weeks. (These figures are for hardcover copies sold in the United States during the best-seller weeks. The current totals are substantially higher, because Arthur's books have continued to sell in hardcover.)

It is obvious from this that a book can sell faster than any other book in the bookshops, but its life on the best seller list can be short. This is usually the case when a writer builds up a vast audience of readers who are looking out for his next book. When it appears, it goes fast and, as it were, burns itself out and drops off the lists early.

Also to be remembered is that in the U.S. approximately eighteen hundred novels are published in a year. The competition for those top ten places on the best-seller lists is enormous. Many authors have highly respectable sales without ever being on the list.

The way best-seller lists are compiled, too, has been labelled inaccurate and misleading. There is no question that, in this electronic age, there must be more efficient ways to arrive at the weekly list than by telephoning selected bookshops for—at best—educated guesses of the previous week's sales.

Arthur has received bouquets for his books and, of course, brickbats. Some think it is a cinch for him to produce a best seller time after time. But an author is only as good as the next book he writes. He must always compete with himself. If he slackens his own standards, his public will be the first to tell him.

For Arthur's public has come to regard him as an author who, in the words of the *New York Times*, 'gives readers their money's worth'. If they enjoy his books they will tell their friends, who will buy them. If they don't, the verdict will be 'Don't bother!' It is, I firmly believe, word of mouth that sells or kills a book—or a film, for that matter. A publisher can launch a massive promotion campaign to sell a particular book—but if the public doesn't like it, it won't buy it. Of course an author needs promotion and advertising to get his new publication known. After that, though, he is on his own.

Every author wants to be read. If he says he doesn't care, he is fooling himself. It's the readers who matter most to an author. That's why their letters mean so much . . . as I will tell you later.

CHAPTER 7

Three Oranges, Two Apples and a Banana

In *The Final Diagnosis* Arthur had a moving scene where a young father, John Alexander, stares incredulously at a tiny three-and-a-half-pound premature baby lying in an incubator . . .

> For the first time the thought occurred to him: This is my son, my own, a part of my life. Suddenly he was consumed by a sense of overwhelming love for this fragile morsel, fighting his lonely battle inside the warm little box below. He had an absurd impulse to shout through the glass: *You're not alone, son; I've come to help.* He wanted to run to the incubator and say: *These are my hands; take them for your strength. Here are my lungs; use them and let me breathe for you. Only don't give up, son; don't give up! There's so much ahead, so much we can do together—if only you'll live! Listen to me, and hold on! This is your father and I love you.*

I was pregnant with our third child when reading this passage, and was close to tears. 'Honey, this is beautiful,' I cried. 'But why, in heaven's name, can't *you* be like that?'

He grinned and replied flippantly, 'I can't waste my best lines on ourselves!'

When we were first married, Arthur had a real phobia about having children. He had known that a woman can become overly possessive about babies, while her husband gets left out in the cold. He was convinced that having children would end our special relationship, and that they would dominate our lives. So he approached the debut of our firstborn with apprehension bordering on indifference.

I announced about four o'clock in the morning of April 30, 1954, that I thought we should go to the hospital. He was as excited as if I had told him I had a headache. He drove me to the Toronto East General Hospital, waited for my clothes, then vanished. I have to admit I told him to go. 'There's no point in waiting. You can't do anything. And a first baby takes ages to come, I'm told.' He saw my point at once, and needed no persuasion. So with a slight twinge of disappointment, I saw him scuttle down the hall to go home to sleep. Events confirmed my common sense, for Jane did not arrive until eighteen hours later. Still, whenever I see a nervous young man pace up and down in the 'father's room' of any hospital, I feel a pang of envy because no one ever paced for me.

The next day, in the semi-private room, the girl in the next bed was embraced by her husband, kissed, patted and crooned over for the whole of the visiting hour. Arthur, who hated showing any kind of sentiment in public, stood beside my bed at ramrod attention, before leaning over to give me a peck. Then, 'How was it?' he asked.

'Oh, fine!' I lied. Eighteen hours of labour, a dry birth, a baby who had to be pulled out with forceps, to emerge bloody and bruised—it was a picnic.

'The baby okay?'

'Oh, sure! She has a couple of gashes on her forehead, but she's nearly eight pounds, and everything looks normal. Er . . . you can see her between three-thirty and four.'

He twitched uncomfortably. 'Do you mind if I don't? I'd feel silly standing with a whole crowd of men and grandmothers cooing and ah-ing.' (He would have, too, so Jane was six days old before she met her father.)

My next thought was, 'Did you bring anything?'

'No . . . why? Did you want something?'

'Well . . . I thought . . . maybe some flowers . . . or fruit?' I said tentatively, picturing in my mind those huge baskets you can buy at gift shops, full of every available fruit in season, wrapped in coloured Cellophane and topped off with a large satin ribbon bow.

The message got through. Slightly garbled. Next visiting hour and Arthur arrived carrying a supermarket brown paper bag. Inside were three oranges, two apples and a banana.

When we got home, I was determined that Jane would not upset our lives too much. Poor kid, when Arthur returned from work at six o'clock each night, she had been bathed and fed and put down for the night. Everything suggesting 'baby' was stashed away in her room, and I appeared smilingly at the doorway with hair combed and new make-up, and changed out of my daytime dress with the baby-burp stains. In the dining room, the table was set with its usual two places and the candles, ready for dinner.

Okay, I overdid it. But I was dealing with a complex, screwed-up guy who was less than happy with his job in industry, and also had visions of his second marriage going sour.

My plan to keep Jane in the background worked. Gradually it dawned on Arthur that the baby was not going to take us over, and that he and I were still solid. He began to spend time just looking at her in her cradle, then stroking her head, and finally picking her up to nuzzle that sweet, soft face—after he had checked that she was clean and dry and in good humour. But he never was enthusiastic enough about babies ever to change a nappy, or spoon-feed that sticky baby cereal.

When Steven was ready to be born two years later, Arthur was in Montreal. He had been 'borrowed' from his employers by a Royal Commission on Canada's Economic Prospects; he was helping to write the transport section of the Commission's report. I phoned him at 7 A.M. and announced I was going to the hospital that day. He wished me well and asked me to phone him the results. Then I called my friend and neighbour, Jean Moyse, herself eight months pregnant and enormous, to drive me to the hospital. We should have practised beforehand, because she had difficulty getting behind the wheel of my little car. 'Here, I'll drive!' I said, and I did. When we got to the hospital we had a tough time persuading the admitting staff that it was I who was in labour, and not Jean. But I finally got bundled into a wheelchair, and Jean drove home as best she could.

I phoned Arthur from my room at midday, and interrupted him in a meeting. 'You have another son—and he's beautiful, and I'm calling him Steven.'

'Wonderful!' he cried, 'but I'm not sure about the name . . . anyway, I'll be home at the end of the week.' Next day I registered Steven's name.

Two years later, Diane was born in the easygoing fashion which has since become her stock-in-trade, at six o'clock in the morning, after a short labour. This time I had an epidural anaesthesia, witnessed the whole thing in the mirror above, and felt marvellous. Our doctor, Jim Bell, who had by now delivered five of Arthur's six children, said: 'Well, Sheila, you got your wish . . . another girl! I'll go and phone Arthur.'

'Oh, don't phone him yet. He's only had about four hours' sleep. You'll wake him.'

'Good!' he said.

The following year Arthur was researching *The Final Diagnosis* and had the opportunity to witness the birth of a baby. White-gowned, rubber-gloved, and masked, he actually held the child's head before it emerged.

The experience affected him profoundly. When he told me about it later, he emoted: 'Sheila, it's like poetry . . . I was all choked up . . . Birth is so beautiful.'

I looked at him. 'I know,' I said, 'I've had three . . . remember?'

When a father works at home, he is keenly aware that he has small children. And Arthur has always been the kind of writer who must have ivory-tower silence and solitude. This is easy to achieve now that our children are no longer at home. But in the early days it was tough on everyone—particularly me.

How do you keep three children under four years of age quiet all day? For a start, we went for a long daily walk, although this was difficult to squeeze into a busy schedule. Two of the kids were in nappies; the baby had to be fed at different times from Jane and Steven; Arthur liked his lunch quietly with me, after the children were put down for a nap. He was also used to getting his morning coffee at precisely 10:30 A.M. One morning Steven, age two, discovered the wonderful thrill of flushing a toilet. He chuckled with delight as he dropped in a nappy from the bathroom pail, and watched it gurgle its way around the bowl and down the hole. Five nappies and two flannels later, the bathroom was awash. As I mopped the floor and struggled to retrieve the nappies from the plugged toilet, Arthur appeared on the scene. It was 10:35 A.M. 'Oh,' he said. 'I was wondering when we were going to have coffee.' I could cheerfully have flushed him down the toilet too.

As the children grew, the days were easier. Summers were a cinch. I just sent them out to play, preferably in a neighbour's garden. But in

Canada summer quickly becomes winter. Getting children dressed for outside play in subzero weather is like preparing an army for battle. First, there are snowsuits to be struggled into . . . how come I never broke one of those tiny arms as they were shoved into sleeves? . . . then thick socks over shoes, for extra warmth, before thrusting awkward feet into rubber overboots. Hat and scarf next, and finally mittens . . . and make sure they are pinned or sewn on to the snowsuit, otherwise one—always just one—will be lost forever. When all three are dressed, it's 'Out you all go to play in the snow. What fun!' But at the last minute, blow three noses . . . if you don't, they'll be back that much sooner. Even so, in twenty minutes or less—you've barely tackled one washload of laundry—there is a clamouring at the door. 'We're cold, Mummy!' . . . and they are. Cheeks bright red, noses running, mittens sopping wet, little fingers stiff, overboots encased in snow. Whining voices . . . they are miserably cold . . . and then Arthur's call: 'Sheila, can't you keep those kids quiet?'

Is it any wonder our children were all enrolled in nursery school by their third birthday?

I had fondly imagined that when all three children were at school full time, life would be a breeze. I celebrated the first morning by shopping in downtown Toronto. Returning at noon, I found Arthur so exasperated he exploded: 'Have you any *idea* how many times I have had to stop work this morning to let out that damned yapping dog? And five minutes later she barks to come back inside.'

I had forgotten Maxie. She was a two-year-old we had had since puppyhood. The trees in our garden were full of squirrels. That dear, dopey dachshund would go berserk until she got outside to try to catch them—as futile a task as trying to stop a rocket once it has been ignited. But she never learned.

Arthur had an ultimatum: 'I cannot be left alone with that dog again. Either get a dog-sitter or let's get rid of her.' We gave Maxie away—to a family that lived in the country. It was a ruthless decision, but the children were brave and soon got over the loss, and Arthur and I faced the reality that we were not true dog-lovers.

The children's school was less than a block away, and it was the custom for kids to come home for lunch. But Arthur never enjoyed watching them eat. There always seemed to be at least one glass of milk that was spilled, and it was more than he could stand in the middle of a working day. So I used to prepare two meals every noon hour—the noisy, chatty, sticky ritual in the kitchen, and then an elegant, quiet lunch in the dining room after the children were back at school. It was a real chore—and I was glad when the children later changed schools and took their lunch with them.

As the children developed from babies to individual personalities, Arthur made amends for his earlier aloofness by taking them separately on various trips.

He and Jane, aged ten, flew to England one time to see her grandparents. She had had an assignment from her schoolteacher that while in England she should collect some chalk from the white cliffs of Dover. Arthur rented a car and drove her there from London. It rained all day, but Jane insisted that she break the chalk from the cliff itself, not just look for a piece on the beach. As Arthur waited, shoulders hunched in the rain, he recognized one of his own kind—a perfectionist.

He once phoned me from New York. 'I'm through with most of my work here,' he said, 'and it occurred to me that Diane has never seen New York as the other two have. How about putting her on an aeroplane and let her spend a few days with me?'

That poor, underprivileged child! Six years old, and never been to New York! So I put her on a Trans-Canada Airlines flight at Toronto airport, and some two hours later her father met her in New York. That trip was memorable for Arthur because Diane wanted to go to the top of the Empire State Building, as Jane and Steven had done on earlier trips. The weather was grey and foggy, with visibility about fifty feet. Diane peered down from the top and said optimistically, 'Daddy, I *think* I can see the sidewalks.'

When Steven was nine, I got a similar call from Arthur in Detroit, where he was researching *Wheels*. 'I've got a great idea. I'm going to see the Daytona 500. Steven would love it! How about putting him on a plane and I'll meet him in Florida?'

Our son, the lone boy between two outgoing girls, was often a bit of a grump as a child, and graciousness was not his strong point. He flew from San Francisco to Atlanta, where he had a four-hour wait between planes. We arranged for him to be met and taken home by a young couple we knew there, who had a two-year-old son. Then he went on to Florida, where he and Arthur watched the classic car race, sharing a treasured father-son camaraderie. The occasion was a big success.

Later we were taken aback to receive a letter from the Atlanta couple saying what a delightful, charming boy Steven was, so polite and helpful, and they hoped their own Christopher would grow up like him. I looked at Arthur. 'Do you think they picked up the wrong kid?'

Over the years I've written countless notes to teachers, explaining why one or other of our children had missed days at school. Usually these 'Dear Miss Smith' communications were written on scraps of paper immediately after I'd made up the peanut-butter-and-jelly sandwich lunches and the kids were ready to depart. No sweat; it was always a last-minute job; it did the trick and everyone was happy. But not if you get a professional writer into the act. He has to prove to the teacher that *his* notes are something special.

I was away, visiting my family in England. Steven had been ill at home, in the care of a temporary housekeeper, and a note was needed on his return to school. As the only resident parent, Arthur had to write it—and being Arthur, he planned ahead and did it the night before. He typed it beautifully on his best letterhead, and sealed it in a real, unused, matching envelope which—for school notes—was unheard of in our house. It read:

> *Among the many miseries which the soldiery long endured*
> *In World War One,*
> *Was a painful gum infection, of which few were ever cured;*
> *And now, my son*
> *Has confronted the same symptoms, and the same pernicious*
> *ailment—*
> *Trench mouth its name*
> *And in course of his reaction, he has suffered a derailment,*
> *With gums aflame.*
> *But with aid of penicillin, not available in trenches,*
> *And incessant*
> *Application of an unguent, he's returning to the benches,*
> *Convalescent.*

Instant fame and success with the school! The note was read to the class. It was passed around the staff-room. Steven was a hero.

Several weeks later Diane was sick, and I was back in my role as official school note-writer. But—no, one of *my* notes would not do. She wanted poetry, too.

'Well,' I said, 'Daddy must write it.'

But Daddy was immersed in other things, as I quickly found out when I buzzed him on the intercom.

'For *Chriss*akes, I'm supposed to be writing a novel, not wasting my time writing poetry to schoolteachers,' he exploded.

'Well, you started it . . . and you can't do it for one and not the other.'

Grudgingly, 'When does she need it?'

'Now.'

'Impossible! Tell her I'll write it later today.'

Back to Diane. 'If you want a poem, tell your teacher you'll bring the note tomorrow.'

'But I have to take it *today!*'

'Look! You're ready to go back to school. The school has to accept you. Your teacher won't turn you away because you haven't got a note, and she won't beat you. So what's it to be? One of my notes now, or a poem by Dad tomorrow?'

Her small face set squarely, 'A pome!'

Okay—a pome it is:

> *Diane has had a nasty fever*
> *Which, obstinately, wouldn't leave her.*
> *We took her case to Doctor Wood*
> *Who then prescribed (we'd hoped he could)*
> *Some medication to undo*
> *A temp'rature of one-o-two;*
> *He also made a rigid ruling—*
> *Diane must interrupt her schooling.*
> *A pity!—early on like this,*
> *But man makes plans which bugs dismiss.*

A tradition was born—fortunately short-lived. After a year or so, the novelty wore off, and Steven took the last Arthur Hailey school note after he had broken his leg (which happened during his own scrimmage with four other boys, when he should have been *watching* a school football game):

Steven Hailey's tibia
  Was shattered in a fall—
A nasty little mish-mash
  Alas! It wasn't all.
His fibia fragmented
  Like cruelly crumpled egg;
And with no tib or fib (why, natch!)
  You have a useless leg.
But now the bones are mending
  With nature's healing touches
And Steven's back, resuming work,
  As best he can—on crutches.

I really thought we had buried this cute stage, but some years later Diane came home from school announcing she wanted a recipe for a school cookbook project. Again, I was away—and come to think of it, perhaps that was always the time Arthur seemed to have these extracurricular spurts of creativity. By the time I returned, it was too late to delete this highly original recipe:

HAILEY SANDWICH

Take two slices of bread; place side by side. Butter each slice (on one side only). Then take a slice of ham and trim to fit the bread or (if you like a lot of ham) fold it over. Place ham on right-hand piece of bread, adding cheese, lettuce, sliced tomatoes, or whatever, depending on how much you can get your mouth around at once. Cover with left-hand piece of bread, press down and serve. (Southpaws follow same procedure, but use left slice of bread first.)

In addition, he had quoted excerpts from five of his novels, giving details of memorable meals. He even had the gall to add a postscript: 'Diane: My fee for this piece of writing is $10,000. If agreeable, I will deduct 50¢ weekly from your pocket money until paid.'

The whole thing appeared in print, including the postscript.

I was aghast and embarrassed, and said so. Later, I learned it was one of the more popular contributions to the otherwise conventional cookbook. Lord knows why.

CHAPTER 8

How to Write a Best Seller

Everyone involved with writing books and publishing them has heard it many times: 'I have a wonderful idea for a book. I know it would make a best seller, if only I could get it down on paper. How do I do it?'

The answer is easy: you marry someone like me. A writer needs a person around who can cope: who can write letters, answer telephones, deal with plumbers and carpenters, discourage interruptions, and pay the bills. As friends have heard me mutter time and again: 'Dammit! I do everything around here except write the books.'

But that *is* quite an exception, because writing a novel is a prodigious undertaking. It takes Arthur three years. He bleeds the words a few at a time, six hundred words a day, and it takes about six hours to complete that quota. I once asked: 'Why don't you put the paper in the typewriter and really pound out a rough first draft—fast?' He looked at me with an eyebrow raised: 'Honey, I can only tell you the way I'm doing it seems to be working.'

'Do you write longhand or straight on to the typewriter?' 'Do you use a tape recorder?' 'Do you wait until you're in the mood?' 'When do you write—what part of the day?' 'Do you keep regular hours?'

All professional writers are asked these questions. Obviously, not all successful authors work the same way. Some I know write thousands of words a day; they shut themselves in a room, have their meals brought to them on a tray, and refuse all invitations to come out. Others work all night and sleep during the day.

Arthur tried writing at night when our three children were too young for school. He has always worked at home—even when he found the noise of a baby, a two-year-old and a four-year-old less than musical. So he began writing about nine in the evening. The house was quiet, the children asleep, telephone calls were thinning out. I used to leave him a special snack that he could look forward to eating about midnight, then he'd go on writing until about 5 A.M.

I hated it. In the daytime, instead of shushing the children and saying, 'Daddy's working,' I had to whisper, 'Sh! Daddy's sleeping.' There was no point in making the bed—if Arthur wasn't in it, I was. The arrangement also played havoc with our sex life. He was too tired when he flopped into bed before dawn, and I found it difficult to get all three children to have naps at precisely the time Arthur awoke, so that I could join him. Fortunately, he grew tired of this arrangement. He had elected to be a writer, not a monk.

Writers who can afford it sometimes leave home for a concentrated spell of writing, choosing an agreeable holiday spot. This doesn't sit well with wives or husbands who have to stay home and look after the kids, though it's a great idea if the spouse can go along and relax while the other works.

Still other authors booze while writing, keeping a bottle close by. This is okay if it works—in fact, the notion looks appealing to me as I am writing this right now. I often think I get my best ideas on a five-hour plane trip, taking every drink I'm entitled to. I sometimes ask an air hostess for pad and pencil and start scribbling a few paragraphs—but somehow, when I reread them later on the ground, they don't seem as good as when I dashed them off in the air.

The one thing all professional writers have in common, though, is that they get down to it and write. They don't just talk about it, they don't wait for inspiration, they don't wish they had *time* to write. They *make* time and press on. Oh, there's often some pencil-sharpening and desk-tidying that goes on first. But sooner or later, they write, though never knowing with certainty if they are at work on a masterpiece or a disaster.

There is no such thing as a surefire best seller. Even a writer with a series of successes behind him can fall flat on his face with his next book. Nor can publishers be certain, in advance, which books will be best sellers. Some books for which publishers had the highest hopes and paid enormous advances on royalties have been spectacular flops. Conversely, there are 'sleepers' which no one expected to be best sellers, but which suddenly are.

In my opinion, Arthur Hailey books have been best sellers for three reasons. First, Arthur is a cracking good storyteller. Lots of readers still love a story and want to keep turning the pages to see what happens next. Second, through painstaking research which he later combines with a story, he gives people an unusual insider's view of institutions and technologies which are an essential part of modern living. Third, he has an almost uncanny sense of timing in knowing what will be topical at publication time—almost four years from when he begins planning.

The reason for this timeliness is simple.

Arthur is a newsaholic. Every morning at our home in the Bahamas we get that day's *New York Times* and *Wall Street Journal* delivered to our front door before 8:30 A.M. At the same time we get the local *Nassau Guardian* and *The Tribune*. In addition, we buy copies of several British and Canadian newspapers from time to time. Then there are the news magazines, and the almost hourly radio newscasts from Miami, which Arthur listens to on one of several radios in his study. (There's also TV news, though the picture isn't reliable. Because we're in a fringe reception area—two hundred miles from Miami—channels tend to overlap. Some evenings we get the voice of John Chancellor and the face of Walter Cronkite, or vice versa.)

A day without news is a frustrating experience for Arthur. If we're away on a trip where news is scarce, he can hardly wait to get to a radio or a newspaper to catch up. And wherever we travel he becomes immediately interested in the local news. So the news never gets away from him. Because of this, he is able to judge what is significant and what doesn't really matter. This constant reading, I know, gives him an acute awareness of the various forces shaping the world and a feeling for long-term situations. He picks up seemingly unrelated news items that give him a clue as to what may happen next month, next year, or considerably beyond.

All this, along with that storyteller's instinct, seems to tell him what subject will make a topical novel three to four years from the time he chooses it. An example of this is *The Moneychangers*, which Arthur began working on in 1972. It was the story of a big bank, brought from success and power to near-disaster, along with various other monetary ills. He believed the subject would be timely. What he didn't know was that some of the most prestigious banks in the U.S. and elsewhere would be toppling like tenpins when *The Money-changers* came out, or that an international currency crisis would be grabbing headlines. As Arthur himself expressed it later: 'I like to be topical, but I didn't *need* all that Wagnerian music in the background.'

The same kind of timeliness was true of *Airport*. That novel appeared in 1968 when North American newspapers were reporting the crowded, dangerous air-traffic conditions in and around major airports: aeroplanes in long line-ups waiting to take off, then sometimes circling for hours before landing.

After *Airport* came *Wheels*, which featured the motor industry in Detroit. The novel's emphasis was on small cars. It appeared on American book stands in 1972 and 1973 at a time when public attention was turning to small cars and just before the petrol shortage became acute. And *Hotel*, which featured civil rights, was published in 1965 when that subject, too, had become prominent in the news.

All of these novels were started three to four years before their publication.

The theme of a book, therefore, is important to Arthur. Preferably, it should be a subject that is challenging, complex, and newsworthy. Also, he himself must be passionately interested in the subject in order to sustain his enthusiasm for it over the length of his involvement.

Once the subject is chosen, Arthur reads everything he can about it. This is not to crib from other writers, but to have an intelligent reservoir of knowledge before he goes out to gather information from experts.

His first introduction to the new project is a meeting he either sets up himself, or asks Doubleday, his U.S. publisher, to arrange. If the approach is to a big organization, this may involve a lunch with the vice-president of public relations. From then on, other interviews are set up. Beyond these, Arthur fans out in all directions—to talk with chairmen in board rooms, office workers at a lunch counter, disgruntled employees eager to dig up skeletons, retired executives spinning out empty days at home and longing to relive their careers before an attentive audience. For while public relations personnel may help him initially, he quickly gets away from official channels, making his own investigations in his own painstaking, independent way.

Arthur has a low-key manner and is a good listener. He always assures his sources that the confidences they tell him will not be in tomorrow's newspaper or next month's magazine. In fact, whatever is used of their experiences, philosophies, opinions, and ideas will be so changed and fictionalised that they need not fear embarrassment when the book is eventually published three years hence.

This explains why most people are extremely co-operative when Arthur talks to them. Some are particularly enthusiastic, with a highly developed story sense. He once consulted an inspector of lifts for the Ontario government. Arthur had envisaged a lift accident for the denouement of *Hotel*, but was reluctant to bring up the subject. After listening to a long account of the safety measures incorporated into lifts and the strict inspection codes, Arthur said hesitantly, 'Could there conceivably be a major lift crash, in spite of all these precautions?'

'Oh, good heavens, yes!' exclaimed the inspector and proceeded to recount some of the most horrendous disasters one could imagine. Finally he said, 'There was one crash I remember that would be a dandy for your story. The lift went out of control and shot *upward* at great speed until it crashed against the roof of the building. That was a nasty one.' Arthur instinctively knew this was one more stranger-than-fiction incident that would not be believed, and wisely settled for a conventional downward crash.

Occasionally his strict policy of not identifying his sources has backfired. While researching *Hotel* he stayed for several months as a paying guest at the old Roosevelt Hotel in New Orleans, now the Fairmont. Its managing director, the late Seymour Weiss, was gracious and helpful, giving instructions to all his staff to answer questions with frankness. Arthur was astonished to discover the number of rackets which were firmly rooted among some Roosevelt employees. He later described them in his novel. Not only did he not betray any confidences, but he wanted to save the hotel embarrassment. LeBaron Barker, his editor at Doubleday, had a solution: 'There's the Hotel St. Charles in New Orleans that you haven't been near. Why not call your fictional hotel the St. Something-or-Other, and it will draw attention away from the Roosevelt?'

So Arthur's hotel became the St. Gregory, and that name was used in the film version also. In 1966 we flew to Miami Beach for the film premiere, and there, among the guests, was his old friend Seymour Weiss. He took Arthur aside to congratulate him on the success of the book.

'But, you know, Arthur,' he said in his soft southern voice, 'Ah have one regret . . . and that is, you did not use the name of mah house.'

While Arthur would never reveal the origin of any of his characters, if people wish to declare themselves the real-life counterparts, he doesn't contradict them if it's true. I can think of three individuals who have done this.

Joe Patroni, the maintenance chief in *Airport*, was a 'cocky, stocky Italian American', who continuously smoked long, thin cigars. The novel also reported that 'Joe Patroni made love to his wife, Marie, most nights, the way other men enjoy a pre-dinner drink.' At the publication party for *Airport*, Roy Davis, a cigar-chomping maintenance chief for TWA, announced, 'I'm Joe Patroni.' His colleagues slapped him on the back. 'Say, Roy, is that true about you and your wife?' Arthur knew by Roy's beaming face that no man is offended if it is suggested that his sexual prowess is better than average.

Ginny Henline, a TWA passenger relations agent at O'Hare, was, in part, the real-life Tanya Livingstone. When the airport scenes for the film *Airport* were shot in Minneapolis, she and Roy Davis flew there to meet their film counterparts, Jean Seberg and George Kennedy, and received much publicity.

Similarly, Dr. Harry D. Schultz announced in his *International Harry Schultz Letter* that he was the fictional adviser, Lewis D'Orsey, in *The Moneychangers*. This was true.

In all the research Arthur has done over the years he has never accepted gifts or money—although both have been offered—to promote any point of view. Neither has he given any promises as to how he will portray an industry or a controversial subject. As a result, he has maintained a reputation for integrity and has remained completely independent.

During an interview Arthur rarely uses a notebook or a tape recorder; he regards these tools as too inhibiting. Instead he carries everything in his head until he can get away by himself and jot down key thoughts in a notebook. He has done this over a cup of coffee at a lunch counter, in a parked car, on a busy pavement, in the gents.

Later the same day, he dictates into a portable IBM unit detailed notes of the day's interviews, including descriptions of each person he has seen, the surroundings, and any other facts which, many months later, will help him recall the occasion.

When Arthur researched his novel *Wheels*, he found the motor industry in Detroit to be a highly competitive, superpowered, aggressive environment. Typically, when the public relations departments set up interviews for him, they scheduled them almost every hour on the hour. It was a pace far more hectic than he is accustomed to and it was a strain for him to keep up. At the end of the day he was so weary, he dictated his notes while lying on his hotel bed, and most evenings fell asleep before they were completed.

Although a shrewd businessman, Arthur admits he is sometimes shaky—as he was at school—on actual mechanical arithmetic. The go-go atmosphere of Detroit didn't help either. He telephoned me very early one day in California, where we were living. I was aroused from a deep sleep.

'For crying out loud!' I protested, suddenly wide awake and mad as hell. 'Do you know what time it is?'

'Sure,' he answered. 'It's seven in the morning here, ten A.M. your time.'

'Wrong!' I said testily. 'It's four o'clock here. You've got the time change the wrong way around.'

'Oh, damn! Sorry! . . . Well, since you're awake anyway, do you have a pencil and pad handy? There are a few things I'd like you to do. . . .'

This was in 1968, when Arthur was away from home eight-and-a-half months of the year. He would be in Detroit for three weeks, then come home for about ten days. Each time he'd arrive tense and impatient, snapping at the children, brusque with his secretary, short-tempered with me. I finally blew my top. 'I will not put up with this. My God, you're *behaving* like a motor executive.'

'You're right!' he exclaimed. 'And I'm beginning to think like one. It's time to start writing.'

The hours and hours of dictated notes are typed by Arthur's valued and long-time assistant, Mrs. Ruth Hunter. A highly competent organiser, a superbly discreet confidante, an exacting copy editor with a B.A. (*maxima cum laude*) in English, she has typed each one of Arthur's manuscripts beginning with *Airport*. (Ruth also read this book in manuscript and sent me fifteen pages of notes about small errors and inconsistencies.)

Arthur's research notes are categorised by subject headings, and he files them away in his superneat fashion—for it may be a couple of years before he has need to refer to them. He accumulates so much information he could not possibly remember it all. Therefore, he cross-references each file, detailing related material in other files. It is this ultramethodical approach to writing a novel that astounds me. Arthur is deliberate and—yes—pernickety in everything he does. There are times he drives me up the wall, he is so exacting.

During this research period I never accompany Arthur on a trip. He is single-minded about this work, is irritated by intrusions and in no mood for social chitchat, unless it relates to what he is researching. In short, he is no fun to be with (for me, at any rate), and I am happy to stay home, or arrange a trip of my own.

I finally appreciated this 'Lone Ranger' approach after I did some research for Arthur on his forthcoming new novel, *Overload*, which he is still working on as I write this. I spent a week in New York, talking to doctors and patients—about electrocutions, burns, skin grafts, polio, severed spinal cords, and paraplegics. It was taxing and emotional work, and I made the mistake of cramming all sorts of social activity into the week as well—lunches, dinners, theatres, films, shopping. I had to make time for my notes, so I was late to bed every night and up early in the morning. I finished my week exhausted. Since then I have understood Arthur's adamant views about not mixing research and pleasure. (Except, of course, for the odd dinner out for him—always with an attractive woman. He needs *some* respite, he tells me.)

Over the years I've sometimes helped Arthur in this way, by taking on specific research assignments. I have always enjoyed the work. I spent a couple of weeks in New Orleans for *Hotel*, talking to firemen, policemen, studying escape routes for Keycase Milne, the hotel key thief, and visiting Charity Hospital. For *Airport* I talked to U.S. Army Bomb Disposal personnel and learned how to install a home-made bomb in a briefcase. (That was before hijacking made preflight personal searches mandatory.) I also spent a couple of days with U.S. Customs at J.F. Kennedy Airport, and a whole night watching mail being sorted at the airport post office and loaded onto planes. When I got back home in Toronto, Arthur remarked that far from being refreshed from such a trip, away from the children and household cares, I seemed somewhat tired and irritable.

'So would *you* be,' I snapped, 'if you'd been up all night sorting mail.'

I was even more peeved later when, after I had typed pages and pages explaining how the post office worked, he used only one sentence in *Airport*. I fared better with Customs; he based the first five pages of Chapter Thirteen on my notes.

Still, *I* haven't always been understanding when Arthur has returned from a research trip. I was irascible after his Detroit experiences. Another classic example was when Arthur saw his first autopsy. Before he wrote the TV play *No Deadly Medicine*, it was arranged that he visit a pathologist, Dr. Richard G. McManus, at West Pennsylvania Hospital in Pittsburgh. (This proved to be a fascinating experience, for Arthur spent six weeks in the hospital, wearing a white coat and often being mistaken for a doctor.) But first, Arthur was anxious to prepare himself for this project, so he asked a pathologist at St. Michael's Hospital, Toronto, if he might witness an autopsy.

'Sure,' said Dr. Terence Van Patter, adding the pathologist's traditional joke, 'but we don't schedule them.' However, later the same day he called Arthur back. 'I have to leave for Orillia within the hour. A factory crane operator fell from his crane to a cement floor. There's insurance involved, and his employers want to know if the fall was an accident or caused by a heart attack. Do you want to drive up with me?'

They drove the ninety miles to the undertaker's in Orillia, where the body had been brought. It was a midsummer day and the tiny room behind the parlour was hot and stuffy, unlike the air-conditioned, clinical, hospital laboratories where most autopsies take place.

Arthur saw Terry make a 'Y' incision with three strong knife strokes, from each shoulder to the bottom of the chest, then downward from chest to genitals. As the pathologist cut through the ribs, revealing lungs and heart, and then removed the various organs from the abdomen opening, Arthur's own insides heaved. He excused himself a couple of times for a breath of outside air, to avoid gagging at the sight and smell. Finally, he watched spell-bound as the dead man's flesh was cut across the top of the head, starting from behind each ear above the hairline, so the incision would not be visible if the body were placed on view. Then the whole scalp was pulled down over the face, exposing the skull to the pathologist's electric saw. It was a sickening experience for a layman, and Arthur's stomach was still churning when he arrived home that evening. Just in time for dinner.

Guess what I had prepared. Calves' liver. Arthur took one look at it, turned slightly green, pushed his plate away, and said, 'Sheila, if you don't mind . . .'

I have always been amazed how a man so impatient at home about small things can show infinite patience when researching. When Arthur was interviewing a house detective for his novel *Hotel*, he spent hours listening to the man's woes. All the hotel employee wanted to talk about was his personal problems—difficulties he was having at home with his wife and daughter, some income tax he owed, and the dull routine of his job, which he disliked. Arthur listened patiently to all this and had just about given up, when his informer said: 'Say, I remember a guy you might be interested in. He had a special racket—stealing hotel keys. He did it this way . . .' Arthur's excitement grew as the house detective talked, and so the character, Keycase Milne, was born.

Arthur exhibited the same patience when he studied the motor industry for *Wheels*. In trying to understand what it felt like to work on an assembly line, he talked to hourly-paid workers, management, and union officials. Mel Glasser, a union officer, gave him this advice: 'Don't do what most people do . . . just walk alongside an assembly line and watch a car take shape. Instead, pick a point in the line where a man is working, any man, and stay at that same position for half an hour.' Arthur did this on three separate occasions. Each time, after the first few minutes, he found himself bored and wanted to move on. At the end of twenty minutes he was looking at his watch impatiently, waiting for the half hour to end.

The experience struck home. He thought: 'If I am this bored after a mere half hour, how does a man feel who can't walk away as I am doing, who must stay on that job for the remainder of the shift, who must come back tomorrow, and the day after, and the day after that, ad infinitum?'

Later, when Arthur wrote the assembly-line scenes in *Wheels*, he transmitted this feeling. From some sources he received praise for his understanding. But we also heard that senior motor-industry executives were unhappy about the descriptions of assembly-line monotony, even though subsequent, independent studies confirmed this view as accurate.

Nor was the motor industry pleased with Arthur's revelation that Monday and Friday cars are often poorly assembled because of high absenteeism at plants. Soon after *Wheels* was published, it was difficult to find a car dealer in North America who would admit to having a Monday or Friday car in his showroom. The *Wall Street Journal* ran a cartoon in which a car salesman tells a prospective customer, 'You'll notice that the price includes full power accessories, air conditioning, stereo tape deck, and an affidavit certifying that it was not assembled on Monday or Friday.'

Arthur is a fussy man and pays enormous attention to detail. He notices dust on furniture, tiny spots on clothes. When he writes, everything must be impeccably accurate. He won't write off the top of his head, hoping the facts are correct, no matter how relatively unimportant these minute details are to the main story. If he were going to write a sentence about installing a U-bend pipe under a kitchen sink, he'd ask a plumber how it was done. He argues: if the sentence doesn't ring true to a plumber, then the plumber will doubt the information in the rest of the story.

So Arthur labours to make this kind of accuracy a part of his craft. That's why the research—painstaking and nitpicking—takes the best part of a year to do. Out of it will come hundreds of incidents and anecdotes and a general theme that suggests itself to his storyteller's mind.

After that it's pure imagination—creating characters, situations, and plot—a process that is intensive, all-consuming, and lonely. I cannot share in it, for ideas are only half formed in Arthur's mind, not ready for others' scrutiny. It's an exciting but exasperating time—and it lasts for several months. His mind is constantly on his story. His ideas come at all times of the day and night.

At dinner I might be chatting and suddenly recognise the glazed eyes. 'You're not listening to anything I'm saying, are you?' I ask, and he will irritatingly repeat word for word what I have just said, even though, seconds before, the meaning had not penetrated his consciousness. Or he will come into the house after a swim, snapping his fingers excitedly. 'I've got it!'—the key to resolving a tricky story problem—and indeed he often does get it while swimming his daily laps.

Another fertile idea-spawning area is under the shower. He forgets where he is while he thinks about his story until the water runs cold.

Sometimes I knock on the shower door and shout, 'Do you know you're in there?' We each have our own bathroom, but we do share the hot water tank, and I rebel at having to bathe in lukewarm water. I was delighted a couple of years ago when our forty-gallon tank burst and it was replaced by one that holds sixty gallons. I considered the extra cost of water and electricity a reasonable business expense.

An outline of an Arthur Hailey novel is forty to fifty pages of single-spaced typing. As well, there are two or three appendices, explaining a philosophy or spelling out technical data. Each draft is read and commented on by me, and by Arthur's editors at Doubleday, Sam Vaughan and Walter Bradbury. Each of us points out weaknesses. One may question an unconvincing character, another suggest where the story line could be strengthened. The criticisms are general; the details Arthur works out himself.

At this point it should be mentioned that the relationship between an author and his editor bears little resemblance to the popular notion of an editor correcting the author's written words. It's more an exchange of ideas. A publisher's editor, while not necessarily a creative writer, must have a special talent for structuring a book and, for fiction, a strong sense of story. Many editors never put a pencil on a manuscript but convey ideas verbally to their authors; others have an eye for detail and do suggest changes in syntax. It is strictly a personal relationship tailored to the author's and editor's personalities. Another function of an editor is that he is, in effect, the author's representative within the publishing organisation; he looks out for that author's interest in matters of book design, production, publicity, advertising and sales.

Some writers dislike editors seeing their work in the embryonic stages; most, however, need a 'sounding board' early on as well as encouragement along the way. Arthur is certainly among these, and has always acknowledged that he owes a great deal to the editors he has worked with.

To get back to Arthur's work methods. It is not unusual for him to rewrite an outline four or five times. Each time he does, it is more than just a matter of revising; he takes quantum leaps ahead as new ideas and story facets develop. That's why this stage of a novel can take up to six months to complete; and while none of this writing will ever be published, it is vital to the finished product. It's like preparing a route map for a long journey. Later, along the way and during writing, he may decide to make a detour by changing a character or introducing additional scenes—but he still needs the map to guide him in the right direction.

Other literary descriptions that never get published are the personality profiles that Arthur writes. He does one for each main character in his books. They include physical appearance, family background, education, philosophy, character traits. All of this helps establish these individuals as real people in Arthur's mind. He is going to live with them a long time, so he tries to know them in depth at the beginning.

Their names he chooses with infinite care. His main objective is that the reader can easily identify the characters each time they come on stage. Nothing is more irritating to a reader, he feels, than constantly having to flip back in a book to establish who is who. Therefore he makes sure names do not look alike (e.g. James Roberts and Jane Robinson). He chooses some Anglo-Saxon names, some of other ethnic origin. Perhaps one character is known by initials (D. O. Guerrero in *Airport*).

His source of first names is a list of boys' and girls' names that I brought home from the hospital after Diane was born twenty years ago. It is now yellow with age. Its tattered edges have been Scotch-taped with sentimental care, but it is still legible. Occasionally he checks in *The Oxford Dictionary of English Christian Names*.

Arthur also keeps a list of names (of people he has met) that he particularly likes and might use in future books. Come to think of it—and this is no surprise to me—every single name on the list is a woman's: Melodie, Damaris, Ardythe, Marti, Deirdre, Rosanne, Jenny, Sharlett, and so on. *There isn't a Sheila in the lot*.

The surnames? Easy. He keeps a Manhattan phone book handy. I doubt that there is a surname in the English-speaking world that is not included in that massive two-and-a-half-inch-thick list of New York telephone subscribers. He may decide on a name beginning with 'K', for instance. So, depending on the type of names he has already used, he will choose a simple, one-syllable name (Kemp), a jawbreaker (Kouchakdjian), or a distinguished one (Kensington).

The actual writing of a 500-page book—the average length of one of Arthur's novels—takes him roughly eighteen months. It is during this time that our lives are extremely disciplined. We usually decline invitations to lunch or dinner except at weekends—not because we are unsociable, but because a lunch with a cocktail or wine makes afternoon writing difficult, and a dinner party often means a late night with a sluggish morning after. Arthur is essentially a morning person, whereas I tend to be a night person. Over the years we have compromised—by my going to bed early and my getting up early.

Arthur's day begins at 7 A.M., when he takes the first of three daily Apresoline pills for blood pressure. (The doctor's prescription label states that the other two should be taken at noon and 5 P.M.—so that's *exactly* when Arthur takes them.) He is so compulsive by nature that he automatically wakes at this time without an alarm clock. Heaven help him if he should not take the pill until 7:25!

'Honey,' I have said, 'your stomach doesn't care if it gets the pill right on the dot of seven. It's not on Greenwich Mean Time minus five.'

'But *I* care,' he retorts.

He putters around the house in the quiet of the early morning: walking in the garden, scribbling something at his desk, dictating a letter or two, or reading in the living-room. I sleep as long as possible, but I am invariably awakened about 7:40 by his exercises. For eighteen years, since a reporter on the *Calgary Herald* described Arthur as 'portly' (at over 14st, he *was*), he has followed the Royal Canadian Air Force 5BX eleven-minute physical fitness plan. This, along with good eating habits, keeps his weight at a trim 11½ st. He does these exercises every day religiously, no matter where he is—at home, in friends' spare-rooms, in hotel rooms. The only days he has missed have been when he was in the hospital for surgery. He is, in fact, a compulsive exercise nut. The ritual concludes with jogging on the spot, interspersed every seventy-five steps with 'jumping jacks' involving slaps of hands on thighs. The sound of that slapping really bugs me, and every so often—after a few sharp words—he will confine the calisthenics to an empty bedroom. Later in the hour I retaliate with my exercises—the women's Royal Canadian Air Force 10BX, which I do to selected bouncy tunes, transposed to a special tape recording for me by our son Steven. Arthur has been listening to those same songs—usually I am exercising while he's shaving—for eight years. I think we both put up with these aggravations because we are glad the other is keeping in shape. But at least Arthur gets a respite. I sometimes skip the exercises on weekends or if I've had a late night out and don't feel like doing them next morning.

Breakfast is at 8:45 and Arthur is at his desk soon after 9:30, having read part of the day's newspapers. He looks at his mail first, answers a few letters, but finally cannot put off writing any longer. I have often called writing a love-hate relationship. Basically, Arthur loves to write, but he is reluctant to get started. I understand and sympathise. Writing is, purely and simply, hard work.

He scribbles in longhand first, a paragraph at a time, then swings around to his IBM typewriter to type the passage cleanly on paper. He then revises it, playing with a phrase, substituting a word, cutting away excess 'fat', wrestling with an awkward expression. After this amending, he types the paragraph again and again, sometimes a dozen times, until it is the best he can do. It will usually appear this way in the finished manuscript. It's a slow, laborious process, but is suited to his methodical, meticulous temperament.

For Arthur's writing does not flow fluently from his pen or typewriter. He worries the words onto paper. Since I began this book I have been overwhelmed by the difference between us in the way we write. Arthur must see each separate paragraph typed clean in all its stages; sometimes he'll revert to his original words, but only after he's typed the alternatives several times. I write many pages at a time, correcting minimally as I go along. Then I scribble changes on top of changes before I commit them to the typewriter. I can 'hear' the words in my head; Arthur must see them.

In short, he gets a book written the way he learned to fly—in spite of airsickness—through sheer guts and perseverance. That's why I get irritated if I hear some supercilious idiot talk about him 'churning out' books as though they tumbled from a word machine.

It sounds pedantic—but because he is such a slow writer, Arthur really does count the finished words. His target is 600 a day, and as each paragraph is completed he deducts the number or words it contains from that target. Occasionally, on a bad day when progress is slow, he will go back to his study after dinner to make up those 600 words. But more often he meets his quota between four and five o'clock. Then he will quit, after scribbling down a few thoughts to make the next day's start easier.

Arthur has on his desk a small wood carving of a kiwi, the nocturnal bird that cannot fly, which is New Zealand's national emblem. During a visit to that country in 1976 Arthur was fascinated to learn that this bird eats six hundred worms a day. He felt an immediate kinship with the kiwi, and now keeps the model in sight as an encouragement to do his own six hundred.

From my point of view, the great thing about this orderly method of writing is that it leaves us plenty of free time to be together. Several times a week, for instance, we will take a picnic lunch on our boat, and swim off a long white beach just minutes from the house. We are both able to switch off, are completely relaxed, and understand each other's moods. We talk of many things—politics, the local scene, the day's news, some gossip, the children's lives—or, sometimes, we don't talk much at all. I know Arthur returns to his desk, within a couple of hours, refreshed from the swim, the fresh air, and the lunch.

Our evenings are also free for what we enjoy most—a leisurely pre-dinner drink, comfortable talk, an excellent dinner, good wine. Then we catch up on the day's newspapers, listen to music, read a book, or see an occasional film. This over-all working pattern gives us free weekends—for entertaining, or being entertained.

Every so often we'll take off for a few days—to New York, Toronto, Palm Beach, or London—as a change of scene. A writer—any writer—needs to get away from his writing once in a while for an emotional rest. He can then come back to it with a fresh, objective view. For Arthur gets totally involved in his work. A thrilling chapter churns in him a lather of excitement—as happened, for example, when he was writing the bomb scene in *Airport*.

If he has been writing something that appeals to his sense of humour, he finishes the day elated and buoyant. Such an episode occurred in *The Moneychangers*, when he described one of Margot Bracken's battles with bureaucracy. It was a 'sit-in' demonstration that occupied all the public toilets at the local airport—a real-life incident planned by an activist group in Chicago but never executed. Later we chuckled over dinner, and had a lively, joyous evening. And this mischievous mood continued as he wrote the scene where hundreds of tenants from Forum East besieged the bank to open new accounts with five dollars apiece.

Conversely, he can be sad and thoughtful, not wanting to talk, as he was when involved in a scene in *The Moneychangers* in which Alex Vandervoort visits his insane wife. And he has been so depressed on occasion that it is a real effort to jolly him out of this state of mind.

I remember when he was writing about the drab life of Rollie Knight, a black assembly-line worker in *Wheels*. He had already spent many hours talking to unemployed young men in the ghettos of Detroit. He began to understand what it is like to be black and poor and hopeless. But back in the comfortable, affluent environment of the Bahamas' Lyford Cay, it was not easy to get into that same bleak mood. So he would reread portions of James Baldwin's *Tell Me How Long the Train's Been Gone*, Eldridge Cleaver's *Soul on Ice*, and *Daddy Was a Numbers Runner* by Louise Meriwether. These books affected him enormously and created in him the right frame of mind for writing. I am proud of the number of compliments he received, after *Wheels* was published, on the characterisation of Rollie.

Then there was the time when Arthur wrote about Keith Bakersfeld contemplating suicide in *Airport*. He was dejected himself for days. And the dread of being incarcerated gave him nightmares when he was writing of Miles Eastin's terrifying prison experiences in *The Moneychangers*. This, incidentally, is the reason I am sure he will never write a novel about prisons and penal reform, although it's a subject he cares about and one that has been suggested many times. Even if he could bring himself to do it, I am not sure that I could live through three years of programmed depression.

I enjoy reading Arthur's work.

There was a time when I used to read each day's production of words as they were completed. But I got too close to the project and lost some of the objectivity needed to give a sound editorial opinion. Now I read each chapter as it is finished, and I am always amused that Arthur makes sure I have ideal conditions for this task. No interruptions are allowed, and he intercepts my telephone calls. He is anxious for my verdict and, good or bad, listens avidly to my reactions. He's always been professional about criticism. If I dislike a phrase or passage, he'll sometimes say, 'You're right. I was doubtful about that too. I'll change it.' But if it is a scene he has toiled especially hard over, his attitude may be: 'Well, let's wait to see if Sam or Brad pick that up.' (If the opinions of Doubleday's editors confirm my view, then Arthur begins dissecting immediately. If not, his judgment prevails.)

I have learned over the years to be honest. The last thing a professional writer needs is phony praise from an uncritical relative. But it is difficult to be tough when you know your words can put a damper on the evening that you are going to share together. Fortunately, Arthur has become his own best editor. Success has given him confidence; he has grown as a writer, and will not settle for anything less than the best he can do. The result is that by the time I see a chapter, his own critical eye has been over it so many times, there is little need for drastic comment. Still, I am careful to be positive over the things I am enthusiastic about first, before I go on to criticise the parts I don't like.

Although Arthur has a detailed outline to follow, his story inevitably changes as he writes. A different incident suggests itself that is better than the original one. Or a minor character will develop and 'take over'. Avril, the high-class call girl in *The Moneychangers*, was just such a person. Originally meant to be a two-line bit part, she developed in such a way that Arthur found himself writing a more prominent part for her in the book.

When this happens he has to go back in the manuscript to rewrite the earlier references to that character. Or he must rework a description in the light of these later developments. Arthur always does this as he goes along, rather than wait until the manuscript is finished and then revise the whole. Again, it's the obvious result of a tidy mind; he cannot bear to leave the earlier chapters in need of revision once he has made the decision to change them.

The outcome of this is that when Arthur nears the end of a book, it really is the end. There isn't a massive rewrite job to be done. It's a wonderfully exciting time. The tempo in the house quickens. The output of words each day increases. Arthur is at his desk earlier, and evening sessions are more frequent.

It becomes impossible for him to keep his earlier measured pace. He is too exhilarated by the thought that his three years' toil will soon be over. He is reluctant to leave his desk for social engagements at this time, and I keep them to a minimum. He also finds it difficult to sleep through the night. He is suddenly wide awake and is compelled to pad over to his study to continue writing. It isn't coincidental that the last sentence of most of his novels has been written in the early hours of the morning.

The next day, the joy in our house is overwhelming. We celebrate with champagne and plan a happy, carefree trip, luxuriating in real leisure days with no guilt thoughts of 'I should be working.' Anyone married to a compulsive workaholic shares that luxury too rarely.

But then the doubts begin to set in. Is the book as good as I can make it? Should I have expanded such-and-such a character? Is this or that scene too long?

Arthur always feels 'let down' within a couple of weeks of delivering his manuscript to the publishers. He knows he has a long wait ahead of him—another seven to nine months until publication day. (It's a bit like having a baby, except that conceiving a child is easier and more pleasurable.)

Always surprising to outsiders is that it takes so long after the writing is done to go through the various stages of manufacturing a book: copy editing, designing, typesetting, proofreading, printing, binding, designing and printing the jacket, then scheduling the advertising, promotion, and distribution.

It is a restless time. Arthur is impatient to see his work in bookshops. He's not quite ready to start a new book, so he wants something exciting to happen to fill the void.

It usually does . . .

CHAPTER 9

Change Is Good ...
Well, Sometimes!

Arthur is a man of great energy, enthusiasms and tremendous drive. This drive is what makes him get on with the business of researching and writing novels. I have always admired it—but the same energy and enthusiasm is always driving right into our private life. When he has most craved excitement and change—usually between books— we have often wound up moving to another house. Or country. In fact, the only people I know who have moved more than we have are those whose jobs demand it.

To explain . . .

Our first house was the two-bedroom bungalow in a Toronto suburb which Arthur bought in 1947 for $8,100. It was the type that sprang up like mushrooms, row after row, just after World War II. We spent our first two years of marriage scouring it, painting it, building bookshelves and room dividers, buying furniture on hire purchase. Finally, in one huge burst of effort, we finished the base- ment. It was magnificent. The decor of the main bedroom had proved so successful, we were now ready to turn the second bedroom into a nursery. The wallpaper was chosen, the curtain material bought, and in a few short months our baby would be cooing in it. I was ecstatically happy.

One Sunday morning we were out driving, and we came across four new three-bedroom homes, sitting in a sea of mud on a high bluff overlooking Lake Ontario. The contractor happened to be around and gave us the price, which was $16,700.

'That's a real bargain,' said Arthur. 'Look at the size of this living- room!'

The next day we signed an offer to purchase, and our little house, slicked up with paint and shining like a jewel, was sold within three days—for $13,000.

Seven years and three children later, our new home was positively elegant. We'd landscaped, planted trees and shrubs, built a patio and added a handsome study on the back of the garage for Arthur to work in, away from the noise of the children. The study was so beautiful—oak-panelled with a large red-brick fireplace—it eventually cost half what we paid for the entire house.

Then in 1960 our dear friends Bill and Glenys Stevenson returned to Toronto after six years in Hong Kong; they began house-hunting. The following Sunday the four of us, with our combined seven children, had lunch together.

'Say, why don't you come with us to look at this new house we like?' said Bill.

Well, why not? It was an innocent enough suggestion.

We admired the spacious kitchen, living-room and dining-room, then inspected the four bedrooms upstairs. We went downstairs to look at the unfinished recreation room, which had a stone fireplace. Next door was a small room with an outside entrance. I knew instinctively that Arthur was visualising a book-lined study and that in the next room he saw his secretary entering the door to start her morning's work. It was unfortunate that the wave-length that develops between well-married people was exceptionally efficient that morning and our receivers were finely tuned. We exchanged final approving looks. I knew what was coming next and was powerless to stop it.

'Bill,' said Arthur casually, 'if you don't buy this house, we will.'

Bill immediately warmed to the idea. 'Great, because then we could buy your house. Glenys and I have always admired it.'

Six hours later, the estate agent for the new house was in our living-room, rubbing his hands over the easiest sale of his life. Arthur drew up an offer to purchase, for Bill's signature—and it was all over.

For me it opened up a new era—weeks of packing, unpacking and general upheaval. Looking back on that move, it was in many ways a giant leap sideways.

I say this now because Arthur's disenchantment with Canadian winters began soon afterward. He was in between the completion of *In High Places* and the research for *Hotel*. We were driving to a film in downtown Toronto when snow began to fall. It was April; we had taken off our snow tyres the day before and the car skidded on the slick surface of the road. Then, after parking the car, Arthur noticed that his newly cleaned shoes were getting dirty from the slush. He exploded: 'Dammit! Why do we live in a climate where it snows in April? We could live anywhere!' The first seeds of restlessness were planted, and I knew then that eventually we would leave Canada for warmer climes. But not yet.

We discussed the possibility of moving to a semi-tropical country, and what it would mean to the children. And it so happened that the following week Arthur had to fly to London. The lady he sat next to on the plane lived in Bermuda, so naturally he bombarded her with questions. Later, settled in his hotel room, he impulsively phoned me.

'Sheila, why don't we take a chance? Put the house on the market and see if you can sell it by the time I get back. Then we can just pick up and go.'

Just like that, I thought. Three children, a house full of furniture and books. For once in my life I could not be enthusiastic with him. I was determined to be cagey instead and not get caught up in the approaching avalanche of enthusiasm. I suggested I go to Bermuda on my own for a week to investigate. I did, and had a wonderful time. I rented a motorised bicycle and put-putted all over the island. I met many charming people who were helpful. One of my questions: 'I notice a lot of mildew in these older houses without air conditioning. What about books? How do they fare?'

No problem at all, I was told. You just take them off the shelves and open them up outside every six weeks. My God! I thought, remembering the thousands of books we have. *I'm* the one who'd be worrying about airing them; and I pictured myself staggering out to the front lawn every six weeks with pile after pile of books.

The houses for sale seemed to be enormously expensive. I knew that financially we could not handle that cost of living. I also had the feeling we were too young to be out of the mainstream, that Canada was far better for the children.

I returned to Toronto. My verdict: 'It's a wonderful, beautiful island for a holiday. But, darling, I don't think you'd be happy living there. The current films seem to be about two years old.'

That was the only time I really rebelled about moving. Ever since I had decided to give up my family in England to return to Canada in

1951 to marry him, I have felt about Arthur the way the biblical Ruth felt about her mother-in-law: 'Wither thou goest, I will go.' But there *are* limits. So we stayed in Toronto, and Arthur overcame his restlessness by having an affair, but this isn't the chapter to go into *that*.

The real shock, however, was yet to come. In the summer of 1965 Arthur was in Los Angeles, doing research for a new novel about an airport.

'While you're there,' wrote Ken McCormick, then editor-in-chief of Doubleday, 'why don't you hop up to San Francisco and see my friend Alexis Klotz. He's a retired TWA pilot, and has some good stories about flying you may find interesting.'

So while the children and I were at our summer cottage in northern Ontario, Arthur visited Alexis, who lives in St. Helena, an attractive town in the lovely Napa Valley, sixty-five miles north-east of San Francisco.

Arthur was enchanted with what he saw that Sunday afternoon. On Monday morning a friend of the Klotzes, Dean McNealy, offered to fly him over the valley.

As Arthur climbed down from the plane, he asked: 'If someone were thinking of living here, what available sites are there?' He was shown several, and as he stood on the last one said, 'What a view! How much?'

'Eleven thousand five hundred.'

'Oh, really? I'll buy it.'

He immediately phoned his secretary to arrange the down payment.

'Doreen, wire me a thousand dollars, will you?'

'Hold on!' said she, her loyalties divided. 'What is it? Gambling or a woman?'

'I'll tell you when I get back,' he chuckled.

A couple of days after this phone call, I was relaxing on the beach at Kennisis Lake in front of our summer cottage. The nearest phone was seventeen miles away—so I was blissfully unaware of events taking shape in California. I had just completed a new and difficult project—reupholstering two old armchairs in our living-room. The new material went smashingly with the sisal rug I'd bought earlier. I was reflecting that, with our Toronto house just redecorated six months earlier with new hall and stair carpeting, we were in good shape. All the ugly spots of both houses had been dealt with. In the autumn, when the children were back at school, I could take up again the TV work that was so enjoyable. (I had a weekly segment on a woman's daytime show, answering problem letters—a sort of television equivalent of Evelyn Home.)

A shout from Steven interrupted my lazy daydreaming. 'Mom, Jane has used the last of the peanut butter to make herself a sandwich, and she won't even share it.'

Ah, well! I knew we were low on milk and I hadn't collected the mail for a couple of days, so, 'Okay, let's take the boat to the landing.' The 'landing' was a marina four miles up the lake, a pleasant ride in our little runabout with its thirty-five-horsepower outboard. It comprised a gas pump, a café and a grocery store which was also the post office. Mixed up with the mail was a telegram:

NAPA VALLEY CALIFORNIA IS A FEW FEET THIS SIDE OF PARADISE. IT IS EVERYTHING WE HAVE DREAMED ABOUT AND LOVE. CLIMATE SUPERB. SPRING IN FEBRUARY. ALL YEAR OUTDOOR COUNTRY LIVING COMBINED WITH CITY CLOSENESS. LOCAL SCHOOLS EXCELLENT. SAN FRANCISCO ONE HOUR DRIVE. TODAY I BOUGHT HALF ACRE IN MEADOWOOD DEVELOPMENT ON GLORIOUS HILLSIDE OVERLOOKING VALLEY AND MOUNTAINS. ALEXIS AND PEGGY KLOTZ EXPECTING YOU EARLY SEPTEMBER TO BEGIN PLANNING OUR FUTURE HOME. LOVE.

ARTHUR

Oh! to hell with him, I thought disgustedly, in my womanly, picayune way. I have just struggled for a whole week with needle, tacks and hammer and those two damn chairs. Now he wants to move! And waddya mean . . . 'everything WE have dreamed about and love'? I was still a London-born city girl at heart. And what about all that money we'd just spent on the Toronto house?

I read the telegram to the kids. They were full of questions. 'What's it like there?' 'When will we move?' 'Will we keep the cottage?'

'Look,' I said, 'you know as much as I do. We'll just have to wait until Daddy comes home on Sunday.'

Meanwhile, I suspected, Arthur was biting his nails wondering about my reaction. Good! Let him stew a bit. I certainly wasn't going to wire back and say everything was hunky-dory. I wasn't sure that it was. I had too many questions myself.

By the time Sunday did roll around, natural optimism had asserted itself, and I began to feel excited at the prospect of moving to California. So when Arthur's car crunched into the driveway after the long drive north, the children and I dashed out, all holding hands, singing 'California, here we come!' It was a corny gesture, but the right one. It set the tone for the whole move, for it was complicated, what with selling two homes, moving three thousand miles, putting furniture into storage, and starting to build a large home on that half acre of 'glorious hillside overlooking valley and mountains'.

Six months later, we flew to San Francisco with sixteen suitcases, bought a station wagon and drove down the magnificent California coast road to Disneyland—to spend Christmas with Arthur's three older sons and their mother. Then we rented a tiny house in the Napa Valley and lived out of those suitcases for four months.

I must confess there were times that winter when I wondered why we had left Canada—a country I loved, and still do. The Napa Valley winter was appalling that year. When it rained, it rained for days on end. Even the famed vineyards looked bare and ugly with their branches pruned back to gnarled, misshapen stumps. 'All-year outdoor country living!' Ha!

It was all right for Arthur. He had rented a comfortable Meadowood Club chalet and it was there that he settled down to write the novel he would call *Airport*. He was excited by the concept of the book, and it buoyed his spirits during those dreary months.

For me, there were daily visits to the building site. The progress seemed maddeningly slow. We waited and waited for the arrival of a long ceiling beam so that the carpenters could finish the roof and get the inside work started. I always could envisage day-to-day living there, from the time we okayed the first blueprints—but sometimes it did tax the imagination. For so many weeks it was a sodden mess of wet, raw timber.

I chauffeured the kids *everywhere*. In Toronto they had walked to school and to their music classes or to the bus stop. I missed my weekly TV work. Above all, deep down, I missed the city life.

But I grew to love the Napa Valley. Nine and a half months after Arthur had sent me the telegram, we moved into our hillside home and had a joyous reunion with all our stored furniture and paintings. Spring *was* early, and after all that winter rain the valley was incredibly green. The children thrived in the small-town atmosphere and grew tanned and long-limbed under the California sun.

Above all, we loved the people, their warmth and friendliness typical of the West. They are maverick types in the Napa Valley, all searching for the good life. Some gave up high-salaried jobs in cities to start new wineries on small budgets and large bank loans, or to sell real estate, or to teach—anything to be in the country where you can feel, smell and breathe a quality of life matched in only a very few parts of the world.

Two years after our move to the Napa Valley, Arthur and I were in San Francisco for one of our regular day trips. For all its new highrise buildings and worsening smog, it is still a stunning city that delights the eye. And, though never boasting a population of more than three quarters of a million, it has an international atmosphere. Arthur phoned the beauty salon where I was getting my hair cut and left word that he would pick me up at four o'clock. As I stepped into the car, he grinned, 'Got a surprise for you!' and drove me to the Embarcadero area, overlooking San Francisco Bay.

The surprise was a studio apartment on the top floor of a newly-built complex. 'I've signed a year's lease on it. We can move in in three months. That'll give you time to furnish it.' I hugged him—this dear, wonderful, impulsive man, who knew that a toehold in San Francisco would round off our country life to perfection. We adored it. We would leave the children behind once or twice a week, drive into the city, see a film, dine out in a fine restaurant, then go back to our little apartment and make love. Next day we would sometimes drive back early so Arthur could be at his desk by 9:30—or we would stay until late afternoon and be in St. Helena in time for dinner at home with the children. It was always a mini-honeymoon that we revelled in. All young parents should be so lucky—to get away regularly and keep romance alive.

The next move was even more traumatic and complicated than our move to the Napa Valley. But by that time I was an old hand at changing residences and took it in my stride—just.

It was autumn, 1969. *Airport* had been successful beyond our wildest dreams. It also brought us financial problems because of so much income flowing in over a short period. Arthur did his best to cope but, even with financial and legal advice, it was taking far too much of his time. I became increasingly concerned watching Arthur's dilemma: his involvement with these matters robbed him of precious time in which to write.

'My God,' I exploded one day. 'What are you supposed to be—a writer or a financial and tax expert? You're spending more time with that damned calculator than you are with the typewriter. It's ridiculous.'

We had a long discussion. We needed a simpler financial base than the complicated one we had, with an office in Canada and our home in California. Arthur and I had often talked about spending winters in a warmer climate. The Napa Valley was superb in summer months, but in winter, while the heavy rainfall was good for dormant grapevines, it did little for our moody resident writer, who got depressed during bad weather.

Our philosophy has always been: life is short; you only get one go-around, so live to the fullest. If a change seems desirable, don't wait. *Make* it happen.

Arthur flew to the Bahamas, which our Canadian legal adviser had recommended as a good place to live and one with financial advantages. He returned a week later, buoyant and optimistic. We decided to try it for two years.

In one way it was a selfish decision—we didn't delude ourselves about that—because it involved change and adjustment affecting our whole family. But our children were understanding. Jane, however, did not want to leave St. Helena High School in the middle of her junior year. Steven had just five months to go in eighth grade before entering The Hill School, a boys' preparatory school in Pottstown, Pennsylvania. So it was arranged that they would stay in California, living with close friends: Steven with Stan and Jackie Peterson until he changed schools; Jane with John and Faye Nichols until she graduated from high school. Diane would come with us to the Bahamas and go to St. Andrew's, an excellent day school in Nassau. (The English-type school was a mild shock to Diane, after attending an American elementary school. The first day she reported: 'All the girls wear blue-and-white-striped dresses, and all the boys wear grey trousers and white shirts. The whole school goes into a big room in the mornings to say prayers and sing a hymn, and the headmaster wears his cape. It's just like *Goodbye, Mr. Chips*!')

I might have had second thoughts about splitting up our family if I had not been separated from my own family in England during the war. I know I emerged from that experience strong and independent; I was sure Jane and Steven had the courage to take the separation in their stride too. So I made the final decision to go.

Our initial move came in October 1969 when Arthur and I left the children in St. Helena with our housekeeper. Looking back, I marvel at the speed with which we resettled our lives. During our first three days in the Bahamas we found a house available on a six-month lease. It was right on the sea, the waves lapping against the porch wall that formed one side of the house. It was obvious that this porch should be Arthur's study. The continuous sound of the surf would provide the 'white noise' that time-study experts say is essential for maximum production. I'm not sure what it did for Arthur's production, but at least it insulated him from the normal noises coming from the rest of the household.

We had been told that everything was slow, slow, slow in the Bahamas, compared with North America. But we bought a desk, a filing cabinet, and swivel chair from John Bull, an office-equipment store in Nassau, and all three were delivered the *same day*. (Naturally, Arthur had to have much grander furniture after our house was built—and guess who inherited that desk and chair and is still using it as I write this book.)

Arthur was writing the early chapters of his fifth novel, *Wheels*, so I left him in the Bahamas to continue working in solitude and returned to California. There I sent off our Christmas cards with the new address, which prompted our friend, playwright Bernard Slade, an ex-Torontonian living in Los Angeles (and the author of the fantastic Broadway success *Same Time, Next Year*), to write back: 'My God, don't you people ever stay in the same place?'

There was much packing to do, and a Christmas of sorts to prepare for. Arthur joined me a few days before our typical Christmas—a family gathering of twelve, including our three children; our three older sons—Roger, John and Mark; their mother, Joan; Roger's first wife, Maureen; John's bride-to-be, Barbara; and the first Hailey grandchild, Angela. It was a superb holiday, and when it was over on December 27, Arthur, Diane and I left the Napa Valley by car, and towing a boat.

A *boat?*

Well, it was like this. In a major move, there is always a need to keep something familiar with you. Arthur decided this something familiar should be our boat—a handsome 155-horsepower inboard-outboard which we had used on Lake Berryessa, about thirty minutes' drive from our Napa Valley home. We like boats, and would certainly want one in the Bahamas; since our boat was less than a year old, it didn't seem a bad idea to keep it. I made several phone calls, in between making arrangements for Christmas, enquiring about the best way to ship it. It was going to be difficult. Arthur had a brilliant idea: 'We'll buy a trailer and take it with us.'

'We'll do *what?*' I said. 'Are you out of your mind? My God, we can't get you to drive from here to Los Angeles, which is only five-hundred-odd miles. Now you're proposing to drive over thirty-five hundred miles—in the winter—and towing a seventeen-foot BOAT!'

All our California friends agreed he was mad. One said, tentatively, 'You know, it might be wise to sell it. Or him. I mean, they do have boats in the Bahamas—or Florida—that you could *buy*.' But Arthur has a charming habit of making his impulsive decisions work—he is determined to make them work. He has all the obstinacy of his father, who doggedly lived to be ninety. When his mind is made up, nothing can change it.

Well, by golly, it *did* work. We loaded the boat with luggage so that it didn't shimmy or sway. We hitched it to a heavy Lincoln and we had a surprisingly smooth ride. Most of the way we did sixty-five miles an hour, and sometimes seventy, with no strain at all.

The weather on that long transcontinental journey was terrible. Near Palm Springs, about the time we had to stop for lunch, we ran into a sandstorm. Sand was everywhere—in the car, in the boat, in our hair, in our teeth. In western Texas there was a snowstorm, with snow-packed, icy roads. And during the rest of the journey we experienced mostly rain, high winds, with only a few sunny periods. And this was the *southern* route.

On Friday, January 2, 1970, in the early afternoon, we arrived in Miami at the dockside, where we had to unhitch the boat before it was shipped to Nassau. We transferred the luggage from the boat to the car, cramming it to the roof. Then, with Diane on my knee and both of us wedged in the front seat between suitcases and the door, Arthur drove slowly to the airport.

In his gallant way, he said, 'You check the bags, I'll park the car.'

We had many pieces of luggage. Diane and I approached the Pan American check-in counter apprehensively, followed by porters.

'I have a little excess baggage,' I told the clerk.

'How many pieces?' he said, without looking up.

'Like seventeen.'

He looked up. 'How many tickets?'

I hesitated. 'Three?'

'Lord! Why me?' he sighed. But he was remarkably cheerful as he ticketed the seventeen bags. I could not say the same for the lengthening line of restless travellers behind us. When we finally arrived in Nassau at 9 p.m., we rented a car for ourselves, a taxi for the bags.

Later, I made a trip back to Miami from the Bahamas to arrange to have the Lincoln, which we had hired, driven back to San Francisco. This is the story of my life . . . I mean, you can't expect a writer to give up precious writing time to attend to these mundane tasks.

Within the next few weeks we bought an acre of land at Lyford Cay, an international resort club and residential area at the west end of New Providence Island. The lot is located on a seawater canal which leads through a private harbour to the sea. As well, we engaged an architect—a tall, blonde, attractive young woman of twenty-nine, Anne Webb-Johnson. After we finally approved the plans, construction of the house began in April.

In the meantime, we sold the boat. Though it travelled by road beautifully, and was ideal for water-skiing on a lake, it was overpowered and stern-heavy for rough seas. It took only a couple of dicey experiences to convince Arthur it had been unwise to keep our California boat. But you can't expect a writer to know everything. I shopped around and we replaced it with a seventeen-foot Mako with a 100-horsepower outboard motor.

By Christmas 1970, we started moving out of rented quarters into our almost-completed new home.

I'll borrow the words of writer Rob Elder as he described the house in the *Miami Herald*'s magazine, *Tropic:*

> It is set in a landscaped profusion of poinsettia, bougainvillea, frangipani and hibiscus . . . simple and charming and unostentatious, its airy, bright colours keyed to gold-and-white tile floors. And there are the little details like the wine room, with its four inches of insulation and a separate air conditioner set for a year-round temperature of 58 degrees, and a stand-by generator in case of power failure. But the lifestyle is built around function, not show. The two cars in the garage are small and practical.

Arthur's study—a hexagonal building separate from the main house—combines comfort, organisation and efficiency. It has a large picture window and, from his desk, Arthur can view the blues and greens of the canal, swimming pool, lawn and shrubs—colours which are reflected in the study's interior decor. The cathedral ceiling is a masterpiece of carpentry in pickled fir. Built-in white cabinets and bookshelves line the walls. There are single copies of all the translations of Arthur's books, which occupy thirty-seven feet of shelves. They include all major languages and some lesser-known ones—for example, Gujarati, Serbo-Croatian, Bahasan and Bengali. As well as the main work area, there are two small connecting rooms—a bathroom and a storeroom for files, stationery supplies, and a safe with a notice advising any potential burglars: *This fireproof box contains papers only. No valuables! Key is in the lock.*

Although Arthur dislikes answering the phone, he has two in his study. One, an extension of the house phone, has its bell disconnected, so he speaks on it only if I advise him by intercom that there is a special call. The other is an unlisted number, known only to his publisher and a few others. This way he works in silence with minimal interruptions. In fact, Arthur has the best working conditions he's ever known. In Rob Elder's words, 'It may be as close to heaven as any writer gets.'

We are now in our eighth year in this home, which is a longer period than we have lived together in any house. We stay in the Bahamas because we love it. The Bahamas has its problems—what country hasn't?—but race relations is not one. The winter days are warm and sunny; we swim and I play tennis almost every day. At the end of our garden we have two boats moored. One is a twenty-eight-foot Bertram flybridge cruiser, in which we can go fishing or take off for a few days to one of the outer islands; the other is the Mako, which we still use for waterskiing, beach picnics and snorkelling over coral reefs. We don't feel remote. Among other advantages, the Bahamas has excellent telephone service, with direct dialling to the U.S. and Canada, and a similar link-up with Europe is likely soon. Also, we are eight minutes' drive from Nassau airport, where we can board a direct flight to New York (two and a half hours), Toronto (three hours), or London (eight hours). In these cities, which we visit at least once a year, we try to catch up on the theatre and other urban activities which island living lacks. When we visit our children in

California, we can have lunch at home, fly via Miami and be in San Francisco at dinnertime. We have a comfortable sense of being international; when you've lived in four countries and have once changed your citizenship, it's a feeling that comes easily.

Only, occasionally, I get nightmares. Arthur suddenly appears in my horror dream, stepping down from a plane at Nassau airport. When he sees me, he runs toward me with his arms outstretched, and he is shouting, 'Darling, start packing! I've found the most wonderful piece of land . . .'

CHAPTER 10

The Four Stages of Orgasm

We have enjoyed being parents. Both Arthur and I feel that having children was an essential part of our fulfilment. At times, though, our attitudes to children have been different. For the purpose of this chapter, I asked the six young Haileys to express some thoughts about their father's role in their lives. I am including part of their replies with some observations of my own.

Jane related a memory from when she was eight years old: 'Dad talked about my being a professor—a staggering idea to a child, and yet one that made me know that he respected me and knew I could work hard to be whatever I wanted. That was nice. He has always respected women as professionals, and I know that rubbed off. He still wanted his breakfast on the table at 8 a.m., though.'

None of our children feel that Arthur was a strict father; they thought of me as the disciplinarian. I was certainly the sharper-tongued, showing my displeasure—and sometimes the back of my hand—instantly. Arthur's disapproval was rarer, quieter, more effective, and reserved for large issues. Even so, he usually discussed it with me first. And he always told me when—as happened sometimes—he was hurt by the children's thoughtlessness. At such moments I became a go-between, explaining his feelings to them, then reasoning with him that they were still children and he expected too much. Roger, the eldest Hailey son, reminisced in his letter about an incident that neither of us remembers, but which illustrates this well:

'I stayed with you the summer I had my ninth birthday. I was playing with a bow and arrow set and Dad asked me if he could have a shot, and I said no. I was having too much fun and didn't want to be interrupted. He didn't say another word, but just went back to the house. It was one of the few times we would have been able to do something together, and I ruined it. You told me how he felt later on and I have never forgotten it; you taught me how important little things like that are to him.'

Arthur has also been a softer touch for money than I am. I have sometimes wished that material things did not come so easily to the children as they have, and that we were less affluent as they grew up. Still, I had my way of paring down their allowances to a less generous level than Arthur was inclined to give, and insisting the children help around the house. For years Jane dusted Arthur's study and emptied his waste-paper-basket daily, and she regularly set the table, in the highly organised manner of her father—with the aid of a checklist.

Steven's job was to maintain our swimming pool, testing the chlorine and acid levels, adding chemicals when necessary and backwashing the filter. (Although he was only between ten and fifteen years old when he was doing this, I'll admit that, compared with pool maintenance company charges, he was grossly underpaid at two dollars a week. Knowing Steven, I suspect when he reads this he'll claim back pay.)

When Jane reached thirteen I gave her a monthly clothing allowance. I had taught her to sew and she quickly realized she could have more clothes if she made them herself. As a result she became a proficient seamstress, whipping up a dress faster than I could. Steven, too, could always sew on name tapes, and today makes a neat job of putting patches on his old jeans. Diane, however, loathes sewing and seems all thumbs as she struggles with a button.

If I was inclined to withhold funds as a disciplinary measure, Arthur was adamantly against it, and his opinion prevailed. I conceded how right he was when Jane wrote: 'One thing I respected him for is that he *never* tied money to personal matters . . . I have friends whose parents cut them off financially when they did not conform to their wills. This often meant they had to drop out of school, and in some cases led to a permanent rift between parents and child.'

As a result of my urging Steven to work for his allowance, and Arthur's encouraging him to use tools at an early age, Steven became our Mr. Fix-It around the home. The girls would ask him to repair their bicycles, record players and hair dryers, and Arthur fell into the same habit, so that when Steven went away, his father said it was like missing his right arm. Today, our Bahamian man-about-the-house, Edmond Burrows, who is good with cars and boats, relies on Steven's talents for trickier jobs. On one holiday Steven stripped down the power-mower engine to the last screw, cleaned and oiled all the parts, then reassembled it. Edmond declared that the mower had never functioned better.

However, Steven was not always this successful. When a small boy he had a mania for taking things apart which he found difficult to put together again. Invariably he would hide all the pieces. When they were eventually discovered he would deny ever having touched the broken object, so that punishment would be for failing to tell the truth. He quickly caught on to the fact that when he admitted his guilt, punishment was nil or minimal. We consoled ourselves that these exasperating incidents were giving Steven a practical course in mechanics.

Dinner time has always been the apex of the day for Arthur. It is the setting for family closeness. He wants to know in the morning what we are having to eat, so he can think about the selection of wine from his 1,000-bottle cellar. Wine is a passion with him, enhanced by the four years we spent in the Napa Valley. Everything about the evening meal must be 'just so'. When the children were at home he insisted they come to dinner with hair combed and in clean clothes. As Diane remembered, 'Our disagreements have been over silly things: like the running battle we had over my wanting to come to the dinner table in jeans, and him wanting me to change into a dress.'

We started to dine *en famille* when all the children could eat without slopping food or spilling milk. But Arthur never understood when they were small that they often didn't appreciate the elegant dinner. That kind of dining, for one thing, takes longer than a hurry-up meal in the kitchen. The children would get restless, eager to return to play. They fidgeted, or kicked each other under the table. A wail would go up, and Arthur became the heavy father: 'If you don't behave, you will take your dinner and have it in the kitchen.' Finally, when sometimes all three of them had left for the kitchen, I'd say to him: 'That's not a punishment; it's a reward. The kitchen is precisely the place they want to be, so they can get dinner over with fast.'

Gradually, though, Jane, Steven and Diane came to enjoy the atmosphere of the family dinner table and the expansive mood that appetizing food and good wine create in their father—and mother too, come to think of it—plus the opportunity for conversation. This was always the time the children chose to ask us if they could do something that was especially important to them. Roger wrote appreciatively: 'Dad has always made this a special time, when the whole family feels relaxed, and we are able to share our lives with each other. When I visit with you, I look forward to dinner time every day.'

We have always included the children in our dinner-table talk about Arthur's work. The earliest occasion was when he confided in them after his novel *Hotel* was completed. Doubleday was to publish it, and in due course it was submitted to The Literary Guild and Reader's Digest Condensed Books, both of which had chosen his earlier novels, *The Final Diagnosis* and *In High Places*, as book club selections. However, Arthur learned during a phone conversation with his agent that both book clubs had turned down *Hotel*, offering the opinion that the novel would not be a success.

Arthur was at first downcast, then philosophic. Perhaps, he thought, he should go back to writing for television. He asked Maeve Southgate to line up some TV work for him. We needed the money.

During dinner Arthur talked to the family. The children were ten, eight and six. He explained that the book he had been working on for three years looked as though it would be a flop; therefore we would all have to live carefully and forego some luxuries we had grown used to. The children looked grave. Jane suggested she give up her piano and elocution lessons—a sacrifice because she enjoyed them. Steven wondered if he could take on a newspaper delivery round. Diane cried out, 'I can give up sweets!'

However, Maeve stalled about lining up some TV work because she believed in *Hotel*, as did Arthur's publishers, whose confidence in it—despite the book club opinions—never wavered. In the meantime Arthur wrote a three-page 'concept' of a novel about an airport and showed it to Maeve. She, and then Doubleday, were enthusiastic. Arthur was offered a handsome advance on royalties—a gesture of faith at that point which he still remembers. (As it turned out, The Literary Guild and Reader's Digest Condensed Books reversed their decisions a few weeks later, and *Hotel* appeared on best-seller lists within three weeks of publication.)

When Arthur began *Airport*, he announced during one dinner that he was trying to think of a name for his fictitious airline. Everyone had a suggestion. Finally Steven, aged ten, said, 'How about Air America?'

'Excellent!' was Arthur's response. But on checking, he found this was the name of a Far East airline created by the CIA.

Two lines in *Airport*, as spoken by Libby Bakersfeld, came directly from Diane, who was eight at the time. She arrived home from school one day and informed her father, 'I want a map of February.' He was amused, wrote the line down, and later used it. The same thing happened another time when Diane was in bed and Arthur came to kiss her goodnight; she told him, 'I can feel my heart beating in my knee.'

Jane was the prototype for Roberta, Libby's elder sister in *Airport*. Roberta, like Jane, was thirteen and going through what Arthur described in the novel as a series of 'snotty moods'. I remember Jane suggested, with no trouble at all, some smartalecky remarks for Roberta to make.

Arthur sometimes has guilt feelings about not having been as good a father as he might have. He wasn't. His patience level was low, and he was ruthless about making time for his work—even during holidays and weekends. He was not really interested in his offspring as babies, before they learned to walk and talk and display some personality. He loved them more the older they grew, but was never a romping dad, the kind who plays ball with the kids in the garden. He dislikes watching sports, so was rarely at swimming displays or other events in which the children were participating. (This may have been frustrating to Diane, because she has been the all-round athlete of the family, but typically she never complained, taking it all in her confident stride. Steven, a good swimmer, would have kept his disappointment quietly to himself.)

But Arthur is not alone. That is a dilemma of ambitious young men—and, today, young women. While they are struggling to succeed in their chosen fields their children's needs take second place to the demands of careers. It is too late when the kids are grown; they don't need their parents then.

Our children were aware of Arthur's preoccupation with his writing. They complained about it from time to time. They wished that he were more relaxed, more able to sit around with them and talk about emotions, engage in hypothetical discussions, or indulge in day-to-day chitchat. As Jane put it: 'All of us have been sad at times when his ambition and thoroughness made us feel he didn't have time for us— the kind of time *we* needed and wanted. Yet all of us know and understand that he would not be the kind of success he is if he were not so hard-working. I probably understand more than anyone else the way he is, because I see the same traits in myself constantly. When I am with people who aren't stimulating me or making me think, I get bored and feel I am wasting my time. I keep thinking of the book I could be reading or the work I could be doing. It took me a long time to understand that what I resented and disliked most about Dad were the very same things I disliked and resented in myself.'

Steven said, 'Dad is a very generous person, and helping people gives him great pleasure. He never wants publicity in return for his generosity, but he needs to feel appreciated by those close to him. Yet it is often more difficult to have some of his time than his material generosity.'

Arthur was conscious of this when his third son, Mark, graduated from the University of California, Berkeley, in 1971. Arthur's graduation gift was what he described as 'a week of my time'. They spent it together in New York, much of the time listening to jazz—Mark's great love. I remember Arthur phoning me, 'Honey, you wouldn't believe it . . . we're never in bed before 4 a.m. But it's okay, I sleep in until 8.30.'

Son John, who is an architect with a master's degree in planning, talked about his visits to us when we moved to California. 'What I remember most vividly is the time I was able to spend alone with Dad. Those occasions were especially important because of the sheer sense of being able to monopolise his time, where he was interested in me and me alone.'

When Jane, Steven and Diane grumbled that their father did not spend enough time with them, I often reminded them that they had nobody to compare him with. They have no idea what it is like to grow up in a family where the father is a typical, ambitious company man: he leaves the house early in the morning before the children are awake, and returns with a briefcase full of work just as they are going to bed.

For, to be fair, Arthur was always available if the children had a

113

problem, and he would give them his undivided attention. I remember an incident when Steven wanted to talk to him. He buzzed Arthur on the intercom to ask if he could come to his study. 'Sure,' said his father.

But when Steven, aged ten, was in the study, Arthur said without looking up, 'Just a moment, Steven. I want to finish this thought while it's in my head.' Afterward I pictured Steven standing first on one leg, then the other, fidgeting with his hands, and getting more impatient by the minute. Then Arthur suddenly set down his pencil, stacked the papers neatly on one side of his desk, looked straight at Steven and said, 'Now, what's the problem?' Steven had one hundred per cent of his mind and attention.

Typically, though, when Arthur is in the opposite role, he likes immediate attention, and has been used to getting it. Jane gives a wonderful imitation of her father walking into a room to tell us something; if everyone doesn't stop what they are doing immediately to look up and listen with interest, he'll throw up his hands and say 'Oh, forget it!', then stalk out expecting someone to plead with him to come back. And one of his most annoying habits, when *he* is interrupted while reading the newspaper, is to put his finger on the place where he stopped reading while he looks up to listen.

Soon after Steven's session in Arthur's study, I was preparing the day's lunches for our trio of children while they were in various stages of getting ready for school, including last-minute homework. The conversation went like this:

> STEVEN: Mom, don't forget you have to sign your permission for me to go on our field trip today.
> ME: Okay, I'll do it when I've finished the sandwiches.
> JANE: Where's the Adriatic Sea?
> ME: It's north of the Mediterranean, between the east coast of Italy and Yugoslavia.
> STEVEN: I can't find my tennis shoes. Where are they?
> ME: Outside the back door . . . where you left them.
> DIANE: How do you spell 'trampoline'?
> ME: T-R-A-M-P-O-L-I-N-E.
> JANE: I have to stay late at school today. Could you pick me up at five o'clock, please?
> ME: Make it ten past. I have to drop Diane at the dentist at five.

DIANE: Vicki wants me to stay over at her house Friday night.
May I?

ME: Yes, that's okay. But remember you have swimming practice Saturday morning.

Steven retrieved his shoes, watched me pack the three lunches as I
fielded more questions, then observed: 'You and Dad are so different. Dad has a one-compartment brain; you have hundreds of com-
partments in yours.'

I knew what he meant: my ability to deal with the minutiae of every
day all at the same time, against Arthur's single-minded way of tackling every subject—large or small—with the same intensity, while
pushing everything else out of his mind.

One advantage in having a working father around the house, even
one immersed in writing, was that it gave our children a true understanding of what the man-woman relationship is all about. It also established the fact that this took preference over the parent-child
relationship, because I don't believe in children growing up to as-
sume they are the strongest common denominator of a family. Yet
we have a good rapport with them all.

If I were asked how we have accomplished this, I would say we
simply treated our children as individuals as soon as possible. Steven
told me: 'The emphasis on individuality has been a constant, dominant theme in our family. It was so encouraged by my upbringing that
I used to be distressed when I seemed to be mostly in agreement with
my father. I felt a need to be different, and was pleased when I found
something to disagree with.' We have also encouraged the children to
make their own decisions, given them early responsibility, and we
have been completely frank in answering questions.

Particularly in matters of sex. If children can talk about sex with
their parents, there is very little else they cannot discuss.

Simplistic? Yes—but it works, and here's how: the parent answers
the first question asked, no matter how young the child, without embarrassment. Otherwise, the moment a child realises there is a subject
that makes a parent feel uncomfortable, he or she will not explore
that subject again. Instead, sexual knowledge will come from other
sources—playmates, books, magazines or films.

The first question a child asks, usually at the age of four or five, is:
'Why does that lady have such a big tummy?'

The answer should be simple and straightforward. 'Because she is having a baby, and the baby is growing inside her.' Nothing else—the kid didn't ask for more information, and doesn't want any.

No, of course, it doesn't end there. But two or three years may go by before the next question, which is either: 'How does the baby get *out*?' or 'How does the baby *get* there?' The first is easy, especially if the child has been used to the word 'vagina' instead of those silly, made-up words.

The second question is stickier—only because you're usually unprepared for it and haven't thought out exactly what you're going to say. I remember vividly how it happened in our family.

Jane (aged eight), Steven (six), and Diane (four) were sitting at the kitchen table eating cereal. I was scrambling eggs for them (we've always been big breakfast eaters). Suddenly Jane said, 'I know babies grow inside the mother's stomach—but how does the baby get there?'

Here it is, I thought. If I say I'll explain later, I will be shrouding the subject in mystery, giving it an importance it shouldn't have. Then my mind raced on . . . but if I go ahead and explain, Steven and Diane will be listening, and they haven't asked the question.

I decided to go ahead. I kept on scrambling the eggs until they were cooked and served them with toast, all the while talking as calmly and naturally as possible.

'Well,' I said, 'when a mummy and daddy love each other, they like to be close together so they can kiss and hug. Then they make love and the daddy puts his penis into the mother's vagina. She has a lot of tiny eggs inside her and the daddy has some special liquid called sperm, which can make one of the eggs grow into a baby. That's all there is to it.'

I took a quick look at the faces to see their reaction. Jane looked serious as she digested this information along with her scrambled eggs.

'I see,' she said.

Steven and Diane looked as if they hadn't heard. 'Good,' I thought, 'it's over their heads.'

There were no more questions.

It so happened that Arthur and I were off on a trip shortly after this episode. Our sitter was a Mrs. Hudson, thirty-ish, sensible, married to a policeman. When we returned, she told me that Diane, all of

116

four years old, had asked her, 'Do you know what my daddy does to Mummy when they want a baby?' and then proceeded to explain the whole procedure.

It was Diane, always direct and unperturbed, who asked me when she was eleven, 'Mum, do you take the pill?' I was startled, because we had never discussed birth control.

'No,' I answered. 'I did for about fifteen months, but I didn't like them. They made me feel fat and bloated.'

'Well, what do you use?' she asked.

'A diaphragm . . . here, come into the bathroom. I'll show you.'

I explained some more biological facts, then finished, 'It's good that you're asking me these questions. Is there anything else you'd like to know?'

'Yes, there is,' she said matter-of-factly. 'How many times have you and Dad . . . you know?'

I stopped short . . . 'In eighteen years? Honey, you don't keep count . . . but quite a lot of times.' When I recounted the conversation to Arthur, he smiled. 'I guess she thought: three children . . . three times!'

Diane's direct approach reminded me of myself. I had been fortunate as a child in being able to talk with my sister Doris. She was married when I was ten; and I was an aunt by the time I was twelve. Doris answered all my questions, too, in an unembarrassed way. At school I became the fount of all sexual knowledge, and what I didn't know I did my best to find out.

But never did I discuss anything with my mother. I sensed early she was uncomfortable talking about sex, as so many of her generation were. When I was eighteen, though, I had a conversation with the other girls at the publishing house where I worked. We all wondered if women could enjoy sex after the menopause.

'I'll ask my mother,' I said, with some bravado.

I chose my moment carefully. My mother was ironing. I cleared my throat.

'Mum, the girls at the office were talking about whether women get any pleasure from sex after the change of life. Do they?'

Poor soul! She was bowled over by the unexpected question and did not know where to look. So she kept her eyes riveted on her ironing, blushed to the roots of her hair, and as the iron suddenly went into high gear, said, 'Of course!'

117

There was only one other time my mother had any comment to make about sex. It was when I had returned from Canada to announce I wanted to marry one Arthur Hailey. She said to me cryptically, 'Just remember you don't spend all of your married life in bed.'

Both rejoinders confirmed what I always suspected: she and my father had a superb time in bed, in spite of their incompatibilities in other areas.

Our frank sexual discussions meant that Arthur and I never worried about the girls getting into amorous situations they couldn't handle. I told them early that I trusted they were both smart enough not to let pregnancy spoil their adolescent years.

Jane remembered Arthur's attitude to her growing-up experiences was that she could best learn for herself. 'He never lectured me or laid down a set of rules. When I went out for the first time with a boy, he never asked me about him or about his family. All he did was ask me if the boy had seat belts in his car. He trusted my judgment and knew it was my date, not his. When my friend called for me, Dad went out to inspect the car to see if the tyres were in good shape and the brakes worked.'

I smiled when I read that reference to seat belts. Arthur was so concerned for his daughters' safety when travelling in cars with boys, he gave them instructions to call him if they were ever in doubt about the sobriety of the car's driver. 'No matter where I am or what I'm doing, I will come and get you.'

One summer when we were visiting in California, Diane had an invitation to go away for a weekend with a young man and to stay with a family at Lake Tahoe. She came into our bedroom late one night to ask if she could accept; I said I thought so. Then she casually remarked that her friend was going to fly a rented aeroplane. Arthur shot up in bed.

'Does he have an instrument rating?' he asked.

'Dad, how should I know?'

'Well, get him to come and see me tomorrow and ask him to bring his logbook.'

Diane reported to her friend our reluctance to her accepting the invitation.

'I can understand,' he said. 'After all, you're only sixteen.'

'Oh, they're not worried about my morals,' she exclaimed. 'It's your flying the plane that has Dad upset.'

Next day Arthur discovered Diane's friend had logged more flying hours than he himself had done during all of World War II. So they went off for the weekend with our blessing.

Arthur's concern for the children's welfare was demonstrated when they went away to school. He gave them each an American Express card—not to use willy-nilly, but for emergency. None of them has abused that trust, though we did get a long-distance phone call (reversed) from Steven once to say he was low on funds and could he use the Amex card to buy a shirt?

The children have frequently regarded Arthur as a quasi doctor. They have heard him tell so many anecdotes from his hospital research days for *The Final Diagnosis* that they think of him as being all-wise in medical ways. One day, when Jane was about eighteen, she dropped into Arthur's study to talk to him. She was late menstruating and was concerned.

Her father said to her, 'Well, how about the obvious question?'

'Absolutely no,' said Jane. 'I am not pregnant.' So together they looked up his medical books for information. However, in a couple of days there was no longer a problem. But Arthur was touched that Jane felt close enough to discuss that subject with him.

Steven, too, has let us know in quieter, more subtle ways than the girls that he has coped nicely with the sexual awareness that is thrust upon teenagers. He once burst into our bedroom to find Arthur and me standing naked, embracing each other, an obvious prelude to more activity. It was no surprise to him. We usually sleep in the buff and many times in their lives the children have seen us that way, both in the house and occasionally swimming in pools, lakes and the sea. Still, I didn't appreciate the intrusion. We respect the children's privacy and expect the same from them.

'I beg your pardon,' I snapped. 'How about knocking before you barge in like that?'

'Sorry,' Steven said, continuing his stride into the room. 'Just wanted to borrow your hair dryer.' He got the dryer and, as he marched out the door, threw back over his shoulder, 'Okay, back to your business.'

Jane, being the oldest of our three, was the first to experience the sex education courses offered at college these days. She enrolled in a class at Stanford; it was the largest class of her freshman year—a thousand students. Later she told me some of the things she had learned.

'You know, Mom,' she said. 'You were pretty good about telling us what we should know. But there's a lot you didn't explain.'

'Such as?' I asked, bridling.

'Well, for instance, you never explained the four stages of orgasm.'

'Jane, I never *knew* there were four stages!' In fact, I don't remember telling her anything at all about orgasm. Like other aspects of sex, it's better experienced than explained.

When the course was over, she insisted I take her file of notes so I could bring myself up to date with what had been going on in the sexual world without my knowledge. I glanced through it, but was put off by the clinical notes and diagrams of cross-sections of genitalia. No doubt about it, in some areas I am definitely old-fashioned. There are things I'd just as soon not have spelled out.

(That has also been my reaction to the recent plethora of sex books, with explicit instructions on who does what to whom. Apart from the kinky and the gimmicky—which I can live without—there's not much in them that Arthur and I haven't groped our way to discovering on our own.)

As the only son who grew up with his father, Steven had a continuous, intimate view of Arthur's work pattern. In his letter to me, he said: 'I see my dad as highly disciplined, hard-working and intensely individualistic. He is very demanding of himself and others around him. His discipline and precision make him an extremely reliable person—everything gets done, quickly and efficiently. The intensity of his discipline—which I could never match—is also the force which keeps him going in his writing. The work is long and arduous, yet he resists temptations to neglect it in favour of more pleasurable activities.'

Then in a burst of frankness, he added: 'Although I have never heard him say so explicitly, I believe that my father lived a lonely and protected childhood, where he was the centre of attention. I don't think he ever had to compromise on any issues, which is always the case in larger families. Even now, he bends very little to compromise, and when confronted by a united defence from the rest of the family drops the subject altogether. But he will often concede the next day. I think he is the classic case of an only child, and this is probably a reason for his success.'

John tried to be analytical: 'My perception of my father is both simple and complex. It is simple in the sense that he can be easily read as a sincere, concerned, honest, warm human being who is terribly diligent in everything he undertakes. He is one of the most generous people I know, not only to his family but to everyone who crosses his path. And that generosity doesn't necessarily equate to monetary terms. He gives both in time and effort. He is complex in the sense that I don't always understand (or agree with) some of the things he says and does because they do not fit into the personality composite I have tried to develop to decipher him.'

Diane, writing from Colorado College in her junior year, was uncomplicated in summing up her feelings: 'I have always thought of Dad as a good friend, particularly in the past few years. We have developed and maintained a close relationship. Since the age of thirteen, when I went away to school, I have seen him four or five times a year; long enough to generate that closeness, without the tension that so often occurs when adolescents live with their parents.'

She remembered an occasion when she and I were in the audience at a talk Arthur gave at Branksome Hall, a girls' school in Toronto. During the question period a student asked her, 'What is it really like to be Arthur Hailey's daughter?' Diane wrote, 'I had no idea how to answer a question like that, so I replied honestly, "I rarely think of him as Arthur Hailey. He's just my dad."'

Her letter ended: 'Frankly, I don't think his fame has affected me much at all, though I couldn't deny the difference his financial success has made, and the opportunities I've had as a result.'

Not all the children have felt this way. Steven said: 'I want to be known as myself rather than as my father's son. I have always tried to keep a low profile and try not to invite searching questions, but I no longer dread or avoid them; in fact I sometimes enjoy their evolution, because I really am proud of my dad's success.'

Jane said her father's being a successful novelist didn't bother her at all while she was living in a small town. Her friends knew Arthur best as Jane's father, who always liked to cadge spoonfuls of their ice cream sundaes. But when she was at college she deliberately didn't mention her father's occupation until toward the end of her freshman year. Then there was some fuss made 'until my close friends got to know Dad as a person'.

John told me: 'Curiously, I began to have a problem in dealing with my father's success only later on in my college career and work experience. It was never unpleasurable to be known as Arthur Hailey's son, but I began to feel that I was better known as the son of an author than John Hailey. This began to develop into a bit of paranoia, which resulted in my becoming close-mouthed about who my father was. This "complex" remains with me still, but in a controlled state. If someone is genuinely interested in who he is, I offer the information without embarrassment.'

I should add here that it is incomprehensible to Arthur why the children should ever have had a problem of that kind at all. He doesn't regard himself as anything special. In fact, he was not happy about my including any reference to that subject in this book. But I insisted. 'If four out of six children have brought it up with no prompting on my part,' I told him, 'then it's a fact of life and a part of our story.'

CHAPTER 11

'Who'll Take Out the Dustbins?'

I have always been a liberated woman. I have been treated as an equal, with total respect, by my husband ever since he realised that I was strong enough to carry out large bins of rubbish. It never occurred to me to ask him to do it. It was a domestic chore that, with my British upbringing, I somehow felt was my responsibility in the marriage contract. I was the one who would be most affected if the rubbish was not picked up, so automatically I put it out each collection day.

But one day, early in our marriage, it suddenly dawned on me that I was the only woman on the block doing it. A seed of discontent was planted.

'You know, honey,' I said, 'I think taking out the rubbish is supposed to be a man's job here in North America.'

Arthur's eyes glazed over, as they often do when a subject is raised that he doesn't want to discuss. At the precise time, he is suddenly 'working', thinking out a knotty problem in a complicated plot. For there is one thing a writer's spouse must understand: a writer can be working in every circumstance conceivable to man—gazing out of a window, sitting on a deck chair in the sun, standing under the shower, even eating at the dining-table. It is impossible to choose the 'right' moment to present a convincing argument over a legitimate complaint—but I do my best.

I raised my voice a note higher: 'I said I think taking out the rubbish is supposed to be a man's job here in North America.'

'Huh?' he frowned. He knew there was no escape. I repeated the statement a third time.

'What makes you think that?'

'Because, my love, I just don't ever see women around here strug-gling out with the rubbish, the way I do.'

'Since when have you conformed to what other women do?'

What diabolical cunning! He had somehow managed to twist my complaint around so that it became a compliment. But I was not to be sidetracked, so I persisted.

I finally wrung from him the promise that if I reminded him on the appropriate days, he would indeed take out the rubbish.

Well, of course, like many another woman, I have always found it easier to do the job myself rather than nag someone else to do it. So, more often than not, I continued to take out the rubbish—except when I was feeling bitchy. Then I would start early in the morning, reminding Arthur that this was dustbin-day. Sometimes it worked, sometimes not, depending on *his* mood. Occasionally we would wind up having a first-class row over the subject, thereby confirming a phenomenon I have known all my married life: most of our fights seem to originate over the most trivial of domestic affairs, when the real reason for such a fight is biological—the urgent need for one of us to let off steam.

Gradually, our bickerings over the rubbish became fewer and fewer—simply because I reverted to taking it out myself—until one memorable episode soon after we had moved to California's Napa Valley. We were living in a tiny rented house tucked away in the hills, reached by a tortuous, bumpy road. Delivery vans were seldom seen, dustcarts never.

We had two dustbins sitting on the back porch, but they were soon full. I then collected the stuff in brown paper bags which I stacked beside the bins. In the meantime I made some enquiries about what one *did* with rubbish. The answer: if it is not collected, the house-holder must take it to the dump. I was given directions, including a little map. Then I mentioned to Arthur that we would have to drive there sometime soon. The subtle use of 'we' was deliberate; if I had said 'you' I'd be badgering him, and the implication was clear that I was not going by myself.

The glazed look came over his eyes, and he suggested we talk about it later. I realised then I shouldn't have used the word 'soon'. It was easy for him. He never used the back porch and never took out any rubbish from the kitchen, so he could remain oblivious to it indefinitely. The pile of brown paper bags and the stench from them got higher. Even the children began commenting on the smell, but since they were only eleven, nine, and seven, I couldn't ask one of them to drive to the dump.

I was desperate, but also determined not to take care of the problem myself, even though I knew it would be much, much easier. So, later in the week, I started my campaign again, before breakfast. My reasoning was twofold: I would get him before he left the house, and I would shame him in front of the children.

I chose the wrong day.

He was furious. 'How can you expect me to write sensitively if I start my day transporting rubbish? You know the mornings are best for me for writing. How *could* you be so selfish as to ruin my whole mood.'

'Selfish! Ha! *You're* the selfish one. Just who in hell do you think you are? Your attitude to rubbish is like the United States not recognising China. You may not like it—but it's *there*,' I shouted. 'It's part of our *lives*.'

And so on and on. The stupid, foolish, petty, childish back-and-forth sniping between two grown adults who both need a good shake.

His final words as he stepped out the front door: 'I am not taking that rubbish *anywhere*.'

'Okay,' I screamed. 'Then it can stay there. *I am not taking it either*.'

Maybe he detected the note of hysteria in my voice, or saw the determination on my face.

He suddenly said, 'I'll come home for lunch, and we'll take it together then.'

'Right!'

I usually took our lunch to the little rented chalet where Arthur was working—on the beginning chapters of *Airport*. That day I prepared an extra-special lunch. The table was attractively set, the salads ready in the refrigerator when he arrived at 12.30; I just needed to heat the soup.

I then made a fatal error. 'Do you want to take the rubbish before or after lunch?'

He glowered at me. '*Before*,' he said grudgingly. 'Let's get it over with.'

Together we carried the rubbish, bag by bag, and loaded up the

125

I MARRIED A BEST SELLER

back of the station wagon. It smelled so bad, my stomach was heaving.

Together we drove down the bumpy lane to the main road, the rubbish gently sliding from side to side and stirring up the air with still more odour. On the main road, we turned north towards Calistoga, and drove and drove and drove. I had been advised the dump was some five miles along the main road and then another mile up a winding side road. It seemed like fifteen miles.

'I think this is it!' I said suddenly. 'You have to turn in right here.' We did—and found a chain strung between two posts, and *padlocked*.

'I don't believe it,' Arthur cried. 'Do they think someone is going to *steal* their rubbish? What do we do now?'

I made a lot of womanly, placating sounds. 'Perhaps they close for lunch, or this is a half day. Anyway, why don't we just leave it here?'

'How can we do that? You can't leave your old rubbish beside the road just like that.' Then, as though talking to a small child: 'You know we *are* going to be *living* here in the Napa Valley. I mean, we might as well start off *trying* to be responsible citizens.'

'Okay,' I shrugged. 'Then we'll just have to drive it back, won't we?'

The awful realisation of that sunk in. On top of that we hadn't had lunch, and Arthur is at his most irritable when he's hungry. He was ready to explode.

We drove back the way we had come. Neither of us spoke a word until I suddenly saw what looked like a dustcart lumbering toward us.

'Hey, I think it's . . . *yes* . . . it's a dustcart. With real rubbish in it! It must be going to the . . . *quick*, turn around! Let's follow it.'

When you want to go back the way you have come on a main road, there never seems to be a side road or driveway, left or right. We were on a narrow two-lane winding road, and we must have travelled nearly a mile before we were able to turn. Then we drove at breakneck speed trying to catch the dustcart. Tyres squealed, the rubbish bags at the back were tossed around, the air reeked foully.

Thank goodness! We reached the truck just as the driver was climbing into the cab, after obviously having unlocked the padlock and lowered the chain.

It turned out that yes, they did close for lunch. And why did they lock the roadway to the dump? Because people would dump their rubbish without paying! Yes, he would be glad to take it to the dump for us. The driver obligingly helped us transfer our rubbish to his truck. You could tell he was used to the work. He took three bags to every one of Arthur's, who was noticeably foot-dragging. Arthur gratefully pressed a five-dollar bill into the driver's palm.

A wave of relief spread over us. We actually laughed as we drove home. We each took a shower and had a splendid lunch, even indulged in a bottle of wine, a rarity for Arthur in the middle of a working day. Afterward, we made love and had a short snooze.

Since that day, we have never ever discussed who'll take out the rubbish, but I can tell you it is never, ever, Arthur. To him, rubbish is a word, one that he might have to use occasionally, very occasionally, in the writing of a novel.

CHAPTER 12

The Postman Cometh

We get letters.

Boy! do we get letters. And they're marvellous.

They come from readers in every walk of life—judges, schoolteachers, housewives, servicemen, teenagers, secretaries, university professors, salesmen, prisoners, business executives. They are posted from all over the world, for Arthur's books are published in thirty languages. The majority come from the U.S., Canada and Great Britain, but many originate in West Germany, Australia, Israel, Czechoslovakia—to mention a few—and that land of prolific letter writers, India.

Apart from royalty cheques, readers' letters are the most tangible rewards a writer can have, because writing is a lonely business. The playwright can stand at the back of a theatre and thrill to an audience's approval at the end of play. The composer can listen to the applause in a concert hall. The painter can eavesdrop as he mingles with viewers in a gallery. But an author cannot overhear what is said about his books in a classroom, in a beauty salon, at a dinner party, in a film line-up.

We reckon that for every person who actually writes a letter, there are dozens who mean to but never get around to it. Myself, for instance: I've read hundreds of books over the years, and have been moved enough to want to write to the authors many times. In actual fact, I have written four letters to authors whose work I have enjoyed.

Perhaps this is why the letters we appreciate most are the ones from readers who we sense would normally never write. One such note came from a law professor who wrote under *Banking Law Journal* letterhead:

> I use my editorial stationery to underscore my expression of appreciation for *The Moneychangers*. I seldom read novels but was fascinated with this one—the plot, the characters, but especially the authenticity of atmosphere.

Another letter that pleased us enormously was quite short. The writer said he was an avid fan of Arthur's, having read all of his books. He ended:

> The reason for this letter is to congratulate you for being a modern-day Dickens.

This may or may not be true, but it was pleasant to hear.

I liked the letter from a pregnant mother of five, who had real writing skill, and had completed a manuscript. She wrote to Arthur for advice:

> . . . Actually, writing and motherhood have a good deal in common. They are both refined forms of masochism, and a story wanting to be written down nags as persistently as a child wanting to be born. They both demand a goodly slice of dedication, as you can no more 'half' write a story than you can 'dabble' in raising a child—not if you wish to do either very well, can you? . . .

I wrote to her at some length because I liked the sound of her, and knew she needed encouragement. Then she wrote back to me:

> . . . I hope you and your husband have a lovely Christmas, and a very happy and successful New Year, and may your husband continue to produce his super books. Some books are like eating a soufflé, or strawberry mousse—delicious but not satisfying. Your husband's books have the richness of Christmas cake and plum pudding and turkey with all the trimmings. They are a veritable feast! You can tell I am a fat lady from the way I always think of food . . .

Some of our most joyous letters are from children. Indeed, it meant a great deal to Arthur to be receiving letters from thirteen-year-olds at a time when our daughter Jane, aged thirteen, had not got around to reading one of his books. When she finally tackled *Hotel*, she looked up at her father in amazement after reading the first fifty-odd pages, and exclaimed: 'Daddy, this is *good!*'

What I love about children's letters is their spontaneity. They tell you exactly what is on their minds:

> I think that having the bomb explode in *Airport* was a good idea because it was a bit gory and that makes it more interesting. Why didn't you make some of the people die on the plane? . . .

> . . . I liked your book *Flight Into Danger* . . . The characters spoke as if they were alive.

> I am eleven years old . . . The only thing I don't like about your books is that a little bit too much happens.

> . . . I would like to have further data on how you write up your books. How much money did you make on *Airport? Wheels? In High Places?*

> I am sixteen years old . . . If you any day comes to Germany, we would be very happy to see you in our house in Bavaria. Our family invite you very cordial . . . Excuse my bad English, but I have English at the High School only since two years. My first foreign language was Latin. I think you prefer a bad English letter than a something better letter in Latin language.

> . . . My favorite part was when the bomb went off and the man who had the bomb got sucked out. How did they film the man getting sucked out? . . .

> . . . I live in Caracas, Venezuela. I have to write to you as an assignment for my English class . . . When did you begin writing? What was your first book? How did you get writing as a career? What ideas do you have for your next book? How do you get your information? What is the average time you take in writing a book? Please airmail the answers back to me.

Children are as demanding in their letters as they are in their homes—if they can get away with it, that is. We have received hundreds of letters from teenagers who have to write a report for school and cannot find any information about Arthur Hailey. They want the material by return airmail because they have a deadline, usually about a week away. (I refer them to an excellent article in *Current Biography*, a publication found in most libraries. Or I send biographical material that I have on hand.) Some of their comments:

> ... This letter I am writing you is not exactly my own idea. It is a class assignment from my English teacher. I am presently acquiring a 'B' average. With your help it would probably go up. Without your help, 'el-boom-o' (the sound of my grades dropping) ... but time is running out for me so please write back straight away ...
>
> ... My paper must be in by a week next Monday, so you see my life is in the balance ...

Then there are requests for autographs—on cards, book plates, first-day-issue stamped envelopes—and also autographed photographs. Arthur agreed most reluctantly to my ordering some postcard-size prints for this purpose. 'I'm not a film-star pin-up!' he grumbled.

One day we got twenty-nine letters from a small town in Ontario, and all of them mentioned *Flight Into Danger*. It was easy to guess that a teacher had given her pupils an assignment to write to the author of the play they were studying in class. One girl wrote:

> I am writing a story which is now thirteen pages long and getting longer. I was wondering if you could give me a few hints on how to write a story? ... Please write as soon as possible because I've never really had a letter from someone real important.

Sometimes Arthur receives some dubious compliments:

> ... I am now in the middle of *Wheels*. It is more confusing than *Hotel* but just as good.
>
> ... I am fourteen years old. I thoroughly enjoyed *The Final Diagnosis*. The book couldn't hold my attention for the first 50 pages. After that I couldn't put it down.

The youngest reader we have ever heard from wrote:

> ... I am eight years old, and even though I'm in third grade I read your books. Right now I am reading *Airport* and I am enjoying it like millions of other people did ...

The shortest letters we ever received was from a boy in Connecticut, whose entire letter contained twenty words:

I read your book *Airport* and I really enjoyed it. I liked the part when he blew up the plane.

Many readers identify themselves with characters in books, and Arthur received one letter from a lady who had a medical problem similar to Edgar Kramer's in *In High Places*. She wrote:

I was astounded to read that Kramer had the same urology problems as I have. Like your man, I have to urinate about every 50 minutes . . . I keep telling various doctors of all kinds that it is both physical and emotional; they all say go to a psychiatrist. The psychiatrist says to go to a urologist, who in turn usually sends me back to a psychiatrist. I showed one doctor a paragraph in the Kramer chapter of *In High Places*. He sounds like he believes me . . . I guess what I am trying to say is—it was a relief to see that one of your characters had something similar to my own problem, and I know I am not imagining it . . . It has been nice chatting with you. Good health to you and yours.

The most poignant letter Arthur has received, and one which moved him as few others have done, was from a U.S. sailor who had been on active duty in Vietnam. He wrote in April 1968:

Last summer I was reading *Hotel* while on active duty in the Navy, attached to a squadron operating off the aircraft carrier *U.S.S. Forrestal* in the Gulf of Tonkin. We were working from twelve to eighteen hours a day. I had borrowed *Hotel* from a friend of mine who worked the night shift. He would read it during the day and I would read it during the night.

On the morning of July 29, just minutes before a large number of bomb-laden aeroplanes were to be launched for an attack on Viet Nam, one of the planes caught fire and its bombs exploded. This started a chain reaction. Within ten minutes 15 planes, with their bombs and rockets, had burned and exploded, creating the worst naval disaster since World War II.

One hundred and thirty-four men were killed; most were on the night shift and asleep at the time. Our berthing compartment caught the full force of one blast and my friend with whom I was sharing *Hotel* died along with others.

Days later, when the fires were out and most of the bodies removed, we began the gruesome task of going through the rubble, trying to salvage personal belongings. I looked particularly for *Hotel*, to have something special to remember my friend by, but never found it.

It was a month and a half later before we got back to the States, and I could get another copy. There was a new meaning to the book as I began reading where I had left off a short time before. I will always remember your book, not only because it was a fine story, but because it reminds me of my friend and the good times we had together.

Arthur has never spelled out sex in graphic detail in books. *Playboy* Magazine once complained that a Hailey sex scene consisted of a three-word sentence, 'They made love.' Just the same, we have had letters from readers who have been shocked by what he has written. One letter received in 1969, which was signed by both husband and wife, stated:

We were so delighted with the *Reader's Digest* version of *Hotel* that we bought a copy of *Airport*, anticipating another exciting story. Our expectations were fulfilled until your crude handling of the sex interest became so disgusting that we laid the book aside in favour of more rewarding literature. What a waste of fine talent—and of our six dollars!

Another man wrote:

I was shocked to find your book *Airport* in the public library. You are the kind of author who has an inferiority complex, thinking that your book won't be interesting unless you use foul language or unless you tell filthy stories of sex . . . Do you think you could write a clean book?

Then along came a letter from a man in Florida, who said:

I have read all your books and must say I find them all so entertaining . . . But when you write you should put more sex into your books.

We have received hundreds of letters from readers over the years asking for advice or information, because they have regarded Arthur as an authority on the subjects he has written about. (He is quick to point out, 'I am not an expert on anything; I just know which experts to ask.')

After *Wheels* was published we were inundated with letters asking how one could order a new car that was not manufactured on Monday or Friday. The answer: There is no way, unless you happen to know someone at the factory who can schedule the new car for assembly on a Tuesday, Wednesday or Thursday.

The most bizarre of the post-*Wheels* letters was from a man who was convinced his car made him feel sick. His letter was intelligent and serious:

> Perhaps I shouldn't bother you with such nonsense, but since you wrote *Wheels*, and being an auto expert I thought I'd write and ask a few questions. I've had problems with my car. I'm constantly getting sick in it. No mechanic can find anything wrong. There have been some maybes—this or that?—but nothing concrete. Now about ten per cent of the time it seems things go fairly well. And by the way, so far my doctors have found nothing physically wrong with me. Mr. Hailey, is there such a thing as auto sabotage? Can someone tamper with an auto's engine or the exhaust system to cause the driver to feel ill? Have you in your exhaustive research come across such cases? If so, how do they do such things? And what should I tell my mechanic to look for?

Arthur's reputation for in-depth research into a subject has made him the target for countless suggestions for new book titles. We get them by the dozens.

The topic most often suggested is a story about a university, followed closely by life aboard an ocean liner, and what goes on behind the scenes of a large department store. Other ideas have included: prisons, newspapers, trade unions, shopping centres, the CIA, insurance, local politics, the building industry, horse racing, the U.S. criminal justice system, and the Alaska pipeline. The most colourful, oft-repeated suggestion is gambling. As one reader put it,

> If you haven't already chosen the field for your next book (though I imagine that within that active mind of yours you already have), let me urgently suggest that you consider the exciting, interesting, fascinating, popular, widespread, pulsating, challenging, sometimes dangerous field of gambling. If the public would eat up a book about the relatively dull subject of banking, you can only imagine what they would do with your treatment of gambling.

I have often pointed out in my letters to readers that Arthur himself must be wholeheartedly enthusiastic in order to sustain three years of solid work on a subject. Although he has often gambled with personal decisions—who hasn't?—he has absolutely no interest in gambling for money; in fact, he has a distaste for it. Two other subjects that were seriously suggested, and for which Arthur would never have the smallest glimmer of enthusiasm: beauty salons, suggested by a woman who owned a chain of them; and ballroom dancing, predictably prompted by a former teacher and studio owner.

I particularly liked the letter from a fifteen-year-old boy who had an idea for Arthur:

> Unlike most of my letters I will tell the point right away. Would you be interested in writing a book about a marching band? Before you start thinking, what a dull idea, I would like to say that in real life there is enough going on to write a book . . . As you probably already know I am in a marching band . . . .

Arthur received an intriguing letter in February 1974 from a woman in England who claimed he was the father of her son. She wrote:

> I know you will be surprised to receive this letter . . . But the years are passing, and human nature being what it is, I can't keep things to myself any longer.
>
> You will have to think back a very long time to Luton, Christmas 1942–43. You were on leave from the R.A.F. and I was a telephonist in Church Street, Luton, and for a week of your leave you took me out, ringing me at the switchboard where I worked to do so. . . . Well, the outcome of that week was that I had a son on October 2, 1943.
>
> I've no need to go into details of what this meant to me. . . . To save my parents from shame, I moved away, but kept my son, and we had thirteen moves in the years that followed, because I did not want him to know the circumstances of his birth.
>
> I never went back to Luton to live, but have always known your whereabouts. I almost came to see you in 1947, when I heard you were thinking of emigrating to Canada. My son went abroad to live . . . he comes to see me whenever he can. I've no motive, or any reason for telling you this, I am very happy now, but felt I couldn't let any more years pass without writing. You

135

may deny this, but I know it is the truth, as you must do if you think hard enough. The enclosed photo was my son at twenty three years' old. If you can remember yourself at twenty three, you surely must see something.

Apart from the fact that the photograph bore no resemblance to Arthur, the letter was sufficiently coherent that, at first, I almost took it seriously. Arthur dismissed it immediately, not only because he had never heard of the writer, but because he had been in Canada with the R.A.F. during the entire period referred to. The neat hand-writing in his wartime pilot's logbook confirmed this.

I decided to answer the letter myself:

Your letter to my husband has been forwarded to us and I am re-plying because he is deeply involved in the writing of a new novel . . .

I think you may have got my husband mixed up with another man—though as a woman, I find it astonishing that one could be so confused about something as personal as the identity of the father of one's own child. But the fact is that my husband was not in Britain during the time you mention—Christmas 1942.

What a pity you have kept all this to yourself for so long! It is obviously going to be extremely difficult to trace your son's father after so many years have elapsed. Sorry not to be of more help.

We never heard from the lady again.

Later we learned this is not an unusual racket. The woman sends a mild letter first—always to someone well known. He may answer for a variety of reasons: he doesn't want any publicity; he has a wife who might be upset; his past has been racy, and he is not sure that the claim may not be true. The next letter requests money; she has had a difficult time, and so on. The victim then suddenly realises the woman has in her possession a possibly incriminating letter from him, and he is now an easy blackmail target.

Is there a writer out there somewhere who once wrote a novel starting with this paragraph?

It all began one day in April when I went round to change a library book. At least, this is the time when it seemed to me to begin, though I know you people trace things a lot farther back, and I'd like to say that I don't believe in all that. Whatever a man does, he's got to take responsibility for his own actions, that's what I believe. I don't see how the world can run any other way. I have to say that, even though I know it may be against me.

If there is, or if someone knows who he is, then Arthur Hailey would like to contact him to commiserate. Not that there is much either of them can do about the situation. I'll explain . . .

We received a letter from a reader in India:

> Dear and Learned Sir,
> I wish to introduce myself as one of your millions of faceless, silent admirers. I am a voracious reader of fiction and in particular, I am crazy about your novels . . . I recently bought a copy of *The Sinner,* which has your name on it as the author. I do not believe for a moment that you have written it . . . and I am most ashamed to see some of my countrymen resorting to this cheap trickery . . . Please, dear Mr. Hailey, I implore you to write to your ardent fan, and tell me you did not write this book.

We were intrigued, and anxious to see this 'new title' of Arthur's. So I sent some money and asked our correspondent to please buy a copy and send it to us. In due course we received it. Sure enough, the yellow-and-black paperback proclaimed in large letters: ARTHUR HAILEY, author of *Airport, Wheels & The Moneychangers*; and underneath in equally large letters, THE SINNER. The book included an accurate biography, a photograph of Arthur on the back cover (with a credit given to our daughter Diane), a Library of Congress Catalogue Card Number, and even a note that the copyright belonged to Arthur Hailey. Nowhere in sight, of course, was the name of the printer or any clue as to where the book was produced.

Since this episode more fake Arthur Hailey novels have appeared in India; among them *Hospital, A Flight to Remember, Surgeon* and *Holiday Makers*. The *Hindustani Times* speculated in its July 2, 1977, issue that fake novels are being produced because old-fashioned piracy is no longer as lucrative as it used to be. Said the *Times*: 'The Macmillan Company of India, Ltd., who are the Indian distributors of Pan Books, are so concerned about the rash of fake books that they ran an advertisement in Bombay daily last month alerting Arthur Hailey readers and listing authentic Hailey books.'

Over the years we have accepted the fact that Arthur's books have been pirated. Unscrupulous printers in Taiwan and India have been copying best sellers for years and selling them at cut-rate prices. But this new caper involves a sharp operator who not only steals a story, but also puts another author's name to it. Everyone but the crook loses out—the author of the story, who doesn't get paid and whose name is unacknowledged; the well-known author who gets the credit for something he'd rather not; and the unsuspecting book buyer who thinks he's getting a new novel by a favourite writer.

It is reassuring to know that some readers get so involved with the characters in Arthur's books that they have to write to find out what happened to them after the novel ended. The letter that most often pops up in my memory was from a woman who had to know whether Gwen Meighen, the stewardess in *Airport*, married Vernon Demerest, if she was able to give birth without complications—and was it a boy or a girl?

After *Wheels* was published, Arthur received an urgent letter from a reader in Denmark. She wanted the address of Sir Perceval McDowell Stuyvesant, the man who, in the novel, headed up a company in California which was converting advanced scientific knowledge into practical inventions and technology. It was imperative, she said, that she discuss with the company details of energy-saving inventions that were being developed in Denmark. Sir Perceval, of course, existed only in Arthur's mind, and his scientific activities had been dreamed up to provide an extra dimension in the novel.

Many readers have written to suggest that Arthur write sequels to his books, because they are sincerely interested in what happens to the characters. One such reader in England really spelled out everything she wanted to know after reading *Airport*. She listed the points:

1. What happened to Inez Guerrero and her children? Was she evicted from her slum?
2. Did Gwen Meighen fully recover? Did she lose the sight of her left eye?
3. What did Vernon Demerest tell Sarah, his wife, about Gwen and how did she take it?
4. Were insurance policies still sold at the Lincoln International Airport?
5. What did the inhabitants of Meadowood do about Elliot

Freemantle? Was anything done for them about the noise from the airport?

6. Was another long and wide runway built beside Runway Three Zero?
7. Did Cindy Bakerfeld marry Lionel Urquhart?
8. What happened between Tanya Livingston and Mel Bakersfeld?
9. Did Keith Bakersfeld continue to work in Air Traffic Control at the airport?
10. Did Anson Harris, Vernon Demerest and Cy Jordan receive any form of recognition for coping in the situation on Trans America Flight Two?

I am sorry about all of these questions but I feel they are important to the story. Perhaps you could write and tell me, or even write another book.

The letter arrived in December 1976, almost nine years since I had read *Airport* in its completed manuscript form. I looked up from the letter and said to Arthur, 'I've got a question for *her*. Who's Lionel Urquhart?'

Readers are always delighted to be able to point out boners that the author has made in a book. And no matter how careful a writer is, no matter how many people read the manuscript, no matter how many times a book gets proof-read—somehow, somewhere, a gremlin gets into the printing press and an error appears.

Several readers wrote to tell Arthur that in *Airport* he described D. O. Guerrero as checking the time by a cheap alarm clock because he had long since pawned his own watch. Yet, at the airport, in the line-up waiting to buy flight insurance, 'he checked his watch again, for the twentieth time, comparing it with the terminal clock.' Arthur took out the reference to pawning his watch for the next reprinting.

In *In High Places*, when Milly Freedeman, the Canadian Prime Minister's secretary, arrived home one evening, she changed from a grey tailored suit and a white blouse into orange slacks and a black sweater. Later that evening, her lover, Brian Richardson, began to unbutton her blouse. After a reader pointed out the mistake, Arthur corrected it in subsequent editions, and Richardson 'began easing her sweater upward'.

I am still amazed that Arthur let that one slip by. And he was a lot younger then.

The Moneychangers, too, had a boner which was spotted by a sharp-eyed reader in—of all places—Turkey. Arthur described the big downtown branch of First Mercantile American Bank as being modern, 'rebuilt a year or two ago when FMA's adjoining Headquarters Tower was erected'. In the very next chapter Arthur wrote, 'It was ten years earlier . . . Wainwright presented himself in Roselli's office on the 36th floor of FMA Headquarters Tower.' Again, this was changed in later editions.

Does an author take notice of the comments of his readers? In Arthur's case, the answer is, 'Yes, up to a point,' especially when he receives several letters expressing the same view. Even if he doesn't take direct action, he does some hard thinking. *The Moneychangers* is an example.

In an era of explicit sex and violence, where anything goes from orgasms to orgies, Arthur had a reputation for writing 'clean' books. The local bookseller could safely recommend a Hailey book to the most conservative of readers without repercussions. No longer, apparently.

When *The Moneychangers* was published, Arthur received much comment—oral and written—about his homosexual rape scene in prison, and the torture of Miles Eastin, that became known as 'the crucifixion scene'. Some of his regular readers were shocked. 'How could you resort to the same sensational sex and violence that is engulfing us from so many sources?' was their sentiment. Even good friends confided: 'I couldn't stand the torture scene . . . so I skipped it.'

One reader wrote:

> In my opinion, the violence, torture and brutality portrayed in *The Moneychangers* is not only disturbing, but totally unnecessary . . . In the future, I will never purchase or read another one of your novels.

Another reader told Arthur how much she enjoyed the novel. But, she added:

> There is just one little thing, though, that I didn't like at all and that was the perfectly ghastly, sickening, violence that you put into it. Was that really necessary? Please, please, won't you

make your next book a little bit less violent? I didn't really read all the bad parts, but skipped over them when I saw how awful they were going to be. I'm still trustfully looking forward to your next book.

Yet, a thoughtful woman in Oklahoma wrote:

I cannot remember reading any book which moved me more than your novel, *The Moneychangers*. You presented an important social problem—the need for prison reform—in such a sympathetic way. You made an excellent point for prison reform and the story illustrated so vividly the need for separate cells and perhaps separate wings of prison buildings for homosexual inmates. Also, perhaps, fewer rapes would occur if all prisons permitted conjugal visits. In my opinion, there is a real need for separating 'white collar' criminals from those who committed more violent crimes. Miles Eastin was a very sympathetic character who showed how prisoners can reform and become normal, law-abiding citizens once again . . .

I knew that Arthur felt it would be dishonest to write about prison life without including homosexuality, since it is so much a part of incarceration in an all-male environment. It was a personal breakthrough for him to write about homosexuality at all. A strong heterosexual, he had always been uncomfortable when the subject of homosexuality came up, and objected strongly to the downgrading terms used by others, such as 'pansy', 'fairy', 'queer'. In fact, he almost liked to pretend that homosexuality did not exist. The writing of the scenes between Miles Eastin and Karl taught him a great deal of compassion and understanding on that subject.

I asked Arthur to tell me frankly how he felt about the criticism of rape and violence, so that I could include his reaction in this book. Would he, for example, have written those chapters differently if he had anticipated the objections from some of his devoted readers?

His answer was an emphatic 'No.'

He recalled how he had discussed his treatment of these scenes with his editors at Doubleday, knowing it was a departure for him to write about such raw stuff. In the end it was his decision, since he was the author of the book and must be the final judge. He felt that the violence had a place in his book in the context in which he was writing—prison life and big-time crime.

141

'Like it or not,' he told me, 'violence and terrorism have become a part of our society to a far greater extent than when my other books were written ten, fifteen, twenty years ago. If you want proof, open any big city daily newspaper. As a contemporary novelist I am writing about life as it is today, not as I—or others—would like it to be. In the circumstances I described in *The Moneychangers* there would, of course, be violence, and I felt I must include it.

'I'll admit that the letters I have received have caused me to think. I am sorry that the scenes offended some readers. But, obviously, others found them realistic and did not object.

'This is not to say I will always make a point of including violence in a story, even though we are living in violent times. It might not be necessary to the story. But if an honest portrayal demands it, then I'll write about violence again.'

In many letters we receive there is a warm feeling that readers care about us. We heard from an eighty-three-year-old lady, an avid reader, who had watched the film of *Hotel* on television. She wrote:

> . . . If I were you I'd sue—very little of your story was in it. I got more angry by the minute . . .

I didn't agree with her; I thought the film of *Hotel* was an ingenious adaptation of the book. But it was touching to hear this complaint from a loyal fan.

Another reader from Berkeley, California, wrote:

> Take time to enjoy life with your family. Reserve a little niche for some private ruminations and time for yourself. Don't burn yourself out for us (your readers). Nevertheless, keep the big books coming as often as you can. We'll snatch them greedily off the counters as they arrive.

And an ophthalmologist summed up his sentiments:

> I delight in your achievements and success—as much because of your positive attitude, as your skill as a writer. And I wish you more of it—tempered by just enough frustration to keep you humble.

In late 1977 our mail contained something new—a variety of 'get-well' cards and letters.

Arthur had been afflicted with a kidney stone, a condition so relentlessly painful, it has been described by women who have experienced both as more harrowing and debilitating than childbirth. After four days of intense agony with no relief in sight, Arthur was sent by our Bahamas doctor, Teddy Laidlaw-Thomson, to Miami Heart Institute, flying there in a private jet generously supplied by our neighbour and good friend, E. P. Taylor, the well-known entrepreneur and racehorse breeder.

It is the custom in many U.S. cities for the news media to monitor ambulance calls. Because of this, we were greeted at Miami Airport not only by an ambulance which Arthur dazedly staggered into, but by a television crew which recorded the event for local news programmes that night. The item was repeated on radio, picked up by wire services, and published in newspapers across North America. From points as far distant as British Columbia and Maine, we received enquiries and condolences—from strangers as well as friends and acquaintances.

Afterwards Arthur was genuinely moved to know that so many people cared about his welfare.

There *was* one sour note, unusual in its insensitivity.

Within minutes of the television news item going on the air, a young man phoned directly to Arthur's hospital room and demanded to speak to him personally.

'May I ask who's calling?' I said. 'This is Mrs. Hailey speaking.'

'Umm—he doesn't know me—but I just saw him on TV, and I hope to be a writer some day, and I want to ask him what's the best way to go about it.'

'But,' I said incredulously, 'he's in great pain and in no condition to speak to anyone.'

'Well,' the voice persisted, 'perhaps I could come by the hospital later and talk to him then.'

I told him patiently that I didn't think that was a good idea. Finally, and reluctantly, the young man realised he wasn't getting anywhere and hung up.

One unexpected development has arisen with the publication of Alex Haley's *Roots*. Arthur and I know Alex, and are delighted that his book has been a sensational success. A nice thing about the writing game is that there is room for everyone, and one successful author

143

can be genuinely pleased about the achievements of another. However, the similarity of Haley/Hailey (both with the same initials) has confused some readers.

Within the past few years Arthur has been getting his name spelled correctly—with an 'i'—after earlier years when, lots of times, it wasn't. But since *Roots* was published, the spelling H-A-L-E-Y has crept back into letters we receive from readers. A few have even complimented him on his new publication—and, said one reader, 'I didn't know until now that you were black.'

For many years—right up until 1972, in fact—I personally answered letters from readers. I explained that Arthur was busy writing, and he could not possibly answer them himself. Sometimes I would let the letters pile up, then spend several days replying to them one by one. I answered questions, explained why Arthur couldn't read manuscripts, thanked readers for suggestions, and sometimes got into a lively discussion about something that particularly interested me. My letters were obviously too friendly, because I started getting replies to my replies, followed up by Christmas cards, and photographs of readers' families.

One day I rebelled.

'This is madness!' I said. 'Here I am, practically chained to the typewriter, writing letters to people I've never met, and am never likely to, while my three children are complaining because they don't get letters from me often enough.'

I arranged for an assistant to acknowledge the letters, but I was not happy with this set-up, and it only lasted a couple of years.

Then I devised a printed form letter which said, in four short paragraphs, that Arthur couldn't answer letters, but that anyone who took the trouble to write a letter deserved a reply; that we appreciated their kind words. This worked well, but it didn't cover requests for editorial help with manuscripts or suggestions for new books, and I found myself adding a P.S. to the form letter to cover these extra topics. The P.S.s got longer and longer before sanity prevailed.

I drafted a longer form letter which dealt with just about every major subject a reader was likely to raise.

Some letters I don't answer at all.

First, there are the obvious crank letters—though, happily, these are few. Then there are the roneoed letters which seem to be sent out by the hundreds to so-called celebrities asking for items to be auctioned for charity. At first I complied with these requests, but the letters came too frequently, and I was spending a ridiculous amount of time parcelling up autographed books.

Arthur has always disliked the growing cult of collecting personal items owned and used by 'celebrities'. There is a Famous People's Eye Glasses Museum in Nevada which collects and exhibits old spectacles. We, too, received a letter from the director, but we declined to send a pair. And even as I was writing this chapter, along came a letter asking for an old button from a garment worn by Arthur, with a statement attesting to its authenticity. I cannot think of anything less exciting than looking at collections of old spectacles and old buttons.

I am not overly thrilled, either, with requests for favourite recipes to be included in celebrity cookbooks. But then, I think publishers have gone bonkers in recent years, tagging cookbooks to every subject one can conceive. I was once given *The Ballet Cook Book*, which seemed to me an incongruous combination.

A memorable letter we received in 1975 was from a mother who asked for fifteen hundred dollars. She was making summer plans for her three teenagers and needed the money, she said, to make up the amount required to send one child to Europe; another to Mexico; and the third, a budding tennis champion, to John Gardiner's Tennis Ranch in California. That year our own three children had arranged to work through the summer months: Jane as a volunteer teacher of underprivileged children in San Francisco; Steven in the economics department of a bank in Toronto; Diane as a girl Friday in a lawyer's office in Montreal. I was certainly not going to help finance the summer activities of our correspondent's children, but I did not feel like explaining why, so ignored the bold letter.

It's been said that everyone has a book inside him or her. I know that a lot of people who think they do have written to us. Their letters go something like this:

> I have had the most fascinating life. My father was an immigrant and I grew up during the Depression. We were penniless. Now I have a large company that employs hundreds. All my friends tell me I should write a book. But I am not a writer.

> In your hands, though, Mr. Hailey, I know my story could be a best seller. You would not have to do any research. I have all the information you would need. Perhaps we could meet. If you ever get to our town, I would be happy to entertain you, and I could give you some details. Or I could travel to, say (name of nearest big city), and meet you there. Please let me know which you would prefer.

Occasionally, the clincher comes in the last paragraph.

> If you write my story, I would be willing to take only a small percentage of the royalties—say, 20%.

Some correspondents are not so generous. They feel a fifty-fifty split would be fairer.

Many such letters are genuinely moving, and we know that the stories suggested would indeed make good books if handled well. I remember one from a former Roman Catholic priest:

> For a long time, my desire has been to promote a story depicting the true struggles and victories of a priest whose lifestyle must straddle the law of celibacy as he seeks freedom and fulfilment for himself and others . . . I still cherish the ideals that led me to the priesthood . . . Behind-the-scenes glimpses would include my first love affair and the consequent struggles to remain a good priest and still be a warm, real person—finally culminating in my present marriage.
>
> I would like to work with an author who has the greatness of spirit and sensitivity to handle the story respectfully. Long before I had read all of your published writings, I felt your warmth and compassion . . .

I personally would like to see Arthur tackle something along these lines. Although he discarded all religious beliefs by the time he was twenty-five, he is a devout believer in the dignity of the individual and the sanctity of life. He is opposed to capital punishment, abhors abortion and, as another priest once said to me, 'Your husband is more truly religious than most people I know.'

In my replies to these letters I have explained that my husband has more ideas of his own for new novels than he has time in which to write them, since each book takes him three years to complete. However, I have thanked them for thinking of him, and—if their letters are well written—have suggested they tackle the writing of their life stories themselves.

146   *   *   *

The best letter of all came from a fan in England. She was Arthur's mother and she wrote it after she had read *Wheels*. She was eighty-four, and this was the last of her son's novels that she read. (A month before she died, Arthur took with him to England a copy of the finished manuscript of *The Moneychangers*, but it was too late. She was already dying, and unable to read it, though she tried.) She wrote:

> *Wheels* is a jolly good book. When I got into it I did not want to put it down. I'm afraid I stayed up late some nights reading it. You've got a brain, Arthur. You must have done a lot of research. I was so glad Erica and Adam came together in the end. They were good characters. I guessed Rollie Knight would come to a sticky end . . .
>
> We are very proud of you. Dad said he's going to read it. I don't know if he will, he does not read like he used. He'll be eighty-nine next birthday. I hope I never get tired of reading. I think it keeps the brain active. Now, Arthur, don't laugh at me—I know I am old-fashioned—but I don't like you using the word BULLSHIT.

CHAPTER 13

The Magic of a King-size Bed

If I meet a couple who tell me they have never had a cross word in all the years they have been married, I immediately suspect: (a) they are lying; or (b) they have an incredibly dull marriage; or (c) one of the two is totally repressed or dominated by the other.

In our family, fights are inevitable. During times of pre-menstrual stress a good argument is almost necessary for my physical welfare. I rather enjoy the verbal battle, but Arthur finds it totally draining.

Therein lies our dilemma. Arthur is easily irritated by small things and is inclined to nag. Most of the time I take little notice of these pinpricks, or tell him he's behaving like an old woman. But sometimes—at an unexpected moment—I blow my top. If he is in a good mood, nothing much comes of it. He hears me out and either says, 'Yes, you have a point,' or jokes me out of my ill temper.

But moodiness is an occupational hazard. A writer is preoccupied with thoughts of his work so much of the time, he is impatient with the mundane chatter that is a necessary part of everyday life. Fortunately for me, Arthur is an upbeat man most of the time, but when I am scrappy and he is moody, then we are all set for an argument. Each goads the other into saying too much. Like many women, I am facile with words when I am mad, sometimes play dirty, usually score the best point and have the last word. (Arthur storms, 'You should have been a criminal prosecutor. You would always get the defendant behind bars!')

After the row I am quick to recover and am usually the first to say, 'I'm sorry. Let's get this over!' I have no capacity for sustained rage.

But it takes Arthur longer to return to normal, because he is mentally exhausted.

Yet he, too, can recognise the wisdom of our family adage: 'A quarrel will be settled sooner or later. Why not now?' So he will sometimes be the first one to come around.

I remember when Arthur and I had been bickering during a wine tour of France in May 1976. We were attending a large, formal luncheon at the Wine Institute in Bordeaux, seated two places apart. I studiously ignored him. Then, during the second course, Arthur passed along to me a scribbled note, which I still have. It read:

> I think you are being unreasonable and I think a week from now you will say so. However, I am *thoroughly miserable* at being at odds with you, so the above *doesn't matter*. I apologise for whatever, and I love you, you bitch!

I smiled down the table, we reached behind the chairs between us, and locked hands momentarily. It was all over.

If one of us can say, 'I'm sorry'—whether right or wrong, it really doesn't matter—then squabbles get nowhere. But sanity does not always prevail, so a small clash can become a big fight.

I can remember several, one of them involving the whole family. It was while Arthur was writing *Airport*. I have forgotten why we were arguing—I am sure it was something trivial, as usual—but whatever it was, I was extremely angry. I towered over Arthur's desk as he was working. Suddenly, in exasperation and rage, I snatched up two pages of typed manuscript—the product of a day's work. I scrunched them in my hand and ran from the study down to our bedroom, where I stuffed the papers deep into a drawer. I felt a glow of smug satisfaction. I knew of no sweeter act of revenge.

Having hidden his day's work, I changed into a swimsuit, dived into our pool, and swam hard for several lengths. For me, swimming is the best therapy for a bad mood. Water flowing over the body somehow cleanses the mind and refreshes the spirit. By the time I returned I was ready to apologise to Arthur for my outrageous act, but the sight of our bedroom stopped me short. It looked as if it had been burgled. Every drawer was out, the contents strewn all over the room; every garment I owned was out of the cupboard; all my shoes were scattered in every direction.

I was furious, but had the sense not to direct my outrage at Arthur. Seldom violent, he must have been in a worse state than I. I roared out my fury, and the children came running, wide-eyed, to see what was wrong. They were shocked at the scene, for they had not seen anything like this before.

'What happened?'

'Your father did it!' I wailed. 'He's gone mad!'

They looked at each other in surprise, then offered to help me straighten the room.

'No!' I said, 'I'll do it,' and settled down to my great punishment.

Later, Jane came back and looked at me accusingly.

'No wonder Daddy did that, after what you did to him! That was unforgivable.'

Kids have a knack of putting their parents' fights into perspective.

Poor Jane—she has a childhood memory that I am ashamed of. During a row Arthur and I were having once, she tripped up the stairs while carrying a heavy Scotch-tape holder. The cutting edge dug into her hand. The jagged wound cried out for a stitch or two. We actually argued, while the poor child was bleeding, which of us was to take her to the hospital.

However, there is hope for all you fighting couples out there, for Jane has told us she knows of no marriage that is as fulfilling as ours.

We must have done something right.

Arthur loves symphony concerts, is lukewarm about ballet, and would rather stay home with a good book than go to the opera. My preferences are reversed: I adore ballet, enjoy some operas, but seldom get excited over the symphony.

Looking back over the years together, I feel guilty that I spoiled much of the pleasure Arthur derived from attending symphony concerts. For if there is one thing I have learned in life, it is that one person cannot be all things to another, and that there has to be an element of 'open marriage' in even the best of unions. I believe it is unfair that a husband or wife should feel compelled to give up sports, hobbies, interests, clubs, or friends because the other doesn't like them. I now realise that it is futile to try to make yourself 'enjoy' an activity when, deep down inside, you know you would far rather be doing something else.

150

While we lived in Toronto and also during the four years we were near San Francisco, Arthur had season tickets to the symphony. I went with him to most of the concerts. Some evenings were real successes—sometimes because we had a particularly good restaurant meal, or the programme was special. I remember an outstanding evening in Toronto when Seiji Ozawa was conducting and Artur Rubinstein was the soloist. The obvious respect each had for the other, the very young and the very old, the exhilaration and excitement felt by the audience—I shall never forget that magical evening. But usually I was bored at symphony concerts, and often fought to stay awake during the heavy passages, much to Arthur's annoyance. If we had kept a chart, and thank goodness we didn't, I think it would have shown that somehow, subtly, we had more arguments during those evenings than any other.

Arthur would exasperatedly say to me sometimes, 'Look, you don't *have* to go to the symphony. Why don't you let me take someone else?' I knew the someone else would be a woman, and I would think, 'Dammit, no, I will go and learn to love it.' But, of course, I never did, and only succeeded in putting a crimp in the evening.

He paid me back for this dog-in-the-manger attitude one memorable night at the opera. The first night of the opera season in San Francisco is a gala affair, the dressiest social event of the year. I wanted to experience the occasion at least once. But Arthur has always frowned on the social implications of 'first nights'. I knew I would never get there if I asked him ahead of time if he would go. So I bought tickets and presented them as a *fait accompli*, and hoped I could bulldoze the evening through.

It didn't work. He did not balk initially, and went along with my plan to drive into San Francisco during the day and stay in a motel. But I was sure he would have made specific plans for dinner ahead of the opera. He loves to dine out in elegant restaurants, and I assumed it would be the part of the evening he would enjoy most. I was wrong. As we drove into the city, black-tie togs and my new white dress hanging over the back seat, I asked mildly where we were going for dinner.

Hostility set in. 'I'm not planning to go anywhere. This is your evening.'

I was determined to keep cool.

'Well, we could go to Trader Vic's,' I said. It is a favourite restaurant of his and a traditional eating spot for opera first-nighters.

'No,' he said. 'It'll be too pretentious there tonight.'

I suggested one or two other restaurants. None of them was right, and I gave up temporarily. We drove the rest of the journey, and checked into our motel, in silence.

Then I flared up. 'Are you telling me we are not going *anywhere* for dinner?'

'Looks like it, doesn't it?'

I don't remember what I said, but I know I indulged in a tirade which got me nowhere. Finally, I slammed out the door, got into the car and roared off Van Ness Avenue onto Lombard Street on screeching tyres.

As I cooled down I realised how hungry I was. I knew Arthur would be, too, which would make him even worse during the rest of the evening. At that moment I passed a fish-and-chips shop. Fantastic solution! I parked the car and ordered two pieces of fish each, plus french fries. In the same block I bought a bottle of gin, some tonic water and limes. I returned to the motel, mixed the gin and tonics and, without a word, handed Arthur one. Then I 'served' the fish and chips in their paper containers with the plastic knives and forks and paper napkins.

It was delicious. The drinks mellowed us and, as we caught sight of each other licking our fingers, we laughed aloud at our incongruous first-night opera dinner.

The evening should have ended happily after that—but as Arthur got into his dinner jacket, the black mood returned. It was a disastrous evening. We avoided everyone we knew, and Arthur became more and more sour. Afterward we started to walk back to the motel. I was in tears and hurried on ahead, Arthur trying to keep up with me, embarrassed that I might make a scene. To this day I wish I had. There was a marvellous opportunity as we skirted the motel swimming pool. One quick push and he could have been in it, flailing about in his black threads and fancy suspenders. But I lost my nerve.

Perhaps the memory of the two cracked ribs stopped me.

This was not an incident one can be proud of, but at least it established me as a woman not to be trodden under foot. We had had an argument in the kitchen, and I became so enraged I pushed Arthur with all my might across the room. He fell against an open cupboard door and bent over in pain. I was sure he was exaggerating, so I ignored the histrionics.

Two days later he returned from an appointment with our doctor to announce the damage to his ribs. I was full of sympathy and apology, and vowed never again to strike out in anger.

Several weeks later, Arthur strained his back and had to go into the hospital and spend a few days in traction. The obvious comment came from our friends: 'Sheila, *now* what have you done?'

The only time I ever tried to 'go home to mother' was several years after that dear lady had died.

We had been invited to a superb Hallowe'en fancy-dress party, given by a friend in the Napa Valley. Some two hundred guests arrived during a dark, rainy evening, imaginatively dressed in appropriate carnival garb. I remember two attractive young women, both hugely pregnant, were dressed as large, round, orange pumpkins, supported by long, shapely, black-stockinged legs.

It was the sort of evening that could have been great fun. But Arthur loathes 'fancy dressing'; to him a costume party is some kind of nightmare. Yet he is a smart dresser and selects his wardrobe with great care. I knew he was already in one of his depressed moods when he put on an old sports jacket, some tired trousers, and a ho-hum tie. I wore a long, ethereal robe in Hallowe'en colours—not strictly a costume, but in the right mood.

Arthur did not enjoy himself, for he had made up his mind not to. He wore a long, bored face, engaging in conversation only when cornered. I tried to ignore him, but found it difficult to pretend all was well. There was a magnificent spread at midnight, and after sampling 'Witch's Brew' and 'Pie à la Rodent', I suggested to Arthur that we leave. He was clearly relieved.

But on the way home I began to feel sorry for myself and upbraided him for his ill humour, his selfishness, his bad grace. Tears of rage and self-pity were falling as heavily as the rain outside and, when we got home, I was determined to *go*.

Once in the house, I went straight to the fireproof safe in his study where we kept manuscripts, insurance policies and other valuable papers. But, although I consider myself a reasonably bright woman, I had not at that point mastered the art of opening a combination lock.

There I was in my flowing robe, turning three times to the left and stopping at 70, twice to the right and stopping at 25, and so on. For almost ten minutes I struggled, but never did I hear that elusive click which miraculously opens a safe.

Suddenly Arthur was at my elbow.

'Do you need some help?'

'Yes, dammit!' I spat. 'I can't get this bloody thing open.'

'Here, let me do it.'

After a few deft flicks of his wrist, the door gaped wide.

'What is it you want, anyway?' he asked.

'My passport,' I hissed. 'I'm going home to England.'

He reached into the safe, retrieved the passport, and handed it to me. I was furious. I wanted him to plead with me not to go, to say he couldn't live without me, that he was desperately sorry.

So I flounced into the bedroom, took off my long dress and started to put on a wool suit I often wore for travelling. I think that shook him.

But he only said mildly, 'Look, it's one o'clock in the morning, it's a filthy night, and you're all wrought up. It's madness to drive to San Francisco in this rain . . . besides, there won't be any flights going to London until tomorrow.'

The last thing I wanted to do that night was to drive to San Francisco, so I mumbled, 'Okay, but I'm going in the morning!'

We slept back to back, as far apart as possible without actually falling out of bed.

In the night I woke up and, forgetting how mad I was, reached out automatically for my nice, warm, cuddly man. He put his arms around me, and although I suddenly remembered my rage of the night before, I was too sleepy and comfortable to fight—and it was all over.

Such is the magic of a king-size bed.

Unfortunately, sleep doesn't always have the same effect on King Arthur.

I remember once being so mad with him, I literally kicked him out of bed. I am a strong woman of about ten stone, and all that weight was behind the large thrust of my heel into his back.

He lay on the floor and groaned softly, hoping to elicit some remorse from me. I ignored him and he continued to lie there.

'How stupid!' I thought, and I padded around to his side of the bed to pour myself a glass of water from the carafe we always keep on his night table. I deliberately spilled one or two drops on his face.

One eye opened and glared at me.

'I suppose you think that's funny.'

'Oh, I'm terribly sorry,' I lied. 'That was accidental.' Like hell!

After a while Arthur got fed up lying there, climbed into bed, and we eventually fell asleep, back to back.

Sometime later I awoke, no longer hostile to anyone, and reached out for him. He wasn't there. I sat up, suddenly concerned, to realise he was sitting on his side of the bed, pouring himself a glass of water.

As I usually do, I murmured, 'Pour me a glass, hon, after you.'

'Yes,' he said. 'I'll pour you a glass,' and threw the contents into my face.

I gasped for breath. My hair dripped onto my shoulders, my soaked nightie clung to my breasts.

As we looked at each other, we quickly saw the slapstick side of it—and burst out laughing.

The cause of our fiercest and most passionate fights has always been jealousy. Yet we both profess to be broad-minded and I have often said—and meant it—that adultery is the silliest reason for divorce I know. To me it would be unrealistic to pretend that when Arthur has been out of town, he has never taken a woman out to dine or spent a night with one. After all, he is an attractive man who delights in women's company. And he has often quipped, 'As a writer, how can I write about other women if I don't get to know some?'

I was never jealous over this kind of infidelity. Call it self-confidence, tolerance, or just plain stupidity—whatever it was, I recognised it early. To be exact, three years after we were married.

Arthur came back from a business trip to Vancouver, grinning broadly.

'What have you been up to?' I joshed.

'What do you mean?'

'You *know* what I mean. You met someone while you were out West, didn't you?'

If he had denied it, I would have known he was lying.

'Yes,' he said. 'A nice girl. I took her out a couple of times. She was fun.'

I was truly surprised to realise it didn't bother me. He was back with me, wasn't he? He had told me about the girl; therefore, it couldn't have meant that much. I did not ask any more questions.

I was determined there would be no double standard in our relationship, for I have always enjoyed men's company as much as Arthur enjoys women's. So we foolishly slipped into the habit of . . . well, not telling all, but hinting at the flirtations we indulged in, perhaps with the idea that we were still essentially true to the other by being open and honest.

We hurt each other from time to time. Where there is love there is, inevitably, jealousy in some form. One vivid recollection I have of this devastating, mind-blowing, unreasoning emotion, was an episode during the breezy early 1960s.

Arthur was in London for a week or so, on business. I was to fly directly to Paris and meet him there for our first visit to that magic city. Only he jumped the gun and got there ahead of me—four days ahead of me—with someone else.

He might have got away with it except that a few days before I was to leave Toronto I had occasion to call him at his parents' home, where he had been staying. His mother told me he had left London, but she did not know where he had gone. If it was urgent, my brother-in-law Frank had his address.

I was immediately suspicious—men in collusion, I thought, one covering up for the other. I had no intention of checking with Frank. But as the days went by I grew more angry and jealous by the hour. I could think of nothing else and found it difficult to sleep. I have always had a short fuse and my outbursts of rage are short-lived as well. But if I suppress my anger, it becomes more intense.

My plane arrived at Orly Airport early in the morning. Arthur was there to greet me; we were all smiles, but I sensed he knew I was on to something. He'd probably found out I had tried to call him in London.

Once in our hotel room he tore off his clothes and made passionate love, hoping that would disarm me. It did—for a while. But sooner or later I knew I would have to open up.

At first I pretended sophisticated nonchalance, and he admitted that yes, he had spent the last few days with a woman. It was not whom I had suspected, which made me feel only slightly better.

We had to go back to the airport to meet my sister Gina, flying in from London. Arthur had impulsively invited her to spend that weekend with us—an act of self-protection, I think. She would be a comfortable buffer between us.

That evening we were to meet her in the hotel lobby before going out to dinner. Normally punctual, Arthur and I were twenty minutes late. The reason: as I was getting ready, the inflamed wound inside me burst. I became an enraged tigress. I shouted at Arthur, shook him, threw things at him (not breakable objects—there is always a shred of sanity inside me that prevents my doing anything that would cause inconvenience or embarrassment afterwards).

Arthur had never seen me as violent as I was in that Paris hotel. The room became a shambles. I let forth a torrent of abuse. How *dare* he bring someone else to Paris—of all places. A city for lovers—didn't he have the gumption to *know* he and I should have explored it together? How could he be so *stupid* and *insensitive?* And why the hell did he invite Gina? I love her dearly—but who needs a sister along on a woman's first visit to Paris with the man she loves?

I gradually calmed down, put on more make-up to hide the tear stains, and together we went down to the lobby and calmly apologised for our lateness. A few years later I told Gina of my outburst in our room. It is a tribute to my acting ability that she never knew I'd had the most memorable temper tantrum of my life.

I chuckle sometimes now to realise that I objected more to Arthur's choice of city than I did to his indulging in a few days off from marriage. Arthur later apologised for his colossal 'error in judgment'. His reasoning had been that the lady in question knew Paris well and he could learn from her the best things to do and see, in readiness for my visit.

It would be unfair to give the impression that I have never been guilty of indiscretion. A then-painful but now-hilarious example immediately springs to mind.

I once made the mistake of telling Arthur the name of an extremely attractive man I had met during a convention in southern California. I had gone there to give a luncheon speech.

It was something of a success, and one of the members who came up to congratulate me was the handsome man of my story. The attraction between us was immediate. We laughed and chatted easily, and over the next few days had fun getting to know each other.

As a result of my talk, I was asked to speak to another group at the

St. Francis Hotel in San Francisco a few weeks later. My friend phoned me to say he would be attending some of the meetings and asked if I would have dinner with him the evening after my luncheon address.

I accepted immediately. Arthur and I had been going through a dull, scratchy, flat spell, and the prospect of a superb candle-lit dinner with my witty friend was delicious.

Arthur had, in fact, refused my invitation to drive into San Francisco the afternoon before the luncheon, to take in a film and dinner, and stay the night in a complimentary suite at the hotel. I suggested he could drive back to St. Helena early the next morning so he would not have to miss a day's writing. He was difficult, and would have none of it, so I drove in alone, telling him I would not be back until late the following evening.

I was miserable that night, rattling around in two huge, luxurious hotel rooms. The management had thoughtfully left a box of chocolates and a bouquet of flowers—but I wanted to share it all with someone. What a shame, I thought, that my friend was not arriving until tomorrow.

Arthur must have done some thinking of his own, wondering why I wasn't going to be home until late the following night and, I bet, deciding that he really was a bit of a heel not to have come with me into San Francisco for the night.

I gave my speech the following day, returning to my suite about three o'clock to check out. Four telephone messages were waiting for me—all from Arthur. I called him.

The voice was phonily bright and unconvincing.

'Darling,' he cried. 'I've had such a good morning's work, I thought—oh! I'm sorry! First of all, how did your talk go?'

'Okay,' I said flatly. 'They seemed to enjoy it.'

'Great!' He pretended enthusiasm. 'Now, as I said, I did some good writing this morning, and I thought I would drive into the city and we could go to a film and have dinner together tonight.'

'Oh, you did, did you?' I replied icily. 'Well, it was *last night* I wanted you. I'm busy tonight!' And I hung up.

To hell with you, chum! You're not going to play with me like some puppet on a string.

So I met my man—even drove to the airport to pick him up—and put all thoughts of Arthur out of my head. My friend checked into the Fairmont Hotel while I parked my station wagon, and by the time I joined him in his room he had ordered a bottle of champagne.

We sipped the bubbly, delighting in each other's company, and planned our evening. Should we dine at Alexis or L'Etoile across the road, or—what about room service? We decided on Alexis; after all, we had the whole evening—no point in not stringing it out pleasurably.

Suddenly, as we sat smiling at each other, the phone rang. My friend answered, looked somewhat startled, and blurted out the truth.

'Yes, she is here,' and handed me the phone.

I couldn't believe it.

'Whatever is it?' I cried, afraid something horrible had happened to one of the children.

Arthur's voice was flat, even, full of suppressed rage.

'Be down in the lobby in fifteen minutes,' he said. 'I'll be at the main entrance to pick you up.'

'I don't believe this is happening,' I said. 'This isn't like you!' I was truly flabbergasted.

'Just *be* there!'—and he hung up.

I turned to my friend, embarrassed for him, for me, and—most of all, for Arthur.

'He's so upset, he's out of his mind. He has *never* behaved like this before! . . . He's picking me up in fifteen minutes and . . . I'm sorry! . . . I have to be there . . . He means more to me than any one in this world. I must go to him.' I sounded like someone in a soap opera, uttering unreal lines.

My friend was a gentleman and, being married himself, understood completely. 'Let me come down to the lobby with you, and you can introduce us,' he said. I liked his class.

Arthur was indeed waiting at the main door in our green Mustang convertible. He was white and tight-lipped. I bent down and said, as normally as I could, 'Honey, I'd like you to meet the friend I told you about.'

He looked directly at my escort and spat out the words, 'I have no wish to meet you!' Then to me, 'I just wanted to break up your evening.' And with that, quite unexpectedly, he roared off.

I became frantic. I dashed out, running into the traffic, absurdly trying to catch him.

Suddenly a small MG sports car stopped beside me, the door swung open and a very English voice said, 'Can I help you?'

'Yes,' I cried, as I jumped in. 'Will you try to catch up with that green Mustang ahead. I can't explain—but my husband's in it—we've quarrelled—and I've got to stop him!'

'Righto!' said the English one, obviously enjoying himself. 'Hold on to your seat.' And he shot off as though he were in a Grand Prix.

Arthur had no idea he was being followed. He was just driving uncharacteristically fast because of his rage. The two cars whizzed up and down the steep streets around Nob Hill, like a scene out of the film *Bullitt*.

I was sure we had lost the chase when, luckily, a green light ahead, at the bottom of a hill, changed to amber and then red. Arthur had to stop. My driver smartly came up beside him, and smoothly nosed his car in front of the Mustang to block it off.

'Oh, thank you so much!' I cried, kissed the astonished man impulsively, got out of the car, wrenched the Mustang door open, and jumped in beside Arthur.

'What on earth is the matter with you?' I cried desperately. 'How can *you*, of all people, behave like this?'

'I don't want to talk about it! I don't give a damn about you! And I don't care what you do the rest of the night. I just wanted to spoil your evening. And by God, I've done it, you bitch!'

I have never seen Arthur Hailey as white-faced, and ugly, and angry, and jealous as he was that night. I hope I never will again. He was a madman, someone I did not know.

Shaking with anger, he drove me back to the Fairmont and left me at the garage.

There was absolutely no way I could have returned to my friend for the rest of the evening, and Arthur knew it. Instead, I collected my car and drove back to St. Helena. I cried with frustrated rage all the way, tears blurring my vision.

'You bastard! You bugger! You rotten sod!' I yelled to no one, delving back to my childhood for all the English swear words I knew. 'It's bloody *unfair!* You get away with it all the time—because you're a *man*. The same old bloody double standard!' and on and on.

Fortunately, the children were all in their rooms when I arrived home—so I went quietly to our bedroom and went to bed. But, of course, I could not sleep, or read, or do anything. Instead, I waited and waited until, finally, I heard Arthur come in about 2 a.m. (He told me later he had tried to get drunk in several bars, which I found difficult to believe, and still do. A moderate drinker, it is not his way to drink alone to deliberately get drunk. I did believe him, though, when he told me he had tracked me down by phoning all the likely restaurants to see if there was a reservation in my friend's name. When he drew a blank, he started on the hotels.)

He marched into the bedroom and paced the floor as he spoke with passion: 'Sheila, listen to me! I know you're not asleep! You and I have slipped into a pattern where we are hurting each other and it's got to stop! We've been too damn clever by half, thinking we're so sophisticated we can indulge in affairs and flaunt them before each other. I love you, goddammit! And I want you *here* having dinner with *me*. Do you hear?'

It was wonderful! Here was my man, showing me he cared. My anger dissipated and I jumped out of bed, put my arms around him, and we both broke down and cried.

CHAPTER 14

Hollywood! Wherefore Art Thou, Hollywood?

Hollywood!

What excitement, what magic that name used to conjure for me!

In the early 1940s Deanna Durbin was my heroine. I sang her songs; I tried to float on air as she seemed to; I even fancied I looked like her. I thought: How wonderful to be a film star!

Apart from my two-day visit to Los Angeles in 1950, my first encounter with Hollywood was in 1956. The film rights of that breakthrough television play *Flight Into Danger* had been sold to an independent film producer, Hall Bartlett. Arthur was to spend six weeks in Hollywood writing the screenplay. When he suggested I join him for two of those weeks, there was only one snag—I was still breast-feeding our baby son. No child was ever weaned to a bottle faster than six-month-old Steven. A baby-sitter was hired and I was on my way, flying from Toronto to Los Angeles.

Even before I got there Arthur had experienced his first disappointment. He had envisaged glamorous parties, flowing champagne, beautiful starlets. But Hall Bartlett put the kibosh on that right from the beginning. He had written in a letter:

> I have made reservations for you at a motel within walking distance of Westwood Village . . . . It is a very modest place, and has nothing fancy or Hollywood about it. However, it is rather quiet. I know the place fairly well because my parents stay there when they are visiting us.

'And,' as Arthur said when discussing the experience afterwards, 'by God, it *was* quiet!'

But, after all, he was there to work, to produce a screenplay in six weeks, and he was being paid a thousand dollars a week plus expenses to do it.

During my stay it was arranged that I visit a film studio with actor Jerry Paris, who has since become a television director. I watched a segment of a film being made, met actor Edmund O'Brien, actress Ruta Lee, and others whose names I don't remember. We all went off to lunch, on the way meeting actor Michael Wilding at the studio gates. I shall never forget that meal. I sat silent—not because I was tongue-tied, but because I couldn't get a word in. Some actors, I know, are never really offstage, but I was unprepared for the totally histrionic atmosphere. I was fascinated by the conversation and listened to a series of stories being told by each of the actors and actresses. Every joke was longer and contained more ethnic dialects than the one before. It was like a Johnny Carson show without cameras.

In the afternoon I made a tour of the studios and saw the various permanent sets—the Old West main street, the big-city ghetto, the pastoral small town. I enjoyed it all—but I suddenly thought of Deanna Durbin and saw her as she must have been: a young girl with a glorious voice working hard from dawn to dusk, amid an atmosphere of controlled chaos.

I filled the rest of my days exploring Westwood and its surrounding neighbourhoods—Brentwood, Beverly Hills, Bel Air, Santa Monica and Pacific Palisades. I shopped in the smart stores on Wilshire Boulevard, enjoying the luxury of spending some of the money Arthur was earning. I bought food from a nearby delicatessen for our lunch each day, so Arthur didn't have to take too much time out from his writing. I had my hair done a couple of times . . . and I remember being struck by one overwhelming fact. Hollywood seemed to be full of young men and women who were working as hairdressers, waiters and waitresses, garage attendants, and shop assistants, but who lived for one goal only: to get into films. They made the rounds of studios for work as extras, and they eked out a living as best they could. They chatted with me. Where are you from? Why are you here? As soon as they heard my husband was writing a screenplay—and, yes, I was bragging a bit—they were angling for a

163

job. Did my husband have any influence over casting? The answer was, is, and probably always will be: *No!*

The writer of an original property—whether a novel or play—is a peculiar breed in Hollywood. He commands respect, but as a physical presence he is often regarded as an unnecessary nuisance. Therefore, the tendency is to consult him as little as possible.

When Arthur had completed the screenplay of *Zero Hour*, which was the eventual title of the film, everyone seemed happy. Hall Bartlett and his then wife, Lois, gave a delightful dinner for us. There were flattering speeches. Finally, as we said goodbye at the airport, Arthur was presented with a beautiful silver pitcher inscribed: 'For Arthur Hailey with our admiration and gratitude—Hall Bartlett— *Flight Into Danger*—1956.' I was given a silver powder compact engraved: 'For Sheila—affectionately Lois and Hall—1956.' Along with Arthur's gift was a handwritten note from Hall:

> This is just a small remembrance to carry my deep appreciation for the wonderful job you have done on the screenplay of *Flight*. Your talent, your patience, your understanding, and your attention to the job at hand are most admirable—and these qualities of yours have made me anxious to look ahead to the time when we can work together again.

It came as quite a surprise, then, several months later, to learn that a 'new' screenplay had been written. The writing credit: Hall Bartlett, John Champion and Arthur Hailey—in that order. When we read the script we found that, yes, changes had been made, but the bulk of it was Arthur's original work. What's more, he had kept all his rough notes and discarded pages and could prove it was essentially his screenplay.

Arthur's agent, dear Maeve Southgate, was as incensed as we were by the credit billing. There were some testy letters back and forth; then Maeve appealed to the Writers Guild of America, of which Arthur was, and is, a member. She wanted to have the screenplay arbitrated. The Guild took several weeks to study the new screenplay, the old, and Arthur's notes. Their decision: the Bartlett-Champion contribution was collaborative and could not be separated, but that Hailey's contribution was the most significant and his name must precede the other two. In the film business, that decision was recognised as final.

Arthur wrote to Hall Bartlett:

> I am satisfied that the ruling was fair and impartial and I hope
> you and John Champion feel the same way . . . we have had a
> difference of opinion and now it has been settled. For my part, I
> would be very sorry if it became a permanent personal barrier
> and that is why I am writing this letter.

Hall wrote back graciously, too, but the incident obviously put a
crimp in the relationship. Although Arthur tried to get in touch with
him the next time he was in Hollywood, we never heard from him
again.

The movie *Zero Hour*, starring Dana Andrews and Linda Darnell,
was duly released in late 1957. It was a so-so film, neither a disaster
nor a box-office smash.

Arthur sold another teleplay, *Time Lock*, as a movie—this time to
Romulus Productions, a British company. But he declined to write
the screenplay. The result was a harmonious relationship.

Television writing was different. When Arthur worked for 'Studio
One' and 'Playhouse 90' on CBS, there was a mutual and healthy
respect between writer and producer. It was a happy time for Arthur.
He would take several months to write the script, then stay with a
production right through to air time. He learned much from his
friend and mentor Herbert Brodkin, who produced two of Arthur's
big TV successes: *No Deadly Medicine* and *Diary of a Nurse*.

Live television was frantic fun. 'Studio One'—a weekly series of
original dramas—was sponsored by Westinghouse. The opening
shot of *No Deadly Medicine* showed a large wall clock. Some four
minutes before nine o'clock, when the show was to go live on the CBS
network in the United States and, simultaneously, on the CBC network in Canada, someone suddenly noticed on the face of the clock a
large GE—for General Electric, Westinghouse's competitor. A step-
ladder was swiftly hauled onto the set, a studio painter scrambled up
and airbrushed over the offending GE. The sweep-second hand
moved to nine o'clock, the painter jumped off the ladder. As the play
went over the network the sound of the ladder falling was heard on
everyone's TV set. Someone had pushed it over to get it out of the
camera's eye a split second before the first shot.

I remember another play, *Death Minus One*, set in postwar

London. One of the scenes showed a bombed ruin near St. Paul's Cathedral, overgrown with weeds. The play was televised from a New York studio, and the weeds were a problem. You could buy plants and flowers—real or plastic—in New York, but not weeds. And there are precious few weeds growing in Manhattan. CBS sent out a crew in a truck to the countryside to dig up fresh weeds. These were packed in pots and 'planted' on the set, but wilted under the hot TV klieg lights. Minutes before air time, while actors and cameramen were readying positions, there was the incongruous sight of prop men watering weeds.

Diary of a Nurse was produced in Hollywood. Rehearsals were in progress. Arthur was working at CBS Television City on last-minute changes in the script. Unusually, a contract had not been signed because Arthur's agent was disputing a minor clause.

Herb Brodkin talked to Arthur: 'Your agent's being most difficult. She's holding out for some obscure clause in the contract. Arthur, you're good—but you're not Hemingway yet. Can't you make her more reasonable? We go on the air next week.'

Arthur was embarrassed and telephoned Maeve Southgate in New York. 'Maeve, they're restless out here . . . rehearsing with no signed contract. Look, it's a good deal . . . I'm being well paid. Can't we sign?'

Maeve's voice came back firmly: 'Sweetie, you go back and be nice to them . . . and leave the negotiating to me.'

The clause in dispute involved residual payments if the play subsequently became a TV series. Maeve held out for more compensation, in that event, than the network wanted to give. In the end she won her point. The following year a television series, 'The Nurses,' based on *Diary of a Nurse*, went on the air. Arthur was paid a fee for each episode. The series played for two seasons, then appeared on daytime television for a further year—during which time Arthur was again paid for every week it was on the air.

No Deadly Medicine was a two-hour television drama. Later Arthur rewrote it as a novel, *The Final Diagnosis*, and later still the film rights of the novel were sold to United Artists. A film *The Young Doctors*, was produced by Stuart Millar and Lawrence Turman, and directed by Phil Karlson.

We visited the set, met the cast—Frederic March, Ben Gazzara, Ina Balin and Dick Clark. We had a good feeling about the production. Again, Arthur did not write the screenplay. He liked it, with reservations. For example, in his novel a baby with an Rh blood factor died; elsewhere in the story a young nurse whose leg had to be amputated was jilted by her doctor friend. The film had happy endings for both incidents; Arthur thought that was Pollyanna-ish to the point of being unbelievable. But, in all, it was a sound, well-produced black-and-white film which, while not spectacular, was a reasonable success.

Arthur's next encounter with Hollywood was in 1965, when *Hotel* became a film. The film rights to the novel were sold to Warner Brothers, and this time Arthur decided he would like to write the screenplay. This was agreed to by Warners, and Arthur went to Hollywood to do so.

I joined him for almost a month. I remember that when Arthur met me at Los Angeles airport he handed me a telegram he'd received from his publishers. It announced that *Hotel* would be on the *New York Times* best-seller list next Sunday in tenth position. It was the first time he'd ever been on the list.

'Wouldn't it be wonderful if it hung on for a few weeks?' he said.

It stayed on the list for a full year.

We rented a car and an apartment at the Chateau Marmont just off Sunset Boulevard. Each weekday I drove Arthur to Warner Brothers, where he was assigned an office in the Writers' Building.

Mentioning Chateau Marmont reminds me of our reunion with Arthur's three older sons and their mother, Joan. They had moved to Los Angeles a few years earlier. As we were still living in Toronto, three thousand miles away, we had not seen the boys for some time. I had never met Arthur's first wife, so we decided this was a good opportunity for the two families to get together. We invited them to our apartment for a Chinese dinner.

It was a great evening. I think both Joan and I had been nervous, but within minutes of meeting each other we were relaxed. Everyone felt good and we were exchanging funny anecdotes. Then we got onto a more serious topic. Arthur made a statement that both Joan and I vehemently disagreed with. I will always remember Arthur's face as he looked first at me—his wife—and then at Joan—his ex-wife—as we spoke up forcefully in stereo.

'My God!' he moaned. 'Not *both* of you. I can't stand it!'

Since that time Joan and I have remained firm friends with a mutual respect. I have always admired her for the superb job she did in raising three boys in a household of three adult women—herself, her mother, and her sister. And I am proud of the fact that she treats Arthur's and my children as her own, with love and affection. They in turn are fond of her and never fail to visit when they are in her area.

Working with the Warner Brothers principals, Arthur wrote a screenplay for the film *Hotel* that everyone concerned seemed to like. However, at this point no producer or director had been assigned, and there isn't a producer or director alive who doesn't have ideas of his own about the screenplay of the film he is going to help create.

So, several months later, when Wendell Mayes was named producer, of course he wanted to change the screenplay. Being a writer, too, inevitably he wanted to tackle the task himself. He wrote a completely new script, which Arthur eventually saw. The writer had ingeniously devised one character, Jeanne, to combine the three women Arthur had created in his novel—Christine Francis, Marsha Prescott, Dodo Lash. The screenplay differed from the original story in other elements too. In the novel the hotel survived; in the film it didn't. Also, the character of Albert Wells, the elderly hotel resident who owned a gold mine—a favourite with readers—had been eliminated.

Thereafter we received no communication at all from the film makers of *Hotel*. Perhaps this was because of an embarrassed sensitivity to the feelings of the original screenwriter. Still, it was frustrating to hear nothing about the casting, the shooting, or anything else. After all, we cared passionately. It had been Arthur's baby for three years; of course he was interested in how one of his stories was being translated to the screen.

All we knew was what we read in newspaper showbiz columns. We had not been invited to visit the set or to meet anyone connected with the film. Then we heard there was to be a big publicity party after the filming. We were not invited to that, either.

I was furious. I wanted Arthur to phone and say we were going to be in Los Angeles and ask if we could attend. We were living near San Francisco at the time, hardly the other side of the world. He was adamant.

'No! I'll go with an invitation, but not without. They know where I am if they want me.'

Eventually, we were in Los Angeles and visited the studio—after the sets had been partly dismantled. We walked through what was left of the 'hotel lobby'. It was like an empty old house waiting to be demolished. We were told some of the anecdotes in the making of the film, and I imagined what the set was like alive with actors and technicians. I was seething inside, but outwardly friendly.

I guess that when it was realised we were fairly nice, reasonable people, without malice, we were included in a few pre-release activities. I remember Arthur was on a network radio show with Merle Oberon, who played the Duchess, to help promote the film. She was a gracious guest, and together, she and Arthur contributed much to a relaxed, lively talk show.

We were then invited to the film's premiere—a wingding in Miami Beach. It was exciting, the first one of its kind we had been involved in. We arrived at the theatre in a motorcade; there were searchlights, crowds, and photographers. And we heard the typical snatches of conversation from onlookers.

'Oh, what a beautiful dress!'

'Gosh, he's much shorter than I thought.'

'Who's she?'

'Oh, she isn't anybody!' (The reference was obviously to me.)

We watched the film; Arthur and I were engrossed in it, since we were seeing it for the first time. Directed by Richard Quine, it was easy, comfortable entertainment. The background music, composed by Johnny Keating, was superb. I liked Karl Malden as the hotel thief, Melvyn Douglas as the hotel owner, and I have always liked the looks of Rod Taylor and Kevin McCarthy. As for beautiful Catharine Spaak, elegantly gowned by Edith Head, she was a joy to watch and hear.

As soon as the film was over and the house lights went on, Arthur stood up, leaned over to Wendell Mayes, shook his hand and congratulated him. I liked his gesture.

Now, when people ask Arthur why he doesn't write the screenplay for the film versions of his novels, his answer is heartfelt:

'Writing a screenplay takes a year *of* your life and a year *off* your life. I've done it twice and I want no more of it. The book is mine; the film is someone else's creation. Besides, after I've worked for three years on a project, I've had it—up to here. I am more interested in getting on with a new book on a new subject. Let someone else dissect my novel and put it together again. It needs a fresh mind.'

Our experience with the making of the film *Airport* was a delight from beginning to end. One of the best things that happened to Arthur in Hollywood was meeting Ross Hunter. They respect each other's work and share a similar philosophy: they are both story-tellers whose objective is to entertain.

Ross has often said, 'Why pay a lot of money for a property and then change it beyond recognition?'—a profundity that is appreciated by a novelist.

People often say that Arthur's books will automatically sell as films. Others have gone so far as to suggest he writes with Hollywood in mind. Well, it simply isn't true. One reason: it is impossible to guess what film-makers will want at any particular time.

When the manuscript of *Airport* was finished, the usual copies went out to the studios. In four months there wasn't a nibble from anyone. At that time *Easy Rider*, a made-on-a-shoestring film, was riding high. All the studios were on the lookout for similar low-budget properties that would be box-office bonanzas. No one—but no one—wanted to make a film about an airport involving aero-planes, snow, and huge crowds, that would require a budget in the millions.

Ross Hunter and his associate, Jacque Mapes, finally became in-terested and negotiations began between Arthur's agents—Maeve Southgate in New York and H. N. 'Swanie' Swanson in Los Angeles—on the one hand, and Universal Pictures on the other. A deal was made.

George Seaton, a warm, painstaking gentleman, was named direc-tor and screenplay writer. Later, when Arthur read the screenplay, he liked it with one minor exception, and that change was made wil-lingly.

The novel *Airport* was set in Chicago. But while the officials at O'Hare Airport were keen to co-operate, it was obvious there was simply no way that filming could be done at O'Hare. The traffic there—both aeroplanes and people—never stops. So Ross Hunter looked around for a moderate-sized modern airport in the snow-belt where air traffic dies down at night. Minneapolis was ideal and, for-tunately, the city's airport officials were agreeable.

Arthur and I were invited to watch some of the 'on location' filming at Minneapolis airport—both interior and exterior. It was an exciting time—for us and for Minneapolis, which is not often the scene for a multimillion-dollar film. First of all, hundreds of 'extras' were needed for the crowd scenes. An advertisement in the local paper appealed for help. Thousands turned up—from plumbers to policemen, socialites to secretaries, builders to bankers. Filming was done at night; when the last bona fide travellers had left, the extras swarmed into the airport. It was strange to see the place teeming with life at 1 a.m.

Outside it was bitterly cold; so cold, in fact, that snow refused to fall. But snow was desperately needed for the filming. The remnants of previous snowfalls covered the ground, but they were icy and dirty, inadequate for glorious Technicolor. The production staff had to resort to using pale, pre-roasted cornflakes, which were blown in front of cameras by huge wind machines.

As the story of *Airport* unfolds, a Boeing 707 is 'deeply mired in waterlogged ground beneath snow, near the runway's edge'. We watched the efforts of a professional Flying Tigers pilot 'straining' to get the aeroplane out. It was dark and the temperature was thirty degrees below freezing. The cameramen and the rest of the film crew all wore thick insulated ski suits. But although Arthur and I had lived in Toronto for many years and should have known it would be cold, we had flown in from San Francisco unprepared and ill-clad for the biting cold.

A shivering technician told Arthur, 'For Christ's sake, set your next story in the tropics!'

We stayed until the Boeing 707 roared its way out of the 'mud', then agreed it was time to go back to our warm hotel room and its snugly bed.

Later we learned that after the film crew had left, Minneapolis had a heavy snowfall, so a second crew was sent back from Hollywood for extra exterior shots. I began to understand why film-making is so costly.

In Minneapolis, and later in Hollywood, Arthur and I were impressed by the camaraderie existing among everyone on the set. Ross Hunter's enthusiasm permeated everywhere. This, coupled with director George Seaton's low-key, gentle manner, inspired the cast and made the production an enjoyable experience.

Arthur and I flew twice to Los Angeles to visit Universal Studios

and watch more of the film-making. On the first occasion our son
Steven and younger daughter Diane came with us. We watched a
scene with Burt Lancaster, Maureen Stapleton and Jean Seberg. As
always, we were struck by the incredible patience actors and film-
makers must have; the same lines said over and over, the same shots
filmed repeatedly. After watching for about an hour, Arthur,
predictably, was restless.

'Come on,' he whispered to me, 'let's go.'

I was fascinated with the whole business and could have remained
all day.

In the afternoon we took Universal's studio tour, which was
unique in the industry. Such a tour is the finest way to see the many
facets of a film studio, no matter whom you may know in the business. We bought tickets like everyone else and travelled around the
lot in an open tram. We passed a mock-up aeroplane with TRANS-
GLOBAL AIRLINES lettering on the sides. Our guide, an attractive
young woman, explained over her microphone that this was being
used in the studio's current major production—a film called *Airport*,
starring Burt Lancaster, Dean Martin . . . and so on. Steven and
Diane were aged twelve and ten. They fidgeted, eager for someone to
say their Dad wrote the book and that he and his family were seated
at the back of the tram.

'Tell her!' Steven urged. 'Tell her you're the author.'

'He's right,' I said. 'It'd give everyone a kick.'

But Arthur, typically, kept quiet. He likes his anonymity.

Our second visit to the *Airport* set was downright exciting. Seaton
was shooting the explosion scene inside the aircraft. We saw the
lightweight foam replicas of everything inside the cabin—shoes,
handbags, spectacles, blankets. They were feather-light so they could
be easily sucked out of the cabin by 'decompression' caused by the
explosion. This was created by a giant 'vacuum cleaner' installed for
the purpose.

Dean Martin is a thorough-going professional; he knew his lines
and took direction from George Seaton without question. He is also
naturally good-humoured with a quick, sometimes ribald wit. He
contributed to the happy atmosphere on the set, for he kept everyone
laughing. After the shooting of the explosion, Van Heflin—who
played D. O. Guerrero, the mad bomber—emerged from the aircraft's toilet, where he had set off the home-made bomb. Martin said:

'Van, when you go to the can, you really go!'

The cast and crew broke up.

At the end of the filming of *Airport*, there was a studio party which we attended. The invitations were 'airline tickets'. We 'checked in' with a passenger agent. It was a great party. We had a marvellous table, sitting with Dean Martin, Helen Hayes, Maureen Stapleton, Jacqueline Bissett. The high spot for Arthur was dancing with the beautiful Jackie B, whom he greatly admired and still does.

We were delighted with the finished film. *Airport* was good, solid entertainment. Audiences loved it; it was a box-office smash.

The film rights to Arthur's novel *Wheels* were sold in 1971 to Walter Mirisch, who had just produced the superb film version of *Fiddler on the Roof*.

In the contract for the filming of *Wheels* it was spelled out that Arthur's name should be above the title—Arthur Hailey's *Wheels*— which was considered a major achievement for a writer in show business. However, again, he did not ask to write the screenplay.

Which brings me to a question we've been asked many times: 'When a novel has been sold to the film-makers, does the author have any control over what is done to it?' The answer is generally no— unless he is willing to stay on top of the film production from beginning to end. In this case, various clauses are negotiated at the time a deal is being made. Ususually, though, when film or television rights are sold, that's it—they're sold. The film is basically the film company's property, which it can handle any way it likes.

The attempts to make a film version of *Wheels* proved frustrating. Walter Mirisch had hoped that one of the major motor companies would co-operate in the making of the film. But they all said no. The official line was that filming would disrupt production. But friends in the industry told us the real reason was that the motor companies were unhappy with the description of assembly-line monotony in *Wheels*, nor did they like the disclosure that Monday and Friday cars are sometimes poorly assembled. Perhaps it would have been possible to make a studio set of an assembly line, but only at tremendous expense.

After the thumbs-down from Detroit, Arthur arranged through a friend, Lord Pritchard, who has a house near ours in the Bahamas, to have the filming done in England. A phone call to Lord Stokes, then chairman of the British Leyland Motor Corporation, did the trick. We received word that the film company could do the filming at any British Leyland plant they wanted. Arthur was so delighted that Derek Pritchard had arranged this for him, he forgot the three-hour time difference and phoned Walter Mirisch in Los Angeles, rousing him from sleep. However, the Mirisch film group had other problems and was slow in making plans. The filming-in-England idea fell through too.

The screenplay was a disappointment. Arthur read it one evening, his face increasingly cloudy as he turned each page. Then he slammed down the manuscript.

'This isn't my story. There's scarcely any resemblance to *Wheels* at all.'

It was then that he decided he did not want his name above the title and asked that it be removed. The contract was amended to a single credit: 'Based on the novel by Arthur Hailey.'

Wheels was not made, for what reason we do not know. Walter Mirisch moved on to another project. We learned later from a newspaper film column—which is the way we so often get our information—that Universal Studios had bought the rights from Mirisch and that *Wheels* would be an NBC-TV ten-hour mini-series, starring Rock Hudson and Lee Remick.

It was about the time when the film negotiations for *Wheels* began to get rolling that Arthur got involved in a brouhaha with Paramount Pictures.

The studio owned the film rights of Arthur's old TV play *Flight Into Danger*, which became the film *Zero Hour*, and later a novel which is still around in North America under the title *Runway Zero Eight*—and in Britain under the original title of *Flight Into Danger*. (And if you are a little confused by all that, so are we.)

Anyway, one day during the summer of 1971 we read in *TV Guide* that a new play by Arthur Hailey was being made as a television film by Paramount Pictures for CBS. We realized immediately it was the *old* play.

Arthur objected strenuously. Across the years, *Flight Into Danger* had become something of a legend. But on the basis that legends are best left alone, he did not want to see the story aired again. There were phone calls back and forth between Arthur, his agents in New

York and Hollywood, and Paramount Pictures, but to no avail. The outcome was a press release which Arthur wrote and had sent to the wire services, daily newspapers and radio stations across the country. It was the one and only time he has resorted to such a tactic. He commissioned a small public relations company to handle the news item after several larger PR firms declined—obviously wary of CBS's power. The press release tells the story:

Novelist Arthur Hailey, author of *Airport, Hotel, Wheels,* etc., issued the following statement from his home in Lyford Cay, Bahamas:

I wish to dissociate myself publicly from a CBS Television production, *Terror in the Sky,* which is being misrepresented as 'by Arthur Hailey, author of *Airport*.'

According to reports from my New York agent and lawyers, *Terror in the Sky* is to be aired September 17 on 'The New CBS Friday Night Movies', made for CBS by Paramount Pictures.

Advance publicity is representing this as new material. For example, *TV Guide* reported, 'Hailey, who also wrote *Airport*, is sticking close to his winning subject with this tale of an airliner that's "talked down" when its pilot becomes ill.'

Both the production and publicity represent an attempt to cash in on the success of my earlier novel *Airport* and the current one, *Wheels*.

I have never, in my life, written anything called *Terror in the Sky*. What is being offered over CBS is, I understand, based on an old play of mine, *Flight Into Danger*, televised by NBC in 1956 and subsequently made into a Paramount movie, *Zero Hour*.

The material is being used over my strong objections and despite protests by my agent and lawyers. However, the lawyers advise me that because of an obscure clause in a 1956 contract through which the original film rights were sold, my legal chances of preventing the material being aired are slim.

In my opinion the original TV play is out of date in content—particularly relating to aviation technique—and style, and while it may have been good a decade and a half ago, is unsuitable for presentation now.

If the play has been revised or updated, it is not my work.

The question of money is not involved. While I am not being paid, either by CBS or Paramount, no amount of money would induce me voluntarily to lend my name to this production.

Therefore I have pleaded to have my name removed both from production and publicity, but this has been refused.

I now take the only recourse open to a writer in the circumstances—to dissociate myself from the production as best I can, at the same time letting the public know that what CBS is passing off as an original production is a rehash of material used by its competitor, NBC, fifteen years ago.

The result: The play went on the air, complete with Arthur's name. Friends said later, 'We saw your TV play recently. It was good.' Which all goes to show it's a waste of time getting excited over things you can't control. In the end, the irritation is quickly forgotten.

Early in 1974, while reading a newspaper one morning, Arthur said to me, 'Hey! it says here Universal Pictures is making a film, *Airport 1975*—a sequel to *Airport*. I wonder if they can do that.'

He went to his files and pulled out the contract, drawn up when film rights of the novel *Airport* were sold to Universal. Yes, 'they' certainly could make a sequel. But also, under the contract, the studio was obligated to pay a substantial sum for each subsequent use of the *Airport* title.

Arthur's attitude was: Oh, well—that's fine! Now let's hope it's a good film.

Soon after, we read—again in newspapers—that Charlton Heston would play the lead. Other names followed: Karen Black, Gloria Swanson, Myrna Loy, Helen Reddy, Nancy Olson, Linda Blair. The *Airport 1975* advertising began to feature Arthur's name in large bold type as 'inspiring' the whole thing.

'Wow!' I said, as we passed one poster. 'Your name's bigger than Charlton Heston's.'

Much, much later—though we were never informed officially—we learned that the screenplay writer of *Airport 1975*, Don Ingalls, objected to this advertising, since his name was in small type near the bottom of the credits. His argument seemed reasonable.

The Writers Guild of America, West, held an arbitration hearing on the subject. (Arthur calls it a 'kangaroo court', because neither he nor his representatives were informed about it in advance.) However, the arbitrator decided that, with slight modification, the credit to the original *Airport* and to Arthur Hailey should, in fact, stay.

Payment of the money under the original contract was never in dispute.

Since then another *Airport* sequel—*Airport '77*—has been produced and released. Again, to answer the many questions we have been asked: No, Arthur did *not* write *Airport 1975* or *Airport '77*, nor was he involved in the production of either film. He was simply the author of the original novel *Airport*, which has proved profitable for Universal Pictures—and the Haileys.

There is also a novel, now on bookstands in many countries, based on the film *Airport '77*. Arthur did not write this either, though we have a financial interest in it, due to Arthur's authorship of the original *Airport* novel . . . but, oh my goodness, let's not get into *that!*

The good thing is (and let's be honest about it) we seem likely to have an income forever from a succession of *Airport* films and—who knows?—perhaps an *Airport* comic book, wind-up doll, and instant-food franchise.

Others, of course, may view this differently. Our friend Herb Caen, the *San Francisco Chronicle* columnist, wrote not long ago:

> Most depressing press release of the wk. (from Universal Studios): '"Airport '77" is the third motion picture inspired by Arthur Hailey's best-selling novel "Airport", and there may be a dozen by the year 2001. "If we can find good dramatic stories," declared Producer Jennings Lang, "I foresee doing "Airports" for the next 25 years."'

Well, Herb, I guess it all depends on your point of view.

When Arthur was near the end of his novel *The Moneychangers*, he said to me, 'Well, if this sells as a film, no one can complain that it would be too difficult to produce. I think it could be made with just a few interior sets.'

However, following the trend started by *Airport*, films such as *The Poseidon Adventure*, *The Towering Inferno* and *Earthquake* were still in vogue. So when early copies of *The Moneychangers* were sent to the major studios, word came back from Hollywood: 'Tell Hailey we want disasters.'

Which proves a point I made earlier: no novelist can outguess the film industry as to what it will want at the time a book is published. However, from the beginning, Ross Hunter was interested in *The Moneychangers*. His and Arthur's earlier association had led to friendship and a mutual regard. Arthur respected Ross as a filmmaker, and liked his enthusiasm. More to the point, Arthur had been

177

happy with the finished product of *Airport*. So when Ross Hunter began negotiations for the film rights of *The Moneychangers*, we hoped for a favourable outcome.

However, books for television mini-series (such as Irwin Shaw's *Rich Man, Poor Man* and Alex Haley's *Roots*) were attracting the TV industry. Ross wanted a contract flexible enough to go either route—theatrical film or television production. We were doubtful about TV. Arthur was reluctant to see his story fragmented into short sequences and interspersed with commercials.

But against that was the argument that a television mini-series could reproduce the whole novel over several hours of film. A theatrical film must be condensed to about two and a half hours. Also, the wide public acceptance of television was likely to open up a vast new audience of book readers—always an exciting prospect to a writer.

In the end, we agreed to the dual contract that included television rights—while I secretly hoped it would become a theatrical film.

Television won out.

The script was written by Dean Reisner and Stanford Whitmore. Although Arthur generally liked their work, he felt the script had become decidedly left-wing in its political viewpoint. His novel had two opposing characters: Margot Bracken, the socialist-activist lawyer, and Lewis D'Orsey, the investment news-letter writer, who was conservative in outlook. While Arthur's financial views parallel those of Lewis D'Orsey—he is pro-free enterprise and strongly anti-socialist—his book was fair in its presentation and balanced out both ideologies.

In the film script, however, Margot Bracken's socialist views were emphasised while Lewis D'Orsey was merely a caricature. There was also a complimentary reference to a labour organiser whom Arthur does not admire.

He stated his objections, but by then the filming was well advanced and only a few minor changes could be made. However, at Arthur's urging, the reference to the labour leader wound up, as they say, on the cutting-room floor.

Arthur and I, together with our children—Jane, Steven and Diane—were invited to watch some of the filming. The day we arrived, the principal character, Alex Vandervoort (played by Kirk Douglas) was visiting his deranged wife, Celia (Marissa Pavan), confined to a nursing home. Our old friend from *Airport*, the grande dame of American theatre—Helen Hayes—played the role of the psychiatrist.

As other scenes were shot in real locations—such as the bank and prison scenes—so this portion of the film was shot in a real home, rented for the purpose. Our children were fascinated by the number of people necessary to shoot a tiny segment of film.

Later Diane said, 'There was one man I saw whose only job seemed to be switching the fans off and on.'

It was an incredibly hot day, over one hundred degrees, and huge fans were used to cool the set between takes. They had to be switched off for filming, otherwise the sound would be picked up by the microphones. A persistent helicopter whirred above as everyone was ready to shoot a scene. It caused more delay; then, as they tried again, a siren was heard in the distance. Numerous people were crammed into one room—cameramen, sound men, script girl, prop men, make-up people, various assistants, stand-ins, and of course the actors and the director, Boris Segal. The last thing they needed, I felt, was the Hailey family visiting en masse. I could understand why visitors to studio sets are not welcomed with enthusiasm.

Arthur visited Hollywood again, after all the filming was completed. This time Henry Mancini was conducting his own music, composed especially for *The Moneychangers*. Arthur also watched some of the edited film. He came back glowing with excitement. The casting was magnificent, he told me, especially Christopher Plummer as Roscoe Heywood. (Later, in September 1977, Christopher Plummer won an Emmy award for this performance.)

The finished result (one two-hour programme, and three one-and-a-half-hour programmes) was televised in the U.S. over NBC in December, 1976, and in the U.K. on ITV early in 1978. In both countries, it was enthusiastically received by viewers and most reviewers.

Hollywood still has a little magic for me. It's a great place to visit. I can goggle like anyone else at famous faces. Dining at the Bistro will always be a delicious experience. As for lunch in the Polo Lounge of the Beverly Hills Hotel, I know of no more entertaining restaurant: everyone peering at everyone else to see who's there, where the action is, and who is taking the most telephone calls at his or her table.

But—Deanna Durbin, where are you now?

CHAPTER 15

Women's Lib...
and Me

At a cocktail party recently I was introduced as 'Mrs. Arthur Hailey, whose husband is the famous author of *Airport* and *The Money-changers*.'

The woman to whom I was introduced smiled sympathetically and said, 'How does that make *you* feel?'

'Oh, I'm used to it,' I replied. 'My ego can stand it.'

'But how *do* you feel about not having an identity of your own?' she persisted.

It was *my* turn to smile. No one who has known me for long will ever worry about my failing to have an identity.

Still, the incident pointed up an attitude which the women's liberation movement has accentuated. The unspoken questions are there: what have you done with *your* life? How do you feel about not having a career of your own? What would you have done if you hadn't married a best seller?

Earlier in this book I said I was ambitious. But my ambition has taken different forms. I have always been a pragmatist who comes to terms with life the way it is. My life has turned out better than I ever expected, and I am not given to dreaming about what might have been. Fairly early in our marriage I recognised that a professional writer dominates the household. Writing is such a demanding occupation that everyone in the family is aware of the activity. It has become so much a part of our life that I have long since accepted its drawbacks as well as its rewards.

So . . . what *have* I done with my life? Well, let's go back to the 1940s.

In my teens in Britain I fancied myself as an actress. I was active in amateur theatricals and played the leads in productions at Hendon Technical College and the Regent Street Polytechnic: *Major Barbara, Viceroy Sarah, Dear Octopus, Crisis in Heaven*, to name a few. I wasn't half bad. But even then I was a realist. I recognised that to be successful in such an over-crowded profession, one has to be so motivated that all other considerations—family, love, personal happiness—are secondary.

I was not prepared to make that kind of sacrifice for a theatrical career.

Journalism was my other love. But again, to be honest, I was more attracted to the glamour of the business than to the sheer hard work of writing. During the four years I worked for a London book publisher, I learned a great deal about writing and editing. However, when I undertook to write the school reader *Bayard the Fearless*, it was because I needed the money. I never had the will to give up activities I enjoyed to write in a dedicated way.

What I *really* wanted as a young girl was to be happily married—and the mother of six children.

Women's libbers will groan in chorus. But in the 1940s and '50s, getting married and raising a family was what life was all about. A woman was expected to get a passable education, then find a man with 'prospects', and marry him.

At twenty-seven, I had a vivid dream. I dreamt I wasn't married. Family and friends commiserated. 'Poor Sheila! She's nearly thirty and left on the shelf. She'll *never* marry now.' The dream was so real, I woke up deeply troubled. Then I remembered I *was* married; what's more, I had a daughter. I reached out for Arthur and snuggled into his back, gave a happy sigh of relief, and went back to sleep.

What a ludicrous dream that would seem to a young woman today!

On this subject, let me interject this thought: I am grateful to the early Women's Lib leaders for the opportunity they gave our daughters to *choose* the kind of life they want. As with all pressures for social change, some extreme—even silly—tactics are occasionally needed to overturn old prejudices and let new ideas surface. Within the Women's Lib movement that certainly happened. But none of this should cloud the main issue: all women have the *right* to make their own decisions and be treated equally with men, without the patronising attitudes we so often encounter. Therefore, count me in—in my own way—within the ranks of Women's Lib.

Anyway, in 1951, my future seemed clear-cut. I had found a man with ability and drive. I would channel my own energy, love and ambition through him to help make him successful. We were a team. My attitude was: what's good for him is good for us.

Fortunately, Arthur's attitude towards me was similar, which is why he has always encouraged me to pursue any activity outside the home that contributes to my own fulfilment. However, in our early days any such pursuits were economically necessary.

When I left my $220-a-month job as editor of the Maclean-Hunter employee paper *Newsweekly*, it was to start my own business. With Arthur's help I sold to six separate companies the idea of a monthly employee publication—in the trade known as a 'house organ'. Each month I collected material from the companies, then wrote, typed, and pasted up each small newspaper for offset litho printing. Then I would take the 'master' to the printers, and eventually deliver printed copies to the six companies for distribution. It became a small thriving business, netting $350 a month, yet I needed only to work three or four days a week. The money always went into our joint account. Arthur and I have never regarded any of our earnings as '*my* money'; it is always *ours*. All our married life I have had access to whatever money was available without Arthur questioning my expenses. Because of this arrangement, whatever else our arguments have been about, we haven't had a single one about money.

So, while I was never the main breadwinner, I did not consciously think of myself as playing a secondary role. Nor did I ever regard myself as dependent.

An incident with a salesman demonstrates this independence. I was twenty-five and three months pregnant. Although we were earning money, we had no savings. One evening a conversation with friends turned to the subject of life insurance. Our friends were shocked that Arthur didn't have any.

'I guess we *should* have some,' I said next morning.

'Sure,' Arthur agreed. 'But I can't get excited over what happens after I'm dead. Why don't you arrange it? After all, you're the one who'll be affected, and you know what we can afford.'

I telephoned an insurance salesman and he came around to see me. Arthur was elsewhere in the house. I looked at various plans and figures, then selected a life-insurance policy that required a small annual premium.

The salesman was dismayed. 'But, Mrs. Hailey, that's only five thousand dollars' coverage. You should have more than that.'

'Why?' I asked. 'That would tide me over the funeral and a few months after. I can earn my own living.'

He tried to persuade me to increase the insurance. We had a long discussion. The salesman asked if he could speak to Arthur; I told him my husband left these matters to me.

Suddenly Arthur appeared, thinking the insurance man had gone. He was cornered.

'Mr. Hailey, I do think it would be wise for you to carry more insurance than five thousand dollars. I mean . . , if . . . er . . . you were not here . . . how would you feel if your wife and child had so little to live on?'

'But,' replied Arthur, 'I wouldn't know, would I? I'd be dead.' Then he said, grinning at me, 'She's a strong, healthy girl, she could always get a job. Besides, she'd probably marry again.'

The insurance representative left for the evening, a beaten man.

When he returned next day I felt sorry for him, so I decided on a $10,000 policy with a $19-a-month premium. I should have saved my sympathy. What I didn't realise until much later was that he hadn't told me about term insurance, probably because his commission would be less. *That's* what I should have had.

The baby was due around April 22, 1954. So during the first half of that month I completed all six publications in record time. Alas, Jane did not arrive until April 30. I was frustrated by her tardiness. I had planned to be in the hospital and out again by that date, then use the first week of May to recuperate at home with the aid of a baby's nurse before tackling that month's editions. I had no other help or any relatives to assist me, so when the nurse departed after her five-day stint, I was faced with the task of producing six papers in less than two weeks, as well as coping with a new baby. However, it worked out fairly well; Jane was eight days late, and the May publications only ten days behind.

Jane's schedule fitted nicely into my business schedule; in fact, she was very much a part of it. I used to take her in a carry-cot on the back seat of my little Austin. When I had to collect material for a story I was to write, I frequently arrived with my briefcase in one hand, the carry-cot in the other. The fact that I breast-fed Jane helped save precious minutes; occasionally if I was delayed and she was bawling in the back seat, I would park the car in a secluded spot and nurse her there and then.

I kept the little writing business going until ten-month-old Jane was no longer happy about being cooped up in a playpen. By that time, from early 1952 until 1954, I had produced more than two hundred separate editions. I was ready to quit; I was fed up with writing those papers. I had long since exhausted the number of ways one can describe two employees getting married: 'Joe Brown and Joan Smith tied the knot . . .' 'Wedding bells rang out for . . .' 'They exchanged vows at the altar . . .' 'John Doe and Mary Jones headed down the aisle.'

In the period that followed—most of 1955 and early 1956—I luxuriated as a lady of leisure. Arthur went out to his job with a tractor-trailer manufacturer. I had only one child to take care of; otherwise, my days were free to do as I pleased. I began to paint in oils, enrolling in a local evening class. It's a soothing, relaxing hobby, though I was dissatisfied with my work—except for a still life of children's toys which I have kept across the years. My paintings were flat and muddy, in the manner of most amateur dabbling. I truly enjoyed the days at home alone with Jane, watching her develop, excited at the thought of another child by now on the way. But the luxury of time to spare lasted only a few months. During the summer of 1956, Arthur went into business for himself, working at home and dividing his time between advertising, public relations and TV playwriting.

I was always conscious of Arthur's being at home. He's a demanding man and I felt 'switched on' at all times. But it was logical that I stay home also during the years of Jane's, Steven's, and Diane's early childhood, so the pattern was set for Arthur to rely on me for dozens of extra little chores, from handling telephone calls to paying bills, then passing an opinion on his day's writing.

And what became of the ambition to have six children?

When Arthur and I originally talked of marriage, I told him I wanted a large family. He was alarmed, and I understood this. He was, after all, the father of three sons.

'Okay,' I said, 'let's make it four.'

Although he grimaced, he knew I was serious. And after our third child was born, and life was still good, he began to think four would be just fine.

Until one memorable evening.

The children had been at their worst all day. Jane, four, was out of sorts and whined continuously; Steven, two, had systematically pulled much of the house apart and threw temper tantrums when reprimanded; Diane, just a few months old, was unhappy because she was teething. When all three were finally asleep and we were having dinner, Arthur looked at me across the candles and took my hand.

'Darling, do you *really* want another child?'

'No, I don't,' I cried emphatically. I meant it. I didn't change my mind; I have never had regrets.

(Now, at this stage of my life, I feel I *have* six children. Our move to California in 1965 meant that we saw Roger, John and Mark more frequently. As John said in a letter: 'My visits to you established the close relationship I now have with Jane, Steven and Diane and, of course, you and Dad. I began to feel much more a part of the family than just a guest, and that is probably the richest experience I gained during those visits.')

Inevitably, during the children's early years, I felt the need to get out of the house to do something different and was fortunate in being able to do this. We had a series of German girls—Brigitte, Helga, and Irmgard, all immigrants to Canada—each of whom lived with us for several months. All were intelligent, pleasant and hard-working; they spoke little English but we managed well enough. Under the influence of Helga's, then Irmgard's loving care, Diane's first words were, 'Eins, zwei, drei, vier' as she was 'walked' up the stairs, one-two-three-four. For what now seems an incredibly small wage of $100 a month with room and board, each one was on hand for five-and-a-half days a week as a combined nanny-housemaid. I threw in daily English lessons and was proud that all three got good jobs in offices or shops when they left us.

At that time I joined a local hospital voluntary organisation. I liked the work with patients, but made the mistake of offering to write the group's news-letter. This meant attending committee meetings with about fifteen other women and listening to interminable discussions. Decisions took forever. I was impatient, fretted at the waste of time, and always felt two people could have settled the problems in fifteen minutes or less. When it was suggested that half-day sessions were not enough, that we should start in the morning, bring a packed lunch and continue through the afternoon, it was time to bow out.

To this day I am wary of voluntary work which involves committee meetings. Also, I have not joined women's clubs because I don't feel the need of them. It isn't that I don't like women; in fact, I enjoy an occasional women's lunch, but I don't like to get locked into activities which are too structured. That's why, over the years, I have been grateful that Arthur's work has been lively, interesting, something I can share in and—more important—enjoy. This has been possible because we're good friends who have not tired of each other's company.

On one occasion in 1959 this togetherness was severely strained. Arthur was committed to writing a play, *Diary of a Nurse*, for CBS-TV, at the same time he had agreed to write his first novel, *The Final Diagnosis,* for Doubleday. It is the only time he has ever contracted for two major projects which overlapped. He never will again, for it was an ordeal for us all. His singleness of mind prevents him switching easily from one task to another, and trying to meet two deadlines he was tense and overworked. I tried persuading him to delay the novel, knowing that book publishers are more flexible about deadlines than TV producers. But Arthur has always been superconscientious; it was the first book he had contracted to write alone and he was determined to deliver the manuscript by the agreed date.

His secretary, Doreen Lyon, was overworked too. With a deadline just days away, the novel needed to be retyped completely. It was impossible for her to complete the job alone in time. Helga had left our employ, I had yet to find Irmgard, so I had no help in the house; nevertheless, I pitched in.

As soon as I was awake, about 7 a.m., I pulled on a house-coat and checked the children, changed Diane's nappy, then coaxed Jane into amusing Steven and the baby as best she could. Jane was not yet five, but was one of those children who seem to be mature by the age of two. Then I'd dash down to our basement to type for an hour.

Meanwhile Arthur showered, shaved, dressed and began writing. Noises above would soon signal that the children were restless and hungry. So I ran upstairs, pulled out cereal and bowls from the cupboard, fruit and milk from the refrigerator, and plonked everything on the kitchen table. I popped Diane into her high chair, secured the

186

harness straps, and left Jane to organise the breakfast and, once more, mother the two younger ones. Then—downstairs again for as much typing as I could get done before Doreen arrived at nine, after which I was back upstairs to clear up a messy kitchen, clean up the children, cook Arthur's and my breakfast, and finally attend to my own toilet, dress the children, straighten the house, and do the laundry.

At noon I organised lunch for the whole family. Then, at 1 p.m. I was ready to take over the hot seat from Doreen for more typing while she went off for her own lunch break.

In the evenings, as soon as dinner was over and the children in bed, I was downstairs typing again. Arthur was back in his study writing. We were rarely in bed before midnight. Next day it was more of the same.

What a crazy household! And how glad I was when the manuscript of *The Final Diagnosis* was finished and sent off to New York!

In ways like this our children were made aware that ours was different from other households. As Steven grew older, it troubled him that Arthur didn't go off to work like other fathers. Steven thought writing was a miserable occupation compared to, say, being a doctor or a fireman. Later he would come home from school, visit his dad in the study and enquire, 'How much did you write today?'

When shown two pages of double-spaced typing, he was likely to say, 'Is that *all*? . . . Well, how much will you get paid for that?'

Once Jane told her friends that her father didn't have to work. 'He just stays home and writes money in the basement.'

Although I've never considered my life humdrum, still there have been times when I've been restless with my role. This is not peculiar to women at home. I know plenty of men who have felt that way too. As a dentist friend said to me, 'How could I possibly know at twenty-two, when I was choosing a profession, if I would enjoy fixing teeth at the age of forty-five? There are days when I am so fed up with poking around in people's mouths that I want to chuck it all and start again.' The truth is that anyone with sensitivity and imagination inevitably rebels at being in a rut, which happens to all of us from time to time.

I felt this way in 1961 when Diane went off to nursery school and I had completed the furnishing of our new house. So I wrote an article which was published in a Canadian women's magazine, *Chate-*

187

laine. It was essentially a prologue for this book, a 5,000-word lighthearted piece about living with a writer.

I also wrote what I hoped would be another children's book— *The Story of Steve, the Pickup Truck* (for boys of five to seven). Our Steven, who was in that age bracket, loved it and listened to my reading of it over and over again. Publishers in New York, though, turned it down, saying it wasn't sophisticated enough for children of the 1960s. After studying Dr. Seuss's *Cat in the Hat* books and similar publications, I could see that they were right.

Then I got an idea for television. I was a woman blessed with common sense, inherited from my intensely practical family. Why not, I thought, have a programme which dealt with some of the problems—small and large—that women experience? I worked out a sample 'show', sold the idea to a women's daytime TV programme, and was given ten minutes of air time on a weekly basis.

It was fun. I invited letters from viewers, edited them, read them on camera, then discussed the problems in a general way so as to appeal to a wide audience. (This differed from the newspaper features 'Ann Landers' and 'Dear Abby', where letters form the bulk of the column, followed by pithy answers.) I spent one day a week preparing my script, then gave my talk live on TV the following day.

It was an ideal part-time occupation. It gave me an interest outside the home, yet did not take too much time. I also earned some money—a good feeling for a young, independent-minded woman with small children.

The segment was successful and lasted three years. Only once did I get into trouble. The local show lived up to its name, 'Free and Easy', and no one ever asked to see a copy of my script in advance of air time; my judgment was trusted. But one day I dealt with a letter from a twenty-eight-year-old woman whose husband had deserted her. She wasn't divorced, but felt the need—socially and sexually—of male companionship. In my realistic way, I said she ought to think of herself as single, feel free to date men on that basis, and if the dates developed into something more—so what?

Alas, I was a little ahead of the sexual revolution! As soon as we were off the air, the phone calls came flooding in. There were shocked complaints from viewers, and later I got a rocket from the management. Daytime audiences, I was cautioned, are not as sophisticated as evening viewers, and would I please cool it.

Anyway, at the end of my third season I was invited to do a similar feature on a Canada-wide network show, 'Take Thirty'. I was thrilled and enjoyed my progression from a single station to a coast-to-coast link-up.

I remember one day Arthur went to our oculist, Dr. E. John Wylie, for an eye test. A new receptionist gushed, 'Oh, Mr. Hailey, I'm so delighted to meet you!' Arthur was all graciousness, waiting to be complimented on his recent book, *In High Places*. 'Please tell your wife how much I enjoy her on television.'

Arthur told this story on himself with much glee. He has always been supportive of any venture I have tackled. He helped me with the TV work—suggesting how I could tighten scripts, watching each telecast, then advising me to look less serious on camera and to smile more often. He also let me know, once or twice, that I had on too much make-up. However, sometimes when we had an argument he couldn't resist the retort: 'You're so damn wonderful at solving other people's problems, how about using some of that homespun crap on *us*?'

Possibly, if we had stayed in Canada, I would have gone on to other things on TV. For the Toronto radio and television personalities were a close-knit group, and once you had been accepted it was relatively easy to stay in the charmed circle.

But that's academic. We didn't stay and, instead, in December 1965 made our move to the Napa Valley.

All the young matrons of the Napa Valley were playing golf—so I tried it too. Along with a dozen lessons, I bought shoes, a set of clubs, and a couple of nifty golf skirts. But golf never grabbed me as friends predicted it would. 'You'll see,' they said, 'it will become a passion.' I was told I had great promise as a golfer, and I *was* good at putting, which I liked. It was all that traipsing between greens that got me down. I never *cared* where that little ball went or how many strokes it took to get to those elusive holes. Wednesday was always ladies' day; I was relieved when it rained on Wednesdays.

I was even more relieved when I gave up golf.

Once again, I plunged into the role of full-time motherhood. On the side, I was a part-time editor and assistant researcher.

The children, at the ages of twelve, ten and eight, were at a charming, interesting, uncomplicated stage of their lives ... or so I thought. They adapted quickly to the easy, casual ways of California

189

living. My own adolescence in an English girls' school, while conservative by Canadian standards, was downright cloistered compared with that of my children in California. I was overwhelmed by a pre-teen cult of teased hair, make-up, shaved legs and training bras. Jane came home from school one day saying that one of the boys in her class had given her his ring.

I was flabbergasted.

'His *ring*!' I exploded. 'What does that mean? Are you *engaged* to him? Migawd, you're *twelve years old!*'

'Mom, it just means we're going steady. All the kids exchange rings in seventh grade.'

'Well, then, you can just *un*exchange rings. I never heard anything so preposterous.'

Poor child! She was close to tears, and I guess I was a bit rough. That evening Arthur and I went out to a dinner party. When we returned we found on our bed a long letter from Jane explaining what 'going steady' meant. It was a harmless boy-girl friendship. She implied we didn't understand the social ways of American junior-high-school life—which was certainly true. She was sure that when we realised the relationship didn't mean anything more than a pairing off at school dances, or a Friday-evening meeting 'at the show', we would agree to her keeping her boy friend's ring.

Next morning Jane was bright and smiling.

'You read my letter? Is it okay to keep the ring?'

'No, honey. It is *not* okay.'

The smile changed swiftly to a tight-lipped scowl.

Later that day Jane found her letter. Arthur had corrected it with a red pencil for spelling and syntax. Understandably, she burst into tears. 'You don't care about my feelings at all! All you care about is my grammar.'

Who says *children* can be cruel? I'm not sure *we* handled ourselves all that admirably, though at the time Arthur felt he was putting the entire episode in correct perspective.

Our writing background has, of course, affected the children. We have always demanded they pay attention to self-expression, both written and oral. It pains us both to hear careless, badly structured speech, and our children have grown weary of our reminders to expunge the 'you knows', 'likes' and 'sort ofs' from their vocabularies.

In later years Jane showed us a paper she had written for her freshman English class at Stanford University. She was incensed because her professor had written 'Bullshit' across the page. Arthur read it.

'He's right!' he advised Jane. 'It *is* bullshit. Your thinking's woolly and you're using exhibitionist words to cover a vacuum. You can do better.'

Jane, who is good at taking advice, did do better and now—some six years later, as this is written—we are proud that she is a teacher.

While Arthur and I have been concerned if one of the children failed a subject, whether in high school or university, we have never fussed about them getting As, Bs or Cs. We have simply urged them to do the best they can, for one child's C may be a fantastic achievement against another child's easy acquiring of an A. Something else we have never done, which I know happens in some families, is reward good grades with gifts or money. I cannot see any merit in this at all.

I am nostalgic about those four years of California living. The children were at an important stage in their development. Because I was a full-time mother, my influence was strong and I like to think that it was good. Certainly it was a part of my life which gave me enormous satisfaction.

I won't dwell on this, however, since so much of our life with our children has been described in other chapters of this book.

Except I'll say this: I believe it important for a mother *never to let anyone denigrate her role*, especially if motherhood is her dominant occupation. As a mother (with some help from Arthur) I have given to the world three well-adjusted, mostly happy adults who can think logically, can cope with life, including adversity, and who will, I am sure, make a meaningful contribution to their times. If I achieve nothing more in my life, I am proud of that—and them.

As with all our major moves, our life in the Bahamas, which began in the late autumn of 1969, kept me busily creative for a year or two, what with building a house, selecting furniture and organising a new home.

We led a quiet life at first, but gradually people became aware we were in their midst. There were invitations to homes, a little attention in the press, and then requests to speak to various groups. Arthur agreed to some, but because he was busy writing *Wheels*, I volunteered to stand in, as I had done frequently before. So I spoke to Rotary, American Women's Club, and so on, beginning to understand what Arthur means when he says how easy it is to become a 'talking writer'.

Diane, who was then eleven, had moved with us to the Bahamas, so I gave her extra companionship in the way parents tend to do with an only child. She and I visited Coral Gables, Florida, every six weeks or so for a check-up with her orthodontist, Dr. Richard Starr. On those trips we had fun together shopping, going to films, watching TV in our motel room—the last a novelty, since we didn't then have television in the Bahamas.

At home Diane enjoyed, as did Arthur and I, the luxury of a super-efficient daily housekeeper, Alice Maycock, a dear Bahamian lady who is with us still. Gone were the days when Diane made her own bed. Alice insisted on doing it and Diane did not protest. When Jane joined us in the Bahamas for vacations, she was amused but slightly critical of her younger sister's pampered life and nicknamed her 'The Princess'. Jane, like my own oldest sister, Doris, had borne the brunt of stricter parents and the burden of younger siblings. Diane, like me, enjoyed the privilege of being the youngest child in a more relaxed family atmosphere.

I had mixed feelings, therefore, when Diane suggested she go away for her high school years. She loved the Bahamas, but missed her brother and sister and felt, wisely, she would benefit from boarding-school experience. So at the age of thirteen Diane went to a girls' school—Emma Willard—in Troy, New York, which proved an excellent choice.

Thus, in the autumn of 1971, I experienced the 'empty nest syndrome', somewhat earlier than I expected. Perhaps I should have felt sad or depressed, but the truth is—I didn't. Arthur and I had a wonderful time on our own. I went with him on trips once more, something I had been reluctant to do during the two years Diane was home alone. We no longer had to worry about leaving her at home while we went off to dinner parties. In the months before Diane's departure she had insisted she was too old for a baby-sitter, yet always looked a little downcast as we left. 'Will you phone me during the evening?' she would say, or 'What time will you be home?'

A few months after Diane had left, I became involved in some charity work in an unusual way. Arthur and I attended a charity auction at Government House, Nassau, in aid of the Bahamas Institute for the Mentally Retarded. I made the highest bid ($400) on the right to carry away as many groceries as I could gather during a five-minute shopping spree around the Palmdale City Market. On the way home to Lyford Cay, which isn't exactly a low-income ghetto, Arthur remarked that we should not keep the groceries ourselves but should donate them to a charity.

'That's a great idea!' I said, and decided that the food collected would go to the Persis Rodgers Home for the Aged.

I phoned the store manager, told him the plan, and asked if he would swap the foods I collected in his store for staples—rice, sugar, canned meats, soups, fruits and juices, evaporated milk—that the old folk needed. 'If I go for these low-priced items directly,' I explained, 'I won't be able to collect much in five minutes.'

He was immediately co-operative and we set the date for the following Friday, February 4, 1972, at 8 a.m., before the store was opened to the public. In the meantime, word got around, as happens on a small island, and I made preparations.

First I cased the store, noting exactly where the high-priced items were located, then I paced out various distances from each of these locations to the next. I used a notebook to record details.

Then I practised for my five-minute sprint. Arthur coached. He measured out the appropriate distances in the roadway outside our home, marked them with chalk, then timed me with a stopwatch as I practised with a borrowed pram to simulate a shopping trolley.

For the event I wore comfortable slacks, a loose blouse and tennis shoes. Press reporters and a commentator from the local radio station, ZNS, showed up; so did spectators, some crowding into the store, others peering through windows from outside. The store manager blew a whistle. At the sound I raced first to the gourmet section and swept every tiny jar of caviar, priced at $29.90 each, into my trolley. Then on to the meat counter, where I tossed armloads of steaks, roasts of beef and huge hams until the cart was full, after which I sprinted back for another trolley, to begin again. All the while I was being cheered on by the spectators and supermarket staff.

'Thirty seconds,' shouted the store manager. Then: 'Five . . . four . . . three . . . two . . . one . . . That's it.'

As a cashier tallied the items I had collected in three shopping trollies, the tape grew longer until the total was recorded—$1,419.84,

193

and that was six inflationary years ago. The manager paled slightly; I pictured him explaining his charitable gesture to his superiors.

But never mind! The amount gave us forty-eight individual cartons of groceries worth about thirty dollars each. Over the next few Saturdays I delivered them, with Nurse Persis Rodgers, to individual homes. It was a revelation. We were overwhelmed by the affection and gratitude shown by these men and women who live alone and eke out a sparse existence on a small old-age pension.

The Home for the Aged has continued to be the Bahamian charity I care about most. It is a small building that at present houses only sixteen old people. But there are plans to extend it and give accommodation to some of the dozens of aged citizens who are on a waiting list. In the meantime these people are visited regularly and given a daily hot meal by the Red Cross. Apart from fund-raising, every year I see these old friends who gather for a big Christmas party. Appropriately, my role is to provide food for the feast—cooked turkeys, hams, pies, cakes and biscuits—donated by friends and neighbours. So far no one has gone hungry.

It was about the time I did my supermarket sprinting that I started to play tennis. Like thousands of others, I have since discovered I love the game. Why did I have to wait until I was forty-four to start playing? And why on earth wasn't I taking lessons six years earlier instead of merely organising tennis instruction for Steven and Diane, while I was chasing that silly golf ball around northern California? Tennis is lively and full of action. What's more, it doesn't occupy a big slice of the day, as eighteen holes of golf does.

Oh well, it's never too late . . . and I've tried to make up for lost time. But there is no substitute for years of experience and hitting thousands of balls. So I progressed slowly and impatiently.

Three years after my first lesson with pro Fritz Schunck, I invited him to come back to the Bahamas to team up with me in mixed doubles for the Lyford Cay Club Member-Guest Tournament in 1975. A superb player and fine teacher, he assessed the situation quickly.

'Sheila, do you want to win or do you want to look good?'

'I want to win,' I said.

'Okay, then don't double-fault, and do your best to return the serves. After that, go up to the net, stay close to the sideline. And keep out of the way.'

I did just that . . . and we got to the finals. I knew I had no business being there, and felt a little nervous. Then I decided not to worry and just to be myself. Poor Fritz! He had played and won a gruelling three-set singles match in the hot, humid early afternoon. He deserved more support than he would get from me.

It was a memorable match. Our opponents were Bahamian pro Bertram Knowles and Jinx Falkenberg McCrary, who played a beautiful game in the tradition of her family. If nothing else, I made the audience laugh. I ducked at the net when Fritz shouted at me and let the ball skim over my head. I followed other instructions obediently. At one point the ball whizzed onto my racket, which happened to be poised above the net. It ricocheted off the strings and landed just inside the sideline, well away from Jinx and Bertram. A put-away shot . . . but I hadn't done a thing. Still, I played it to the hilt.

'You see!' I grinned at the spectators. 'I'm not just a pretty face.'

We had no right to win—and we didn't, although it was close. But both Fritz and I received little silver cups for being runners-up.

Arthur was delighted and boasted to friends about how I'd won a silver cup. He doesn't understand the first thing about tennis, so it was a waste of time explaining. I just let him go on thinking I'm dynamite on the courts.

As much as I enjoy tennis, I couldn't devote my life to it. It is too warm in the Bahamas to play more than an hour or two a day and, in any case, I'm too late for Wimbledon.

This book had been in the back of my mind for years. Like thousands of others, I had idly said to myself, 'Someday I'll write a book.' I also remembered the words of the distinguished American novelist, the late Edna Ferber.

In 1962 when *In High Places* was published and we were in New York, our good friend at Doubleday, Ken McCormick, took us to have afternoon tea with Miss Ferber—the author of *Giant, Show Boat, Saratoga Trunk*, et al—in her Fifth Avenue apartment. Afterward she wrote to Ken, 'If I were you I'd watch for that book she'll write someday. Anyone who compulsively, while making the beds and washing the dishes, puts things down on paper and tucks the pieces of paper into drawers and cupboards is a potential writer.'

Quoting all this in a letter Ken added, 'How soon may I sign you up, Sheila?'

I kept the letter and treasured Edna Ferber's encouragement.

However, I spent more time talking about the project than writing, and it wasn't until 1975 that I began to get something down on paper. Even then I procrastinated. There were always excuses—the children were home on holiday, or would be shortly, or we were going on a trip, or friends or relatives were staying with us.

I finally completed four chapters and, although I showed them to Sam Vaughan, president of Doubleday's publishing division, I said I intended to submit them to another publisher also. What I didn't want, I carefully explained, was to have Doubleday feel obligated to produce my book just because they published Arthur's. I was sensitive, not wanting anyone to do me a favour. Sam said he understood my feelings and would discuss them—and the four chapters—with his colleagues.

A week later I received a letter from Nelson Doubleday, who, across the years, has become our personal friend along with his wife, Sandra. Nelson's letter read in part: 'I see absolutely no conflict between you and Arthur being published by the same house. Therefore, my dear, knock off all this chatter about other publishers and come see the one who thinks an awful lot of you and your husband.'

We signed a contract. The agreed date for delivery of the manuscript was February 28, 1977. I missed it by four months, because it wasn't until late summer '76 that I began to write diligently. I discovered that writing a book is more difficult than *talking* about writing a book.

I began to understand what Arthur had tried to explain. Writing dominated my days. I resented interruptions, was impatient with phone calls, and became ruthless about non-essentials. I had a heightened awareness of just why Arthur doesn't like accepting two evening invitations in succession; suddenly, I didn't either. I felt listless the mornings after; too much energy was sapped from writing.

In one of his regular letters to Jane, Steven and Diane, Arthur explained why they hadn't heard from me:

> This house has become a writing factory.
>   Normally, as you all know, I keep going pretty steadily, but

just lately my pace seems pedestrian compared with Sheila's. For her pace, with a deadline drawing near, has become frenetic. She is at her typewriter early in the morning, stays there most of each day, and is still tapping away when I go to sleep at night . . . I must say it's exciting to see—from a different angle than I usually do—a book near completion . . . I'm also pleased because of her sense of satisfaction as the ending nears. None of the satisfaction, though, takes away the inescapable fact that there is still a lot of work to be done with rewrite, rewrite, rewrite, as is always necessary. In a way this pleases me also, because your mother now realises far more than she did before— she admits this frankly—just how much sheer, bloody toil goes into not just the writing itself, but the process of going over it all again and again until one becomes weary of the words being arranged, re-arranged, and re-arranged once more. So we have a mutuality of interest and understanding.

All this writing activity has changed my daily life. I have become more single-minded than I ever accused Arthur of being. And I realise now why a writer needs someone to smooth his life. Without such a person, little chores are neglected. 'That can wait,' I'd say to myself, 'until I've finished the book.'

As a result, our house has been thrown out of its usual order. We have always been essentially an organised family. Oh, there are boxes of undated photographs that have never been put into albums, and never will be. But I usually pay bills and answer letters promptly. Our living-room is always comfortable and tidy.

However, I *work* in an incredible muddle.

I like to cook, but when I do the kitchen appears as if a hurricane swept through it. I need someone behind me to put away ingredients as I use them, to wash spoons and bowls and measuring jugs after I'm through. My greatest luxury since living in the Bahamas has been the daily presence of a cook, Madline Dean, who prepares superb meals and keeps our kitchen organised and gleaming.

If we go out in the evening, I leave my bathroom in a jumble of open drawers, plugged-in hair dryer, toothpaste, face powder, eye shadow, contact lens solution and perfume. I don't have time to put it all away before I go out because—whether I devote an hour or fifteen minutes to fixing myself up—I am *never* ready until three minutes after the time I said we should leave. Arthur has often said, with real feeling, that we have shared a bed for twenty-seven years and it's been great; we shared a bathroom for eighteen of those years, and it was awful. One of the rewards of Arthur's success has been separate bathrooms.

As for my desk—well, it's exactly the kind a writer should have. I like all my papers horizontally spread out so I can see everything at a glance. I am not a list maker. Instead, my desk is littered with little slips of paper recording my latest brain wave, or reminding myself to do something or phone someone. There are bills waiting to be paid; invitations not RSVP'd; letters from friends, my sisters, our children, Arthur's readers; also the last three days' newspapers that I haven't yet read in depth.

Since this book began, the whole room is chaotic. My study sometimes doubles as a bedroom when the house is overflowing with young people. It contains a studio bed, a comfortable armchair, my desk, and a wall of books. The bed and chair are always covered with papers. When Arthur drops in to discuss something, there is never a place for him to sit. I have to gather armfuls of papers and remove *Webster's Dictionary* and Rodale's *The Synonym Finder* from the armchair to make room.

Some good has come out of this activity, though. Arthur has taken over paying the bills. In many ways, I think he's glad to be doing it. The office clerk in him likes to pay them the day they come in, which I *never* do. (I like to see them sit on my desk for a few days.) And he *types* all cheques neatly, which I *refuse* to do.

For Arthur is pin-neat about everything. While his desk may have a few papers scattered across it while he is working, at the end of a day it is miraculously clear. He thinks vertically. He files away every paper; everything has a little home. I mentioned earlier that in California Jane earned ten dollars a month for emptying his waste-paper-basket and dusting his study *every single day*. I told him no one dusts every day unless someone in the family has an allergy. But he could tell when Jane did the job in a rush, or skipped it altogether. Now that we have a full-time housekeeper, Arthur's study—a separate building from our house—gets even closer scrutiny. Alice is his friend. She understands his funny little ways and devotes her working days to pleasing him: folding his shirts just so, making sure his clean underwear gets rotated from the back of the drawer to the front, cleaning his shoes, keeping up a supply of beautifully laundered linen towels so he can have a clean one every time he shaves.

Arthur, in short, has never had it so good. In contrast, my room gets a once-over-lightly once a week. In answer to Alice's pleas to let her clean my study, I'll say, 'Okay, do it this afternoon while I'm playing tennis—but don't move any papers!' Only when preparing to go away on a trip do I take time to really tidy my cosy, cluttered office.

Sometimes I visit Arthur in his study, taking with me some of my own mail or other papers to show him. Invariably I leave behind a paper or two. He gets *so* peeved. 'You're like a molting canary. You're always shedding things,' he grumbles.

When this book is finished, I shall be overjoyed. Afterwards, I know I will feel let down. I shall miss it. For years I have been describing Arthur's attitude to his writing as a love-hate relationship. Only now do I fully understand this.

However, I shall be glad to get back to a more normal household, and to entertain more frequently. We like to give small dinner parties for six to twelve people, with good food, excellent wine and—we hope—stimulating conversation. I have neglected this social side of our lives. Even with efficient help in the house, one person still has to arrange the evening, from invitations to shopping to menu-planning to table-setting, and it takes time. Like a theatrical production, it doesn't just happen.

I shall be happy, too, to have the leisure time to have more tennis lessons. Lord knows I need them. Also, I have a mountain of unread books beside my bed. Since my writing activity began, I have been so tired by the time I go to bed each night that I cannot keep my eyes open for the hour's reading I usually enjoy. My regular delving into newspapers and magazines has suffered too, and I don't feel I'm as knowledgeable about the news and what's behind it as I like to be. So I am looking forward to catching up on world affairs.

But after my life has returned to 'normal'—what then? Well, who knows? Arthur thinks that sooner or later I shall want to write again. I am less certain of this, but one thing's for sure: if the years ahead are as full and varied as life has been so far, I won't complain.

CHAPTER 16

Brief Encounter

Naomi was not her real name, but her presence was real indeed. She loomed large in our married life in the early sixties. The reason: she was the first 'other woman' with whom Arthur was truly emotionally involved since we were married. Oh, of course, there had been romps and skirmishes—but they were for fun and affection, the kind I discussed earlier.

Naomi was different. She captured his heart and his mind for the better part of a year. I don't remember how it all started. She was just suddenly in our midst. We'd met her and her husband a few times at parties, and I liked her enormously. She was an attractive woman, with a quick wit. She always made *me* laugh; I could certainly see why she would captivate Arthur.

My husband was in his early forties—for men the most restless of ages. By the time a man is forty, he knows he must come to terms with what he is and where he is going. If he is busy with a successful career, he worries about his youth slipping away and wonders if his sexual prowess is fading. Is he still attractive to women? If he is not successful in his career, he wonders still more about his sexual powers. For making it with other women often compensates for failure.

A man of some stature—a writer, an actor, a sports figure, a politician or a prominent businessman—has a built-in attraction for the opposite sex. If, as well, he is physically attractive, has an engaging personality, and is comfortable with women (for there are many men who are not)—then he has it made. Conquests can be easy, ego-building, exhilarating.

Arthur had everything going for him. He was also between books. He had finished *In High Places* and was going through that most difficult time for an author—waiting for his novel to be published. He was clearly ready for something exciting in his life—as he always is between books. If it doesn't happen naturally, he makes it happen. And in the climate of that swinging time, when most of our friends were also in their frenetic forties, it was almost inevitable that the diversion should be the breathless, heady excitement of falling in love.

Arthur has never been good at hiding his emotions—except in public—and I could tell early on that he had flipped over Naomi. Not that this was difficult—it's hard for a man to conduct an affair discreetly when he works at home.

He began going out mid-morning for 'a breath of air'. Never mind that it was five degrees below zero outside. He was never away longer than an hour. Naomi lived in the north end of Toronto, and a half-way meeting point for both of them was a suburban railway station, usually deserted. Arthur had been deeply moved by the original film version of *Brief Encounter*, starring Celia Johnson and Trevor Howard, so the station had real significance.

With my earthy practicality, I thought that was madness. I knew this sort of meeting would just prolong the agony—my agony—and I wanted the affair over, fast.

'For God's sake,' I said one morning in exasperation, 'why don't the two of you check into a motel for a night, and get it out of your system?'

As soon as it was out, I realised it was the wrong thing to have said.

He looked at me pathetically.

'How can you be that crude? You just don't understand, if you can even suggest that. This is something beautiful.'

'Okay! Then go off together for a few days—and I really mean that! Do it the beautiful way!'

I was being bitchy, but I really *did* mean that. There was no other way to end the affair.

Arthur had started the research for *Hotel* by this time, and was making frequent trips to New Orleans. It didn't take much imagination to guess that's where they would go. I myself had a budding little friendship going at the time, and so I had no qualms about accepting an invitation to New York at the same time Arthur was to be in New Orleans.

I learned later that Naomi had baby-sitter problems and couldn't make it. Arthur called me from New Orleans to ask me to join him— the nerve of that!—to discover from *our* baby-sitter that I had just left for New York. He was furious that my illicit tryst had been successful while his had not, and when we both returned home I suffered days of his jealous anger, born out of his own frustration. But it didn't cure him of Naomi. The affair continued bitter-sweet and unconsummated, and I alternated between sweet reasonableness and blind rage.

Arthur sold the serial rights of *In High Places* to *Maclean's*, the Canadian magazine, for $7,500, and we decided to blow it all on a trip to Japan. On the first day of April 1962, we left Toronto with stop-overs ahead in San Francisco and Hawaii. We flew over the international date-line on April 4, so that Arthur got three hours of birthday while sitting on the plane on April 5. I gave him my gift and a card, and hoped fervently that, at least for the next four weeks, Naomi would stay in the background.

She didn't. A birthday card from her was waiting on our arrival at the Imperial Hotel in Tokyo on April 6, and it was Arthur's bad luck that the room clerk handed it over as we checked in. I recognised the handwriting immediately. We had another fight. But it was impossible to keep up our hostilities. The thrill of being in Japan for the first time was too much for both of us, and we were soon exploring the city, hand in hand.

Before we left Tokyo for our tour of the Japanese countryside and the smaller cities, Arthur took me to a jeweller to buy me some pearls. I chose an attractive necklace within our modest budget. Then came the clincher.

'I'd like to buy Naomi some pearls, too,' Arthur said casually. 'Would you help me choose them?'

I was all ready to explode—then suddenly saw the funny side of it. This was too much. This dear, naïve, thoroughly mixed-up man was actually asking his wife to choose pearls for his girl friend. I had an overwhelming sense of being needed.

I picked up a crooked string of yellow, misshapen, under-nourished pearls.

'Here, how about these?'

He had the good sense to laugh. 'Come on. You can do better than that,' he said shrewdly. I like to think that I shop wisely, and I knew that he was going to buy Naomi some pearls anyway, and he knew that I could not bear to let him make a bad buy.

I finally chose a decent-looking string, about a third of the cost of mine. 'There! That's a beautiful present with which to end a beautiful affair.'

That gesture truly cleared the air, somehow, and the rest of our holiday was spent in sweet rapport.

Arthur had been told by several writer friends that every man should experience a week in Tokyo alone, and I must say there were times in Japan I felt in the way. We were told not to enter bars unless they exhibited a sign which said 'English spoken here'. But we disregarded the advice and were glad we did. With the aid of a Berlitz phrase book we managed superbly, but I was consistently ignored by the giggling hostesses who gathered around Arthur, even though *I* supplied the appropriate Japanese phrases. Obviously he had to be free to explore the possibilities; after all, a writer must embrace all experiences if he is to write convincingly.

I had arranged to spend the week in Hong Kong, where I met interesting people, ate in offbeat Kowloon restaurants, saw the sights, strolled the streets, and ordered beautiful made-to-measure clothes. I loved it. Then, halfway through the week, I received a cable from Tokyo, saying Arthur was joining me. He had had a superb time, too, his mission was accomplished, but he had had enough and was ready for more familiar companionship.

I enjoyed showing him around Hong Kong and explaining some of the facts I had learned in my brief three days alone there. We both revelled in the sights and sounds of that wonderful city, and shared a closeness that was at its peak the last night, when we had a magnificent dinner at Gaddi's in the Peninsula Hotel.

I had almost forgotten Naomi, but she suddenly burst into our lives again.

We were en route home to Toronto. Our plane, which had stopped in Vancouver for refuelling, developed mechanical difficulties and was several hours late leaving. The longer the delay, the more upset Arthur became.

'What's wrong with you?' I asked. 'You're usually so philosophical about late flights.'

'There's nothing wrong with me!' he snapped, and I immediately knew there was a lot wrong.

When we were at last aboard, and he was still tense and irritable, he finally blurted out that he had arranged a lunch date the day after we were due to arrive in Toronto. (I didn't have to ask with whom.) With the long delay in Vancouver, we were obviously not going to be in Toronto until the early hours of the morning, and he wouldn't be in very good shape for his luncheon.

I was chortling on the inside, but with a blank face and a flat voice, I said, 'Well, you could telephone your friend and postpone the lunch,' knowing full well that this would upset him just as much. (Arthur has always hated changing plans once he has made them.)

Later, when our pilot announced that Toronto airport was closed because of bad weather, and we would have to overfly the city and land in Montreal, I laughed aloud. In return I received some strange looks from fellow passengers and a murderous scowl from Arthur. The gods were on my side, I thought. Couldn't have planned a scenario better myself.

We landed in Montreal about 3 a.m., and were told a bus would take all passengers to a hotel in the city. Arthur was pale with angry frustration, while I was openly gleeful. We collected our baggage and proceeded to the waiting bus. He accosted a passenger agent. What time would the airline be flying us back to Toronto?

'Well, sir,' replied the agent, 'it's hard to say . . . you see, they still have thick fog over the airport and we just don't know when it will lift. We'll keep you informed, though. . . . Well, I guess, sir, the airline could certainly promise that you'll reach Toronto by late afternoon.'

Fresh laughter from me—but not for long. Arthur became a raging lion, ready for action. He sprinted over to the Hertz counter and enquired about renting a car. Jolted by the cost of driving it to Toronto, a shred of sanity remaining, he then leaped onto the bus and addressed the entire busload of passengers in a loud voice. I couldn't believe what he was doing; he is a private, unshowy man who hates scenes.

'My wife and I,' he announced, 'are renting a car and are driving to Toronto. We can be there by eleven o'clock. Is there another couple who would like to accompany us and share the cost?'

No one murmured. They all looked at him pitifully through bleary eyes and, I suspect, thought of the free hotel room and clean bed awaiting them in Montreal.

'Sheep!' Arthur muttered as he wheeled around and climbed off the bus. Then louder, 'They're all *sheep!* The airline says do this, they all do it. Sheep!'

There was no laughter left in me. I was exhausted.

'Maybe,' I said, 'but sensible sheep. It's lunacy driving to Toronto. It's three hundred and fifty miles! And we haven't slept for two nights. Let's *go* to the hotel,' I pleaded. 'You can call Naomi and have lunch tomorrow. Jeez, it's only a *lunch* you're cancelling.' I got nowhere.

We drove to Toronto, and we drove fast—so fast, in fact, that just outside Cornwall, Ontario, we were stopped by the police. Old 'Straight and Level Hailey' got one of the very few speeding tickets in his life. And my flagging spirits revived long enough for a few chuckles.

We continued the rest of the way in silence, as before, and arrived home about 11 a.m. Our baby-sitter, already a day past her assignment, was anxious to go, and left. Arthur hauled in the bags, and prepared to shower for his date.

My rage surfaced, and I sarcastically reminded him that we *did* have three children, that we had been away for nearly five weeks, they would be home soon after twelve o'clock to greet us, and that he would already have left to keep his damned lunch appointment.

That hit home and he was momentarily contrite. Then he suggested I phone the school and explain we were home after a delayed flight, were longing to see the kids, and could they come home early for lunch. I could see he was determined, and I was wrung out mentally and physically, so like a fool I actually did phone. Let *him* explain to the children why he was going out for lunch as soon as he had arrived home, I thought dully.

The trio came home—they were aged eight, six and four then—and there was a wonderful welcome from them. (Years later Jane told me that it had puzzled her profoundly that we had phoned to have them come home early. It was so out of character, she said.) I started to make their lunch in the kitchen, but was interrupted by Arthur asking where in the suitcases were the cigarette lighters we had bought in Tokyo. They were cute little musical lighters, a couple of dollars each, and we had bought several for our smoking friends. Naomi was obviously at the top of the list.

I exploded. '*No!* I am not going to tell you where they are! Hell,

205

isn't it enough that she gets the pearls? She bloody well is not going to get a lighter too!'

Arthur would have liked to hit me, but he has rarely done this. Instead, he snatched up a piece of bread smeared with peanut butter, and threw it into the sink. The children's eyes saucered. What a helluva homecoming!

He hurled out the front door and drove off in his rented car to keep The Luncheon Date. I simmered down, ate with the children and listened to their chatter. Like most children in a warm, secure home, they took the up-and-down moods of their parents for granted and quickly forgot our stormy scene in the kitchen.

Jane and Steven went back to school, while Diane 'helped' me unpack. We did it slowly because I was so desperately tired and dispirited, and because Diane was full of chitchat, as always, which somewhat slowed our pace. I came across the lighters and hid them.

Later that afternoon, I glanced out of the window and saw Arthur climbing the steps to the front door. To my astonishment, Naomi was by his side. It dawned on me as I ran downstairs to open the door that he must have turned in the rented car, and she drove him home. But to invite her in, today of all days—well, it was a bit thick, I thought.

I put on a bright smile as I opened the door. Naomi smiled warmly back—but Arthur stared right through me as if in a daze. I chatted inanely—a weakness of mine in an embarrassing situation—as I led them into the living-room, where we all seemed to collapse in an emotional heap. Then I leaped up and suggested I make tea for us all. Three or four o'clock in the afternoon has always seemed to me to be too indecent an hour to suggest a drink, but it is a sinking time of the day and my old English habit of afternoon tea-drinking has served me well.

Naomi and I made small talk over our tea while Arthur just sat there, looking grey and haggard. Then he excused himself, announcing he was going to his study to look at the mail that had accumulated during our absence.

As soon as he had left, Naomi became serious.

'I guess Arthur has left us alone so I can tell you my news. I am leaving John.' John was Naomi's husband.

My jaw dropped and my face must have registered real shock.

'Oh! not for Arthur,' she hastened to reassure me.

'Gee, thanks!' I said. What an ironic twist!, I thought. She then told me about her new love, and I listened with only half my mind. I thought of Arthur with real compassion. Poor dear! Here he had been carrying a torch for Naomi these many months, and she had been falling in love with someone else—another *writer* yet. No wonder he looked haggard. I wanted to rush to him and put my arms around him and tell him *I* still loved him. And I didn't have long to wait before I was able to do just that.

Naomi left soon afterward. I had given her my philosophical thoughts about divorce. Was she sure she wasn't exchanging one set of problems for another? Was John really that awful to live with? Couldn't she just have an affair? How did the children feel? . . . But her mind was made up.

After her second marriage Naomi drifted out of our lives and our circle of friends. But I spoke with her on the phone two years ago after thirteen years of silence. She was the same delightful woman with that beautiful sense of humour.

'Heard you were writing a book,' she said. 'I hope there's a chapter about *me*.'

'There *is!*' I cried, 'and so far I think it's one of the best I've done.'

She chuckled. 'It seems I've always been a great inspiration to writers!'

I forgot to ask her if she still had the pearls. I hope so. Mine were lost forever several years ago.

Since that time there has been one other affair—at least that I know about—in which Arthur was caught up in a mood of romanticism. It came much later and was more distressing to me because it had lasted for many months without my being aware of it. When this sort of relationship surfaces eventually, a woman—or man—feels truly cheated. The recent trips out of town take on new meaning. One feels: *what a fool I've been!*

The relationship involved a woman more than twenty years younger than Arthur. It is a real ego trip for a man in his fifties to know that a young woman finds him attractive. And if she falls in love with him, it is easy for the man to do likewise. Whether this feeling is real or imagined is hard to say. In many ways it's a game, an indulgence in a bit of fun. For falling in love has to be the most wonderful, spirit-lifting, exciting, delicious experience there is. It's even more so when the love affair is illicit. The couple sees each other at his and her best. They are away from the tedious cares of the domestic household. Every meal is a candle-lit delight in a dark restaurant, a picnic on a deserted beach, or a room-service breakfast.

I knew the girl and her husband socially. And I knew Arthur was fond of her—but I didn't find out *how* fond until I came across some long love letters that Arthur had foolishly kept. It was immediately obvious that the affair had been going on for some time and—for the girl, at least—was heavy and emotional.

Arthur was away the day of my discovery, but he phoned me that evening as a matter of course. He was absolutely bowled over when I let fly: 'You stupid fool! Don't you ever learn?' I raged on that this time he had gone too far, I would not put up with it, and the relationship must stop.

He ended the affair that week. He was abject and begged me to forgive him. I said of course I would eventually, but over the next couple of weeks, inevitably, I had some stormy outbursts. He suffered greatly from my tongue-lashings, but I got everything disagreeable out of my system. There was a period of sweet reconciliation; then we resolved to put the affair behind us.

How sad it is that sound marriages can end in divorce in exactly these circumstances! It would have been easy for me to threaten to leave, but I had no intention of doing so. I loved my man and I knew he loved me too. Why destroy all the good things we had because of hurt pride?

I have a close, dear friend, whom I will always admire for the way she handled this kind of crisis in her life. Her husband had actually left her and their four children to move in with a new love. My friend, her heart pounding, went to the apartment and knocked on the door. Her astonished husband answered it. She told him: 'I just want to tell you there are five of us at home who love you very much and will be happy to see you back when you come to your senses.'

He returned within a few days. They have now been married thirty-two years. They have that warm, easy, comfortable companionship that goes with long years of marriage.

To say that an affair can strengthen a good marriage sounds glib. But it *can*. Not that I am condoning affairs. I am not. But I understand them. They happen all around us, and they always have. There are broken homes in every community to prove it.

I believe it is primarily the way a woman handles a husband's affair—and vice versa—that determines its outcome. It is simply not true that only shaky marriages fail because of an extramarital relationship.

Sooner or later, I think, indulgence in affairs leads to pain. I know personally that it is possible to have a light-hearted, affectionate relationship outside marriage, without emotional complication. But emotions are unpredictable, and I suppose it is easy to get more deeply involved than one intended.

It's safer never to get entangled in an affair at all.

And yet . . . and yet . . . Arthur has often insisted that he cannot write about life unless he has experienced it. He is fond of quoting Tennyson's *Ulysses:*

> *I cannot rest from travel; I will drink*
> *Life to the lees: all times I have enjoy'd*
> *Greatly, have suffer'd greatly, both with those*
> *That loved me, and alone . . .*
>
> *I am a part of all that I have met;*
> *Yet all experience is an arch wherethro'*
> *Gleams that untravell'd world, whose margin fades*
> *For ever and for ever when I move.*
> *How dull it is to pause, to make an end,*
> *To rust unburnish'd, not to shine in use!*

Arthur has had, in effect, a built-in excuse to 'drink life to the lees' and 'to shine in use'. He also has had an understanding wife.

There is no doubt that over the years he has gained much insight from some of the friendships, platonic and otherwise, he has had with women. And in the novel which Arthur is currently working on, *Overload*, the main character—Nim Goldman—experiences some of the pleasures and heartaches concerning 'other women' which Arthur has explored himself. There will be many men who will identify with Nim when the book is published.

However, after Arthur's last romantic episode with his young friend, I decided enough is enough. I told him: 'Okay, you've had a good innings. But from here on, your descriptions of other women can be taken from memory. God knows, you've done enough research to last the rest of your life!'

CHAPTER 17

Books: the Sales Pitch

What sells a book?

The author's name, for one thing. If he or she has a history of writing books which readers have enjoyed, there's a good chance that a new work will sell on the reputation of the old. And the name of a well-known personality (who has not written a book before) will sometimes, though not always, guarantee a big sale.

The title, too, is important. Who, for instance, could resist a book called *Everything You Always Wanted To Know About Sex . . . But Were Afraid To Ask?* As it turned out, not many.

An author is not always the best judge of what is the best title. Arthur called his first television play *Flight 714*, which isn't exactly titillating. Someone at the Canadian Broadcasting Corporation—we never found out who—renamed the play. *Flight Into Danger* is a title which has endured across the years.

When Arthur had almost finished writing one of his novels, we were vacationing in Acapulco, Mexico, with our friends Janet and Pierre Berton. (Pierre needs no introduction to Canadians. He is a prolific writer of books, a TV and radio personality and, in my opinion, was one of the finest newspaper columnists ever.) We sat on the beach discussing titles.

Arthur said, 'The one I'd really like is *Grand Hotel*; too bad Vicki Baum thought of it first. At the moment, I've two possible titles: *Full House* and *Main Mezzanine.*'

Pierre thought for a few seconds, then said, 'Call it simply *Hotel*.'

I looked at Arthur and wrinkled my nose. We were not impressed.

When we were back home in Toronto, Arthur passed Pierre's suggestion to his editors. By this time we had eliminated *Main Mezzanine*, so the Doubleday Art Department prepared coloured roughs of two book jackets. Both pictured the façade of a hotel similar to the Plaza in New York. The title *Full House* appeared on one jacket, *Hotel* on the other. There was no question which had the greater impact.

It was Pierre Berton, too, who gave me the title for this book, after my own two suggestions were rejected. (One of them was *How To Live with a Writer and Survive*; the other I have used as a chapter heading.)

When Arthur began writing a story set against the background of an international airport, he named it *The Surly Bonds of Earth*, a quotation from the poem 'High Flight'. He loved it; everybody else hated it. His publishers said, 'How do you expect us to sell a book with such a downbeat title?' Finally, as the book neared completion, all of Doubleday's salesmen were telling bookstores they would soon have a new Hailey novel—*Airport*. The name grew on us; we accepted it as a *fait accompli*.

Next was the novel about the motor industry. Arthur thought: what better title than *Swing Low, Sweet Chariot*? Again, he was the only one who liked it, and he received a list of alternative suggestions, among them *Detroit, Motor City, The Horseless Carriage*. Then two people independently suggested *Wheels*. One was Tom Burns, then sales and marketing vice-president of Doubleday; the other was our old friend Alexis Klotz of the Napa Valley.

The title *The Moneychangers* was an early choice of Arthur's, but Maeve Southgate, his agent, did not like it. *Bank* was suggested, then *Money*. We were lukewarm about both. Sam Vaughan of Doubleday was very big on *The Bank*, because, he said, 'It sounds big, is of a piece with *Hotel* and *Airport*, and because that's what the book is about.' Across the dinner table one evening, our children summed up their reaction to that one with all the candour and eloquence of the young: 'Ugh!' Yet we trusted Sam's judgment and *The Bank* was the title we decided to go with. The jacket was designed; everything was settled. Then while Sam was on holiday, his colleague Ken McCormick phoned us to say Doubleday had just learned that a non-fiction book, *The Bankers* by Martin Mayer, would be published a month ahead of Arthur's novel. Clearly the two similar titles would create confusion, so *The Bank* was out. I, for one, was relieved.

Arthur searched desperately for another title, leafing through books of quotations. Then when he could find nothing else, he went back to the title he had always liked, *The Moneychangers*, with a mental apology to Maeve.

She had died just a few months before.

Although titles are important, they aren't everything. A good book can triumph over an unlikely title. For instance, who could imagine selling many copies of a novel called, say, *Too Late the Phalarope*? Published in 1953, this was the second of Alan Paton's widely acclaimed and successful novels.

The modern way is to promote anything that's for sale. It doesn't always succeed, but it helps. So advertising a book, any book, is important in making people aware that it *exists*.

A publisher will determine in advance how much money is to be spent initially on advertising a certain book, where ads will be placed, and how often they'll run.

Experience guides publishers in estimating how a book will sell and what the initial promotional budget should be. They can be wrong, though. That's one of the charms of the business—no one knows for sure what's going to happen to a book. Sometimes a great deal is expected in terms of sales, but the book never catches on. Other books suddenly 'take off' in a manner wholly unexpected—such as happened with the phenomenal *Jonathan Livingston Seagull*. When this occurs, publishers increase the advertising to maintain momentum.

Mention of a book in the news columns of a newspaper, or a reference to it by a well-known columnist, can be better than advertising.

That's why a promotion tour has become an accepted way for certain authors to help sell their books. However, there can be problems if the author is shy or inarticulate. Just because a person writes well does not mean he or she speaks well, or feels comfortable before a microphone or TV camera.

To answer a question often asked: yes, a publisher pays for most (but not all) promotion tours, including air fares, meals, accommodation, taxis and hired cars. The publisher, too, arranges the media interviews, bookshop appearances, lecture engagements, and literary lunch speeches. The tour can be a comparatively short four-city, two-week affair, such as Arthur did for *Wheels*, or a three-month trek covering every major city in the United States.

Over the years Arthur has formed some definite ideas about book promotion. He agrees that some promotion is needed, but feels a long tour is so physically exhausting that a writer may be better off conserving his energy and getting on with the next book.

The longest tour he ever did was for the original, hardcover edition of *Airport*. He was away five weeks. I had been with him in New York and Toronto for the more exciting portions of the tour—the parties, lunches, network shows. But our children were all living at home then, and I didn't like to leave them too long, so Arthur continued on his own, travelling from city to city. At each stop he was met by a Doubleday sales representative for that particular area, who briefed him on the activities arranged.

Some of the salesmen were super-conscientious—the kind who take command at the airport on arrival, double-check the day's schedule, and smooth the way from one engagement to another.

Then there is the other extreme. Arthur recalled a memorable example for me. First, no one met him at the airport, nor was there a car waiting. It was Sunday, the weather was bad, and the local salesman explained later he hadn't felt like turning out. That same evening Arthur was due at a radio station out in the suburbs. A snowstorm had started; the local salesman still hadn't shown up; there wasn't a taxi to be had. Finally Arthur managed to get transport by paying a hotel waiter going off duty to drive him. When he arrived at the radio station he discovered that neither a copy of his book nor one of his own prepared 'digests' had been received. (More on those 'digests' later.) After the broadcast he was tired, and looking forward to getting back to the hotel and to bed. But it was still snowing and no taxi would travel that far out of town to pick him up. Arthur was obliged to wait until 2 a.m. when a disc jockey had finished his programme and could give him a lift.

The next day began with a 7 a.m. television interview, which meant a 5 a.m. wake-up call—for TV stations are invariably out in the suburbs where land is cheaper than downtown.

No wonder Arthur arrived back home in California grey, haggard, and looking several years older. I was shocked by his appearance and vowed I would not let him undertake such a tour again.

213

'I really am exhausted,' he admitted. 'Every morning I was awakened by the hotel operator, and I'd think, "What city am I in, and where do I have to be when?"'

Something else Arthur told me about that tour: like most of us, he wakes up at least once during the night to go to the bathroom. What with changing hotels every other day, he would get out of bed sleepily, and start off in the direction of where the bathroom had been the night before, with the result that he was constantly walking into walls or tripping over furniture. He had bruised shins to prove it.

The tour Arthur enjoyed most was the one to promote the Bantam Books paperback edition of *Hotel*.

A year or so earlier, when the hardcover edition of the same novel was published, Doubleday had promoted it strongly. At that time Arthur was not well known. However, his publishers regarded him as a potential best-selling author and were anxious to give him wide exposure. So the tour was long and arduous.

Arthur was almost dreading the 'paperback' tour. He was engrossed in the writing of *Airport*, and resented taking the time away from his typewriter. But he had not, at this point, met Esther Margolis.

She is, in Arthur's opinion, one of the top-rank crackerjack executives in the publishing business. In 1966 Esther headed the publicity department of Bantam Books. She wrote to tell Arthur she would be accompanying him on his tour for the promotion of *Hotel*.

When Arthur arrived at Detroit airport, having flown there from San Francisco, he was met by an attractive, slim brunette whose first words were, 'I'm Esther Margolis. May I have your baggage tags?'

It was symbolic of what followed, because from then on she took over totally the logistics of the tour. She was the one who registered at each hotel, tipped the porters, ordered meals, engaged the cars, gave directions to their drivers. In short, she pampered him, relieving him of all troublesome details and leaving him alert and fresh for the TV, radio and press interviews. He found that the eight-city tour with Esther, instead of being a chore, was a delight—though strictly business, he says with a touch of sadness.

That particular occasion will always remain for him the epitome of what a public-relations tour by an author should be. There have been other tours since, conducted by efficient, conscientious people—but none compares with his nostalgic view of that one.

As I write, our good friend Esther Margolis has been a vice-president of Bantam Books since January 1971, with wide responsibilities extending far beyond publicity tours for authors.

I had mixed reactions, however, even to *that* tour. Arthur came back bright-eyed, relaxed and happy, which was good for all of us in the family. But the next trip he and I made together he was standing back, carefree, waiting for *me* to take care of the baggage and organize the airline check-in. That's one thing about dear Arthur: he can very quickly get used to having things done for him.

It is amazing how much can be crammed into one day during a publicity tour. As an example, here is the schedule for a day in Toronto, after *Wheels* was published. It is typical of any day's programme in a large metropolitan city.

6:30 A.M.	Car pick-up at hotel	
7:30 A.M.	CFTO-TV	Toronto Today Show
9:00 A.M.	CFTO-TV	Carole Taylor Show
10:30 A.M.	CFRB Radio	Betty Kennedy Show
11:30 A.M.	CKFM Radio	Fred Napoli Show
12:30 P.M.	Lunch with *Star* reporter	Barberian's Restaurant
6:15 P.M.	CBLT-TV	Weekday—News Show
9:00 P.M.	CBL Radio	As It Happens
10:00 P.M.	CKFH	Bud Riley, News
11:00 P.M.	CBL Radio	Don Sims Show

I remember that particular day because when we got back to our hotel after lunch, looking forward to an hour's nap, a student journalist was waiting in the lobby, hoping Arthur would give him some time in which to discuss how he should go about getting his just-completed novel published. Tired as he was, Arthur admired the young man's enterprise and talked at length with him.

As a friend said to me during that visit to Toronto, 'I got up in the morning, saw Arthur on TV, opened the newspaper and read a write-up on him, heard him being interviewed on radio as I drove home that evening, and again on radio as I got ready for bed. And darned if he wasn't on radio again the next morning. My God! when does he find the time to go to the john?'

Just as Arthur is highly organised at his work, so is he organised about publicity interviews. He realises it is unreasonable to expect every newspaper reporter, radio or TV personality to have read his new book in advance of an interview, because there are so many authors with books to promote. It would be a physical impossibility for a media person to have gone through them all.

Therefore, in advance of any tour, Arthur researches his own book, carefully picking out segments which, in his opinion, may be newsworthy or have some other special interest. He then prepares a summary of those points, indicating the pages on which they appear in the book. Copies of this summary are given to interviewers who can glance through the sheets, then pick out a subject which interests him or her and go directly to it. The interviewer sounds as if he or she has actually read the book—a mild deception which Arthur is happy to go along with.

Some of the potential interview topics he selected from *The Money-changers* were: how to open a Swiss bank account; thefts 'inside' a bank; how bank frauds are covered up; why U.S. currency is the world's easiest to counterfeit; some vignettes about credit-card fraud; some widely held misconceptions about ownership of gold. I particularly liked one thought under the heading, Women's Lib. It read:

> P. 173—Alex Vandervoort: 'No man is whole unless the woman he loves is free, and knows the use of freedom, exploiting it in fulfilment of herself.'

This 'digest' idea was Arthur's own which he first developed for the novel *Hotel*. It has been popular with busy radio and TV personalities. Their job is made easier, their interviews smoother and more interesting. If it prevents one interviewer from beginning with those unimaginative words, 'Mr. Hailey, tell us what your book is about!', then the work involved in the résumé is worth it.

Before any promotion tour, Arthur also gives himself a brief refresher course on his subject. Usually eight or nine months have passed since he finished writing the book, by which time he has moved on to another novel and is deeply involved in the new subject. It is amazing how 'fuzzy' he can become about situations and even characters in the book behind him. For this reason, while on tour he carried around a file of notes and clippings to refresh his memory. He refers to it each morning in the car on the way to the first engagement, then leaves it in the car so he can glance through it at other times during the day.

In any city being visited on a promotion tour he reads the local newspapers carefully to see if there is something regional which ties in with his book. Another point: he tries not to say the same thing on more than one TV or radio show in the same city.

His attitude to the entire promotion business is that the TV and radio shows and press interviewers are doing *him* a favour in drawing public attention to his book. Therefore, in return he wants to do the best he can for them. This is why Arthur gets himself keyed up just before air time, then gives an interview everything he's got. He cannot bear idle chatter beforehand, and en route to a radio or TV station wants to sit quietly and relax.

But what makes Arthur relaxed is not always relaxing to the person accompanying him. Someone who doesn't know him well often feels that he or she should keep up a steady stream of conversation or, worse, engage in what is virtually another interview, asking questions like, 'Where do you get your ideas?' or, 'Do you write in longhand or on a typewriter?' What's more, Arthur has always detested smoking and, now that it's known to be medically dangerous, has become a militant anti-smoker. He requests—always politely—that no one smoke in a car during the time it is on hire. Some publishers' representatives who are nicotine addicts have been pretty shaky by the time Arthur has left town.

While on the paperback tour for *The Moneychangers*, Arthur noticed with great pleasure that not one Bantam Books salesman was a smoker. We non-smokers are truly gaining influence, he thought. Only later did he discover that Judy Hilsinger, who was in charge of the publicity tour, had written ahead asking that smoking be verboten while Arthur was around. One company salesman admitted to Arthur, when saying goodbye at the airport, that he was going to smoke a whole pack of cigarettes as soon as the plane had gone.

Nowadays, I try to go along on promotion tours—and Arthur likes this too. I can smooth the way by explaining his idiosyncrasies in a light-hearted way, answering the telephone, keeping track of extra requests for interviews which always pop up, and finally being firm with a persistent caller if I think the schedule is demanding enough already.

Against that, however, is the fact that Arthur is sometimes so tense he can become irritated with *me*. He is always punctual and is usually ready and sitting in the hotel room at least ten minutes before we are due to leave. Always a last-minuter, I am scurrying around changing handbags, putting in my contact lenses (or looking for a lost one), or making a phone call just before departing. Then, at the lift, I might say, 'Oh, I forgot my earrings!' and will dash back to get them. All of this makes Arthur jittery, and I sometimes think he is better on his own.

Now, about interviewers.

There are good ones, and others who are not so good. Arthur always enjoys the top-notch people, especially if their questions are tough and he is kept mentally on his toes. Occasionally, one comes across an inexperienced or inept interviewer. I have seen Arthur help out by answering one question in a way that leads to another. He is, in fact, always gracious. No one likes a smartass, and if a guest scores off an interviewer, he usually denigrates himself.

In any city there are requests to go to bookshops to autograph books. Arthur used to do this; now he doesn't. He finds such sessions time-consuming and exhausting, and shop appearances sell fewer books overall for the bookseller than TV, radio or newspaper promotion.

I remember we were in Detroit immediately after *Wheels* was launched. Jane and Steven, then seventeen and fifteen, were with us and in one shop all four of us were on the job. Steven went down a line-up, handing out slips of paper so that each person could write the name to be inscribed in his or her book. I accepted each book at the head of the queue, opening it to the correct page for autographing. I also made sure Arthur would be able to read the name on each slip before I passed it to him. He signed, then flashed a smile at each book-buyer and exchanged a few words. Jane then slid the book away from his hands, closed it and passed it back to the customer.

Arthur did a lot of autographing in Detroit. There was an excitement there because of the local subject matter. Journalist Marci McDonald told it well in an article for the *Toronto Daily Star* entitled 'How Arthur Hailey Sells His Books'.

> . . . This was a 14-hour whirlwind day, a day of endless autographs and 10-times-asked interview questions, a day of pump-

ing handshakes and hearty smiles to strangers, the fourth such day in a two-week, four-city promotional tour for his latest book, *Wheels*.

 . . . All of Detroit was abuzz about *Wheels*. At every cocktail party and in every newspaper the guessing game was going on. (Who) was Hailey's handsome, hard-driving auto executive with the young blonde wife? Didn't the book's nagging auto critic Emerson Vale bear an uncanny resemblance to a certain Ralph Nader?

 . . . For two hours, with infinite toothy exuberance, Hailey retraced the signature with the tiny three-dot grin drawn into the loop of the final 'Y' in his name, as they lined up—the women in curlers and expensive coiffures, the kid playing hookey from high school and the lackey of a top Detroit auto designer mentioned in the book.

When asked if he got writer's cramp, he would reply each of the 15 times, as if he had just coined it, 'Every writer should have this problem.'

 . . . By 2.30 P.M., 190 had been sold and signed, more than one a minute. John Genovese, the publisher's sales representative, rushed up to report that Hudson's, who had ordered 10,000 copies, had already sold 6,000, and was re-ordering 3,000. And it wasn't even the end of the week yet.

At the other extreme I remember going with Arthur, at a later date, to a suburban bookshop in Dallas. He had made an exception and agreed to sign copies of *The Moneychangers* for an hour or so. It was a Monday morning, and it was raining—hard. Arthur sat in an almost empty shop, inwardly fretting at the waste of time, while the shop assistants chatted with him, saying over and over that it was a shame it was raining and they had expected such a good turnout. About half a dozen customers trickled in. I couldn't stand it and deserted Arthur to do some shopping.

In Arthur's opinion, it is more important to meet the bookshop sales personnel than the actual book-buyers. A friendly assistant can sell more copies of a book to undecided customers than can a long autographing session. And over the long haul he thinks he best serves everyone—his publishers, booksellers, his readers, himself—by staying home and getting on with the next book.

This attitude is reflected in a standard memo he sends out nowadays when he is asked to make public speeches. Arthur is an excellent speaker. He can spin anecdotes the way he tells stories. He can grab an audience's attention and hold it until the talk is over. And he can always make people laugh. As a result, he gets many requests to speak to various groups. This memo expresses his philosophy:

> Being a successful author has pleasant compensations, not least of which is interest in the author's work, resulting—among other things—in invitations to speak at public functions.
>
> Unfortunately, it is impossible to be two things at the same time—a 'talking writer' and a 'writing writer'. Talking to audiences, however stimulating to a writer's ego, is costly—in terms of time, preparation of a speech, travel, lost writing hours, and simple physical tiredness. Nor, contrary to superficial opinion, does a public speaking engagement make any substantial difference to the sale of an author's books.
>
> For all these reasons, this particular writer has reached some conclusions regarding public speaking:
>
> 1. Quite frankly, he would prefer to stay home and write.
>
> 2. However, rather than be ungracious or become a recluse, he will accept occasional speaking engagements—but no more than three a year.
>
> 3. It is not unreasonable to place a value on his time and energy. Therefore, he will charge a fee for each speaking engagement, namely $2,000.00, plus first-class air fare and overnight accommodation.
>
> 4. He will not, however, keep the fee for himself but will donate it to charity. The charity will be one of his choosing. The paying organisation may, if it prefers, make its cheque payable directly to that charity but, in any event, a receipt will be provided.

Do reviews help sell a book?

Yes, of course. And both kinds of review help—good and bad. This was brought home to us vividly early in Arthur's career. His novel *In High Places* was first published in 1962 when we were living in Toronto. It was prominently reviewed in that city's *Globe & Mail* by William French. It had a six-column headline and occupied half the Book Page, together with a photograph of the author. It was a well-written, thoughtful review, but the message was clear: French didn't like Hailey's novel.

To our astonishment in the days that followed, when *In High Places* was selling madly, friends would say something like: 'Say, that was a good write-up of your book in Saturday's paper. We bought a copy and are looking forward to reading it.'

As a result of that and other similar experiences, Arthur and I have come to the same conclusion: Even 'bad' publicity is good publicity, as long as the names of the book and the author are mentioned and spelled correctly.

There seems little, if any, overall logic to most reviewers' reactions to any book.

When *Wheels* was published in North America, and while number one on best-seller lists, it received the worst reviews of any book since Arthur began writing. There were no more than a dozen good ones. Paradoxically, in Britain, where most earlier Hailey books had been castigated in the press, *Wheels* received excellent reviews, the bad ones totalling no more than half a dozen. As Arthur said at that time, 'I have no explanation for the difference.'

Particularly amusing to us, also in the case of *Wheels*, were the reviews in the Detroit area versus those outside Detroit.

First, the Detroit area:

> . . . a hatchet job . . . an insult to the thousands of decent men and women who are connected with automobiles.
> *Detroit Sunday News*

> Some auto men are smarting over the picture of Detroit that emerges . . . 'It's a collection of all the unfavourable sensitivities about Detroit,' complains one auto official.
> *The Wall Street Journal*, written by the Journal's Detroit Bureau Chief

> *Wheels* won't be purchased by Detroit's car builders as Christmas gifts . . . It doesn't paint them in a favorable light.
> *Saginaw News*

A selection from other parts of the country:

> Auto industry public relations men will love [*Wheels*]. The industry comes off as trustworthy, loyal, helpful, friendly, courteous and kind.
> *Chicago Daily News*

> [*Wheels* is] a salute to the auto industry . . . Hailey plays a diligent Boswell to management's Doctor Johnson. He describes the pox marks on his subject's cheeks, but finds him to be an admirable fellow.
> *The New York Times*

His sympathies clearly lie with the men who make and sell cars.

National Observer

Hailey's enthusiasm about the auto industry which he sees as a kind of number one public servant . . . He puts up the auto people as the knights in shining armor.

Louisville Times

The reviews of all Arthur's books fall into three categories. Using *The Moneychangers* as an example, the first—and admittedly smallest—group includes the unabashedly favourable reviews. Typical is this from *The Chattanooga Times:*

Arthur Hailey, author of the fabulously entertaining and successful *Hotel, Airport* and *Wheels*, has done it again with a novel that offers an in-depth look into the world of banking. There's something for everyone in this blockbuster and Hailey, as usual, has populated his novel with a cast of characters so lifelike and believable that you expect to run into them the next time you go to the bank . . . In a time of soaring inflation, it's comforting to report that you can still get topnotch reading at a reasonable price.

Then, there is the group, again small, that contains the really scathing reviews. *The Macon* (Georgia) *Telegraph* had this to say:

[*The Moneychangers*] is a thick bit of froth in which [the author] works hard to put some suspense and excitement into the banking business but manages only to bore. . . . Along the way we pick up unusual and interesting facts about money or its uses, as spoken by Hailey's characters, but these cannot salvage what is basically a weak plot. The only money-changing that ought to matter to the reader is that he has shelled out $10 for the novel and is left with a dull story.

And the *Washington Post:*

We all know Arthur Hailey. He's the guy with the formula for the instant novel. It's simple: take a setting, invent a soap opera plot, fill in the background with a smattering of soft journalism and as much trade gossip as you can pick up. Stir thoroughly and out pops *Wheels, Airport* and *Hotel*. And now there's *The Moneychangers* . . . Surely there is a good novel in all this. No doubt someone eventually will write it.

Occasionally, in this category, there are reviews which are vicious beyond belief. One doesn't like them, but one learns to shrug them off because they don't seem to discourage anyone from buying the book. In fact, they are self-defeating. The reviewer too often reveals that the attack has its roots in personal frustration.

Finally, there is by far the largest group of all: the reviews that are 'mixed' in their praise and abuse. Some are more generous than others, such as this one from *Business Week*:

> . . . Plainly [Arthur Hailey] is headed toward bestsellerdom again with *The Moneychangers* . . . Hailey's storytelling skills are intact, his mastery of detail hasn't diminished, and his sense of timing is well-nigh perfect—the failure of banks and the foibles of bankers are among the hottest topics of the day . . . Sure, there are better writers in the world . . . Hailey's characters are plastic, one-dimensional clichés . . . His prose seldom rises above the level of that in a B-movie. Given all that, the book still zips along—engaging, and, when you are finally hooked, really hard to put down . . . It will entertain and instruct, and it's just the thing for a long weekend, or a long business trip. For all of its 472 pages, it's a fast read.

There is also the kind that is grudging, like this review from the *New York Times*. After finding fault with *The Moneychangers*, the reviewer confesses:

> Still, I didn't have ridicule in mind while I actually read *The Moneychangers*. What I had in mind was diversion and, to tell the shameful truth, I found it. I found it in Mr. Hailey's sure-handed way of building a solid, old-fashioned story—in his knack for making everything work for him . . . Not bad for a lazy summer afternoon in the hammock.

I asked Arthur, for the purpose of this book, if he had any comments about reviews. He had this to say:

'A review has a brief life, usually one day, then immediately disappears and is forgotten. Books of all kinds last longer, which may account for a regular reviewer's built-in frustration.

'I've never complained about bad reviews. It's all part of the game, part of the book-writing scene, and any author who can't endure criticism, no matter how sharp-edged, should engage in some less public occupation.

223

'I read most reviews carefully, weigh them, learn from a few. I hope each book will be better than the last, and over the course of the books I've written I've learned some things to avoid.

'I know I cannot delineate a character as well as some writers. I read other writers and I might think they use language beautifully, I wish I could use language like that, but they may be deficient in other areas. I sometimes think some fine stylistic writers could have done better in the way of plot, that they could have told the story in a livelier way. I believe story-telling is my strength.

'But I will never be defensive over my work. I've put a lot of time and sweat into it and it's the best I can do. If you like it, fine.'

And he added cheerfully: 'If you don't, that's okay, too.'

CHAPTER 18

'He Was a Storyteller'

In the published words of June Callwood, a perceptive Canadian writer, Arthur Hailey is 'courteous, enthusiastic, boyish, guarded, self-effacing, confident, generous, springy-stepped, unaffected, sentimental, punctilious, prudent, quaint and honest'. Add to that description the adjectives I used on the first page of this book and the reader will deduce he is a complicated man.

He is. But if I were asked to sum him up in one word I would say, simply: he is a *good* man.

Another description was rendered by our friend Alfredo Machado, who is Arthur's Brazilian publisher. I was in Alfredo's company when he was asked by someone who did not know Arthur, to describe him. A man of great wit, Alfredo thought for a second, then said, 'Arthur is a rectangle.' I laughed at this because I knew what he meant. One would never say my husband is a square; but a rectangle—perhaps.

If you were to ask Arthur, today, what is the most important aspect of his life, he would say without hesitation: 'My wife and my children.' And he would mean it. However, one reason for this—to be objective—is that he is fulfilled as a writer. If he had not achieved some measure of success in his writing, I believe he could have become frustrated and a cynic. It is easier to smile on others if fate has smiled on you.

Over the years I have chided Arthur: 'If I mean so much to you, how come you have never dedicated a book to me?'

He dedicated only one of his books—*The Final Diagnosis;* it was to Dr. Richard G. McManus and Herbert Brodkin, who inspired the TV play *No Deadly Medicine*, on which the book was based. Since then Arthur has maintained he does not like dedications. As for dedicating a book to me which might read, let's say: 'To my darling wife, without whose love, inspiration and help this book would not have been written'—well, Arthur, a private man, suggests that's like making love on television. I think that's poppycock. Although in my younger days his reluctance to go public with a declaration of devotion irritated me, I am now resigned to this idiosyncrasy. Besides, he did try to make amends by naming our cabin cruiser *Sheila*, a canny manoeuvre. Obviously he hoped I would share his pleasure in the boat. (In fact, I love the sea and boating, except in rough waters, when my enthusiasm erodes as quickly as my breakfast.)

Arthur has a modest view of himself. This is the reason he has seldom sought media attention, apart from the obligatory appearances when a new book is published. In between books he disappears from public view. Explaining this once in a tape-recorded interview, he said: 'The strength of my life is my marriage and my family. And for people who haven't got this, I guess they need the attention. But I need my marriage and my family more than I need the outside thing. Also, Sheila and the children are balloon-prickers who stick a pin in me the moment I become too inflated.'

The last statement is true—with exceptions. I sometimes have a more realistic view of Arthur than he does of himself, and an incident in Brazil demonstrates this.

Arthur and I visited that exciting, colourful country during Carnaval in 1972. He is always amazed to discover in foreign countries we have travelled to—Germany, the Netherlands, Italy, Denmark, France, Japan, Australia, New Zealand, to name a few—how widely his novels are read and how well-known he is. Wherever we went in Brazil, reporters and photographers would seek him out. The trip was supposed to be for pleasure, not a publicity jaunt, and Arthur soon became unhappy about all the attention. One day we arrived at Belo Horizonte airport, hot and tired, en route to Oro Preto. As we walked towards the terminal we were aware of a TV camera crew, bright lights and lens aimed at arriving passengers. Arthur looked around curiously to see who was so important as to warrant a televised reception. I nudged him with my elbow.

'It's for you, dopey!' I laughed.

Inside the terminal building we were surrounded by half a dozen newsmen who wanted, right there and then, an impromptu press conference. I caught Arthur's eye as he answered questions; he was longing for it all to be over. With him, a little celebrity status goes a long way. But I was not surprised by the enthusiasm we encountered, having seen the Brazilian sales figures for his books, and throughout our travels in that country I cajoled him into a mood of gracious acceptance.

While we were touring Australia and New Zealand in 1976 with Jane, Steven and Diane, Arthur was again overwhelmed by an enthusiastic reception, unexpected by him—but not by me. The highlight of the visit was a large luncheon given by—well, it was difficult to know who *was* responsible! Collins organised the function on behalf of Pan, his British paperback publishers. Also on hand were representatives of Hutchinson and Nelson, who were there on behalf of Souvenir Press and Michael Joseph, his British hardback companies.

The lunch was held at the spectacular Sydney Opera House. During the festivities, Arthur was presented with his second 'Pan' award—a golden statuette of the mythical Greek deity, Pan—for having sold a million copies of the paperback edition of *Hotel*. (The first one, for *Airport*, was presented in London in 1974.) Arthur was delighted by the number of people who attended the luncheon, as well as the public response he received in both 'down under' countries. All of us thoroughly enjoyed Australia and New Zealand; the two countries differ greatly, but each is strikingly beautiful.

In the same way, our trip to the U.S.S.R. in July 1977 was a revelation to us both. This time Arthur enjoyed it all in a state of dazed wonder as we were treated, from arrival to departure, like visiting royalty. In a three-week journey to widely separated parts of the Soviet Union, we discovered that Arthur is one of the most popular and widely read North American authors. High officials, university scholars, writers, as well as taxi drivers, waitresses, clerks—all were excited to meet him. One poet said to Arthur during a dinner party in Tbilisi: 'You are the first writer who has written about technology so poetically. We Russians are hungry for facts about life in America and we love to read good stories. You are a living classic.'

Arthur laughed at this, but it was explained to him later that his work is handled by publishers of classics, not 'modern' publishers. He was even more astonished to discover that a single copy of *Foreign Literature* magazine, which serialised *Airport* and originally sold for 60 kopeks (about 80 pence), was selling for up to 45 roubles (£60) on the black market. The reason for a black market in books is that when one becomes popular in the U.S.S.R., there are never enough copies to go around and each may be read by hundreds of people. One copy of *Airport* we saw had been handled so often that pages were torn and ragged and the whole thing had fallen apart.

Christopher S. Wren, chief of the *New York Times*'s Moscow bureau, told us that when asked by would-be tourists what to take to Russia as gifts, he replies: 'Bring Arthur Hailey paperbacks.' And at lunch at the Canadian Embassy in Moscow, I told Ambassador Robert Ford that Arthur was truly amazed to discover how well-known he is in the U.S.S.R. Said His Excellency: 'I am amazed that *he* is amazed.'

Arthur's lack of vanity was brought into focus when his agent, Maeve Southgate, and his editor at Doubleday, LeBaron Barker, were alive. Maeve regarded Arthur with fierce loyalty and affection. In some ways her attitude was like his mother's: nothing was too good for him. Once he was in Maeve's office-apartment and heard her negotiating a contract on the telephone. She made Hailey sound like the best thing that had happened to publishing since Shakespeare. Arthur, who had listened with acute embarrassment, told her he hoped he would never have to hear that again, and to do her negotiating when he wasn't around.

Lee Barker was a superb, no-nonsense editor, but on occasion could be prickly. He, too, thought highly of Arthur as a person, and respected his patience and professionalism.

Arthur respected and was fond of them both. Unfortunately, Maeve and Lee were, for a while, less enamoured with each other. Lee would complain to Arthur that Maeve was impossible to deal with; Maeve would write Arthur an irritated note describing how inflexible Lee was. After such squabbles, Arthur would either write or phone, to humour one and soothe the other. I said to him one day: 'Honey, don't you realize . . . *you* are the property. The *writer* is supposed to be temperamental. They should be placating *you*.'

My husband, the diplomat, suggested after one of these incidents that Lee and Maeve have a long lunch and get to know each other better. Until then, most of their communication had been by phone or letter. They did meet, talked for four hours, and became firm friends.

It was an immensely sad time for Arthur when, over a period of fifteen months, death claimed the four people outside our immediate family who were closest to him.

Lee Barker's life ended first, in June 1973—an untimely, sudden death from a cerebral haemorrhage. Arthur and I flew from the Bahamas to New York for a simple but moving memorial gathering at which four people spoke: John Sargent, president of Doubleday; Ken McCormick, Lee's colleague for thirty years; Ilka Chase, author and friend; Arthur Hailey, author and friend.

Only two months later, Arthur's father died in England, aged ninety, after two sad years of senility. That year Arthur had flown several times across the Atlantic to comfort his mother, and was at his father's cremation. On that occasion, though it was a great emotional strain, he was determined to speak about his father himself. He said, in part:

My father, George Wellington Hailey, who died last Wednesday, was born in 1883. In that year of his birth, Gladstone was prime minister, Queen Victoria was on the throne and only seven years earlier had been proclaimed Empress of India. Winston Churchill was eleven years old. It was three years before the birth of Charles de Gaulle. The Wright brothers would not make their first flight at Kitty Hawk for another twenty years. The *Titanic* would sink twenty-nine years later. World War I was then thirty-one years away. World War II was fifty-six years distant. It would be eighty-six years before the first human being would set foot on the moon.

I mention these milestones now to make the point that my father's life was long, his experience—both of his time and personally—wide and full.

When my father was a young man he was a sailor in the Royal Navy and fought in the Boer War. Later he became a regular British Army soldier. He served in the Far East, also through the entirety of World War I, in France and in the trenches, surviving where so many of his generation failed to. Of this time, he was proud of the fact that he was an Old Contemptible—the German Kaiser had referred at the beginning of World War I to 'Kitchener's contemptible little army'—and, until last week, my father was one of the few survivors in those thinning ranks.

In between my father's military service he was a merchant

seaman and travelled to most countries of the world, creating memories which stayed with him throughout his life.

Less than two months before his death, at a time when recollection sometimes failed him, I spoke to him of Gibraltar, where I had been myself a few days earlier, and his memories came flooding back so that he spoke with enthusiasm and excitement of his own time in Gibraltar long ago.

Even in old age he was ready for travel and adventure. In his eighty-sixth year, for my parents' Golden Wedding, he flew by jet aircraft with my mother to San Francisco, California—his first flight ever, and a long journey which would have daunted many whose years were not as great. His only complaint during the flight was that the aeroplane did not appear to be moving very fast. His horse in the army, he said, had seemed much faster.

It was this zest for life, and for experience, which made him cheerful, which he always was. Good-natured, too, and generous, and kind—especially with children, as I remember from my own childhood, and as others here today have cause to know as well.

In all the years I knew my father, I do not recall he did an unkind act, or was guilty of meanness in any way. Of how many of us, at the ending of our lives, could the same be said?

A reason for his cheerfulness—a strong one—was that he possessed that greatest of gems: a totally happy marriage and a love affair that lasted to his death.

This is an emotional moment. But let it be cheerful too, for my father's life was rich, and full, and good.

Maeve Southgate's death was sudden, like Lee Barker's. It happened in January 1974, and a few days later Arthur flew once more to New York, to a meeting of the Society of Friends, of which Maeve had been a member. Arthur and others spoke about their recollections of her. He was particularly moved on that occasion by two things. One, the number of people who testified how Maeve had quietly befriended them, including former alcoholics—she had been one before we knew her—and a young man who broke into tears while describing how Maeve had aided and counselled him after his withdrawal from drug addiction. Second, a reading by Maeve's executor of some characteristic words she had handwritten on her will shortly before her death. Four years later (as this is written) Arthur still has those words on a card pinned up in his study, where I went to copy them:

I beg my darling friends to forgive this frigid lawyer lingo. Only the content is my doing, not the language. Saying au revoir (never liked adieu), my heart is filled with love galore for each one of you, as it has been for many years. Bless you for the friendship you have given me.

One thing astonished us. Maeve Southgate had been secretive about her age and we believed her to be in her late sixties. Only after her death did we learn that she was seventy-seven.

That same year, in the summer of 1974, Arthur's mother came to visit us in the Bahamas. She was then eighty-seven. We knew, and so did she, that she was suffering a disease of the lymph glands which was terminal, and she had only months to live. She spent hours under a big ficus tree in our garden, contentedly reading or just sitting there, sorting out her memories.

How grateful I am that she lived long enough to enjoy her son's success! And enjoy it she did. She always got into conversation with strangers—on the bus, at the cinema, in the post office—and managed to bring the talk around to books and, of course, her son. Often, the strangers had read Arthur's books and would comment on them. These 'chance' encounters filled the pages of Elsie's letters.

Knowing that his mother was nearing the end of her life, Arthur composed a letter to her which I know she treasured. This is part of it:

> The purpose . . . is to write some things about you, as I see them. I particularly want to express these thoughts now, and not leave them—as can easily happen—until time has slipped by and suddenly it is too late.
>
> I want to say to you that you have used the years you had exceedingly well . . . For it is not by spectacular, or noisy, or financial successes that real achievement should be measured, but by what we do—much more modestly—in relation to our wives or husbands, family, friends. It is the example we set, the integrity we establish, and the cheerfulness with which we go across our time which really count. And you have done all these things in full measure . . .
>
> Let me make clear to you now that you have been a *fantastic success* as a woman and a mother. I have said on other occasions that I know such talent as I have within me comes from you; that is so clearly evident that Sheila sees it equally as I do. The other thing you have given me is an optimistic nature . . . As to courage and strength of spirit, you have always shown both.

I am not the only one who has observed these merits. Our children certainly have—particularly Jane, Diane and Steven, who have seen you, read your letters and heard Sheila and me speak of you, affectionately and admiringly, as we always do. So you have left your mark on them, have influenced their natures, and that same influence, in time, will extend to other children yet to be born.

What I am saying is that love and virtue have flowed from you, so that when you die there will be traces of you in all our lives and perhaps through generations far ahead.

So let this be said, here and now, and loud and clear, while I can say it plainly and you are alive and alert to understand: you are loved, appreciated, admired and treasured. You have (as the Bible puts it) 'fought the good fight' and won resoundingly.

When Elsie died in England, we were on a few weeks' vacation in California. Her cremation was set for four days later. But Arthur had promised American Airlines that he would speak at a graduation ceremony at the airline's agent-training school in Dallas, where Arthur's oldest son, Roger, would be one of the graduates. The two dates conflicted. We knew the occasion was important to Roger, and after some mental wrestling, Arthur chose to be with the living and went to Dallas, so missed his mother's funeral. From Dallas he flew on to England to tackle the sad task of disposing of her possessions and her home.

I mention these deaths, for they tell something of Arthur. He shed tears on all four occasions. His emotions, usually kept in check, are nonetheless close to the surface. He sobbed when he heard of his mother's death, even though we had been expecting the news for some time. Steven, then eighteen, who has the same sensitivity, crossed the room and put his arms around Arthur and shed tears, too—but more for his father, I believe, than for his grandmother.

In the last year of her life, Elsie told us she was glad that she got her wish and that George, her husband, died before she did. She recognised that he needed her more than she needed him. Arthur, too, has said he hopes to die before me. A morbid thought perhaps, yet I know deep down, just as his mother did, it would be better that way. We women are strong . . . it is a myth that we are a weaker sex in need of male protection.

*   *   *

Arthur has often said that if he has a tombstone, all he wants on it is his name and 'He was a storyteller'. He has told our children, 'Story-telling is an old and honourable profession, as old as the strolling player and the court jester.' In another age he might have been a pro-fessional raconteur, entertaining the court before a blazing fire. He did this once during an evening in Kenya in 1972. We were on safari with four of the six children. With a dozen people seated around a camp-fire, Arthur spun stories while everyone listened with rapt at-tention.

Arthur is also proud of his reputation for in-depth research and accuracy of background. When people say (as they do), 'You must have been in medicine . . . the hotel business . . . an airport executive . . . in the motor industry . . . a bank manager,' he glows.

Never one to cover the walls of his study with framed awards or photographs of himself with other personalities, he has, nonetheless, given prominent place to a small, simple plaque which reads:

In Appreciation for
RECOGNIZING
UNDERSTANDING
COMMUNICATING
The Problems of Modern Aviation
Thru the Novel
Airport
from
Professional Air Traffic Controllers Organization
July 8, 1969

In the same way, he was delighted by some published words of the distinguished scholar and spokesman on communications, Marshall McLuhan. In a 'letter to the editor', commenting on an adverse re-view of *The Moneychangers*, Dr. McLuhan wrote:

> [The] review of *The Moneychangers* missed a wonderful oppor-tunity to explain Arthur Hailey as 'a fabulously successful com-mercial novelist'. *Airport*, *Hotel*, and *Wheels*, like *The Moneychangers*, are not based on a story line. Rather, they follow the path of development and social process. They offer a kind of mimesis or dramatisation of the human learning process itself. The process which Arthur Hailey has hit upon is like the

233

documentary technique, itself a kind of repeat of the stages by which men experience their world. That is why the documentary, as such, whether in the news reel or in John Grierson's famous *Night Mail* or his *Milk Route*, fascinates readers and viewers alike. The incidental ornaments which Hailey adds, and which [your reviewer] finds 'slick' and 'shallow', in no way disturb the basic genetic or development pattern of social action and experience which are involved in the mass of themes of *Airport* and *The Moneychangers*. There are dozens of similar themes which Hailey has not touched, and his audience will be delighted if, and when, he gets around to them.

Arthur is a kind man. I will never forget his reaction when I lost—through my own carelessness—several thousand dollars' worth of personal jewellery, including my wedding ring, those pearls Arthur bought in Japan, and other gifts he had given me across the years. It happened after we had been in New York for several days and were going home to the Bahamas.

I was carrying the jewellery in a tote bag, along with my passport and other items. At the Pan American terminal of J. F. Kennedy Airport we stepped out of a taxi and I took my handbag but not the tote bag. Seconds too late I realized what had happened, then watched with horror as the taxi sped away, the licence number by that time unreadable. I knew instinctively I would never see that bag again, and I was right. None of the jewellery was insured, which was another folly of mine.

I felt the blood drain from my face. I looked at Arthur. 'My bag . . . with all my jewellery . . . it's in the taxi.' I left him to check our baggage in while I flagged another taxi, hoping to catch up with the first. Of course, it was hopeless; there were hundreds of taxis in the area, all of them looking alike. Feeling mentally numbed, I returned to the Pan Am terminal and found Arthur. When he saw me, he put out his arms and hugged me.

'Stop worrying!' he urged. 'What's happened has happened, and it could be a whole lot worse. We're safe, the kids are okay. Let's be glad it wasn't something more serious.' When I reminded him about the wedding ring, he said: 'The ring's gone but the marriage is intact. Better that than the other way around.' I did worry, of course, and blamed myself for stupidity and carelessness. But Arthur never reproached me, then or later.

Instead, during the months that followed he secretly replaced, with time-consuming correspondence and much intrigue, the most valuable pieces—jade, gold and diamond earrings he had given me on my forty-third birthday; an emerald ring and a multi-stone bracelet from Brazil; a diamond eternity ring from Switzerland. Each time he gave me the new jewellery—the duplicate earrings, for example, I found under the Christmas tree—I was reminded again of his generosity and compassion.

After the last replacement, he said with a smile: 'Okay, that's all. But if it ever happens again, honey, you're on your own.'

My forty-third birthday—another example of Arthur's thoughtfulness. We had been living in the Bahamas for a year. Through some fancy undercover work, he arranged with a friend to invite us to what I thought was a black-tie dinner for six at Lyford Cay Club. I accepted innocently, thinking it would be a nice way to spend my birthday. I wore my new jade earrings. I did notice that Arthur was a bit jittery as we were getting ready for the evening, but thought he was just feeling tense. Then as we walked into the Club, he said quietly: 'You've heard of "This Is Your Life". Well, this is your birthday party.'

Some forty guests were waiting to surprise me . . . and what a surprise! As my glance swept around the room, it stopped at one face. I couldn't believe . . . it was my sister Gina. Arthur had planned it all weeks ahead, had sent her an airline ticket, urging her to fly from London and stay right through Christmas. I ran and hugged her emotionally. There wasn't a dry eye in the place. Through the rest of the evening I felt loved and pampered while Arthur beamed, delighted that his surprise had succeeded. A splendid organiser, he loves to introduce some dramatic element to an occasion, and all his talent for suspenseful storytelling was in evidence that night.

I have been proud of Arthur's writings over the years. Though, primarily, he spins a yarn, in every one of his books there is something of his philosophy, much of which I share. He has never been a loud crusader, but I believe he has made people think. He is not afraid to speak up about something he believes in, but never proclaims his views in strident tones.

In May 1969, when we were living in the small wine-country town of St. Helena in California, Arthur was asked to give the town's Memorial Day address. It was during the Vietnam War when passions were running high, producing clashes between young and old, liberals and conservatives, those who believed in the war and those who didn't. Prominent among the townspeople gathered for the occasion were members of American Legion Post 199, most of whom deplored the antiwar activities that were churning on college campuses all over the nation.

I admired what Arthur said that day:

No one ever wants to die in a war. Those who speak of glory, or the nobility of laying down one's life in battle, are usually those who have not made the scene.

What most soldiers in wars have always wanted is to finish the fighting and go home—home to normality of living, to make love or make wine, raise children, and in time grow old, and die decently when the body fails from nature's causes.

These are the things which most of those whom we remember on Memorial Day wanted for themselves. And when they died, in whatever war, these men were not dreaming of glory. A short time before, most of them had been thinking of ordinary things—like mail from home, or chow, or girls, or last night's dice game, or tomorrow's weather.

And soon after, when the time of peril came, there was almost certainly a tightening of the gut, and wondering if this time their number was coming up, though hoping, maybe praying, it would not. For the urge to survive has always been the strongest human instinct, as true for soldiers, through the world's long history, as it is true for you and me this sunlit springtime morning.

Thus, I think, we should remind ourselves on Memorial Day that those who have died in wars were seldom eager heroes, but ordinary people, like ourselves, who departed life reluctantly. There is another thing about them: they were mostly young.

The youthfulness of our dead warriors is something which those of us who make it back from wars—the survivors and spectators—all too easily forget as years go by. We grow older and greyer, sometimes in the head as well as on it, and when we think of our dead we still consider them contemporaries—as being like ourselves, the elder, solid citizens which most of us have since become.

But the fact is: these dead soldiers never did grow old. And, on this day, to remember them as other than they were would be to falsify their memory.

What kind of men—and women—were these whom we are assembled here to honour?

In World War II, which is the only war I was a part of personally, our generation was a yeasty bunch, imbued with urgency
and enthusiasm and ideals. We believed there should be major
changes, both in the way the world was run and in the scales of
values of those times. We asked pointed questions which
annoyed our elders, and ridiculed established ideas and customs
which others before us had taken for granted. We did our share
of hell-raising and, at times, our manners were not the best. In
theatres of war we did our duty as we saw it, but in privacy and
in our minds, were often disrespectful of authority. We usually
thought we knew better than our elders, and as it turned out, we
often did. I remember very well that a large part of the generation which preceded us, and whom we spoke of as 'Colonel
Blimps', did not approve of us at all.

Let us be clear about it: these are the kind of people we com-
memorate today, and what was true of the young soldiers of
World War II has been true—in degree, according to their
times—of soldiers in every other war.

For even in wars, as well as out of them, it is the young who
imbue us with new purpose and ideas, who prod and lead, and
raise our sights toward civilization's higher ground. And even
the young who die leave something of themselves behind.

I wonder sometimes—and especially today—if these young
and dead could scrutinise us now, observing the unrest and fer-
ment of youth which trouble this and other nations, what would
they see and hear, essentially, above the shouting and through
the tear gas, and where would their sympathy most lie?

I think I know. I think we all know.

One more thing. War and violence represent a paradox of the
human situation. Part of the paradox is that most people in this
world abhor war and its consequences, and have learned over
the centuries that after a war, no matter who may appear to win,
all sides lose. Despite this knowledge, we have never learned to
end war.

The other part of the paradox is that despite the tragedy of
war there is some good, always, which emerges. And it is true,
sadly true, that every great forward step in human progress has
been accompanied or preceded by violence or uprising or force
of arms.

We may not, and should not, approve of war or violence or
excess. But until we learn to make a better world, that is the way
it is, and this is the lesson of Memorial Day: Nothing is ever
wholly negative, nothing is ever wholly lost. Despite all grief and
human wastage, even over dead men's blood and bones we
manage to progress a little.

Let us then remember the dead—in all wars—gratefully. And

let us hope that because of them we may become a touch better, a thimbleful wiser, and a handshake more tolerant of this changing world they did not live to see.

Arthur is an agnostic. Yet he lives his life more closely to Christian principles than most people I know. He has given our children hope and integrity and a philosophy that is simple: respect other people's dignity and treat them with kindness and tolerance, no matter who they are or what they do.

On my desk, as I write, is a birthday card which was sent to Arthur on his fifty-seventh birthday. It is from Joan, his first wife, with whom he has not lived since 1949. It says a great deal for him, and for her:

> Dear Arthur:
>   I am sitting in the kitchen, pen in hand, wondering what do I say to someone like you. 'Happy Birthday' and let it go at that? No, there has to be more, even though it may sound repetitious.
>   Whether you believe in our Heavenly Father, or not, you must know that your kind thoughts and overwhelming generosity in the past to all of us will not go unrewarded.
>   All I can give you in return are my prayers and good wishes for a very happy birthday. I will remember you at mass on April 3, which is Passion Sunday. Have a very special April 5, 1977.
>   God bless you . . . Love, Joan

I have tried in this chapter—in my own words, in Arthur's words, and in other people's words—to expose the inner workings of Arthur Hailey. As I joked to friends, 'I've spent most of the book knocking him; in the last chapter I want to build him up.' Overall, I hope I have shown him as he is—warts and all. Of course I cannot be completely objective—I love the guy—but I also know there is no one else in the world who understands him as well as I do.

That's partly the reason I have written this book. A lot of superficial words have been printed about him that are completely off base. He was once described in a newspaper article as 'a pipe-smoking Englishman', when he has never smoked anything in his life. Another interviewer wrote that Hailey didn't care about the quality of his work, only the money he received for it. This is absolutely untrue. How can anyone write a penetrating portrait after a two-hour interview, or less? I also feel the way Arthur did when he wrote to his mother the year before she died: let me get it down on paper while there is still time.

For our life has been good, and I want to share some of it. We have achieved what for most people is an unattainable dream: freedom and independence—the greatest reward which Arthur's writing has given us. We control our own time. We go where we want, and when. Unless something happens that is internationally cataclysmic, we have sufficient money tucked away for us to live comfortably through the remainder of our lives. As well, we are happy and content in each other's company.

I am sure that both of us will go on working—at something—for the pleasure of it and because I believe the day you stop working is when you start to die. Once, Arthur summed up his attitude towards work for a group of students:

> I have tried to apply one rule to everything I have ever done, including writing. That is: whatever you are doing, at any time, give of your absolute best and never, ever, settle for less than the utmost you can do.
>
> Better to decline a task than do it carelessly.
>
> Nothing is wrong with honourable failure—it happens to us all from time to time, and is good for experience and for the soul. Nor can all men and women be as great as some. But dishonourable failure—when one has not given of one's best—is cause for shame, even though sometimes only an individual, within his or her own conscience, knows which is which.
>
> Nothing should be more important, at any particular moment, than the task one is doing right then. We may not be geniuses or epic poets—our lack of talent usually stops us short of that—but we ought to aim at being both.
>
> There is a practical application to this attitude and habit: he who strives constantly for highest quality may some day exceed the limitations he believed he had.

No one who has 'made it' has it made indefinitely into the future. Nor, outside fairy tales, does anyone live happily ever after. Success is sweet—both in a career and in a marriage—but you must work at it every step of the way. Arthur's career is less important to him than it was, yet still he strives to write better than he did. As for our marriage, I have no formula. I hope it stays sweet. With love and a sense of humour . . . it has a chance.